CARELESS WHISPERS:
THE LIFE & CAREER OF

GEORGE**MICHAEL**

CARELESS WHISPERS:
THE LIFE & CAREER OF

GEORGE**MICHAEL**

ROBERT STEELE

OMNIBUS PRESS

London / New York / Paris / Sydney / Copenhagen / Berlin / Madrid / Tokyo

Copyright © 2011 Omnibus Press
(A Division of Music Sales Limited)

Cover designed by Mike Bell
Picture research Jacqui Black

ISBN: 978.178038.0.155
Order No: OP54054

Exclusive Distributors
Music Sales Limited,
14/15 Berners Street,
London, W1T 3LJ.

Music Sales Corporation,
257 Park Avenue South,
New York, NY 10010, USA.

Macmillan Distribution Services,
56 Parkwest Drive
Derrimut, Vic 3030,
Australia.

Every effort has been made to trace the copyright holders of the photographs in this book but one or two were unreachable. We would be grateful if the photographers concerned would contact us.

Typeset by Phoenix Photosetting, Chatham, Kent

Printed in the EU

A catalogue record for this book is available from the British Library.

Visit Omnibus Press on the web at www.omnibuspress.com

Contents

Introduction

"I'm coming out here on my own so that you'll realise I just want to start again . . . It's fantastic to be free. I just want to say thank you for everybody who has supported me in there, it's quite inspirational."

George Michael gives an impromptu press conference outside his London home, on his October 11, 2010 release from prison.

It's a measure of the evergreen popularity of Anglo-Greek vocalist Georgios Kyriacos Panayiotou – George Michael to his public – that he remains the single most played artist on British radio. Nothing, it seems, can derail the affection a large section of the UK public has for the suburban north London boy. Not changes of musical direction or short-lived resolutions to cease recording or live performance; not vast gaps in his output that can be measured in years; neither a copious intake of drugs in someone who once appeared clean-living, nor rumours about his well-guarded sexuality that finally blew as wide open as a broken cubicle door. Against this, his much-publicised reckless behaviour seems to have made less of a dent in his popularity than the front bumper of his car did to a shopfront.

On the eve of what promises to be a major comeback, perceptions of George Michael differ across the pop culture of the West. In his native Britain and continental Europe, he's the perennial superstar who never went away – however embarrassing his behaviour seemed at times; in Australia he's the new pommie in town, and the Antipodean gay scene seems to have adopted him as one of their own; in the USA, which is not (yet) on his major comeback tour itinerary, he's a figure from the past who occasionally crops up on TV. The discredited ghost of the late-1980s *Faith* era, he's remembered less for his music and more for a comical restroom indiscretion with a plainclothes cop – as well as for the sin of satirising an American president (in a video for an undeniably rather silly song).

If George retains much of the fan fervour and goodwill built up among his audience over the years, it's largely because his audience have grown up (and into middle-age) with him. To those of us who are of his generation, recollection of the Wham! years is still a bright beacon of youth for the girls who made the records into hits at the time; for most guys, the appeal of Wham! remains strictly a 'girl thing', tolerated but a wee bit naff – something to be endured if you were buying her their latest record or accompanying her to see them at Wembley. Among nostalgic thirty- and forty-something guys, a liking for Wham! will be recalled as virtual proof that a boy was gay – at a time when few of us knew about George Michael's sexuality, ironically enough.

Even George himself has disavowed his early recordings at times – "What I was then and what I am now – one of them has to be a fake!" he insisted at the time of his 1990 official (auto)biography. These days, he'd probably be less hard on himself and recognise it for what it was – pure pop music for almost desperately upbeat times. Having once shared the general male prejudice about Wham!, your author now concedes that nothing rolls back the years like hearing the joyous stomp of 'Freedom' or the cheesy tinkling melody of 'Last Christmas'.

It made what followed all the more remarkable. Was 'Father Figure', that moodily erotic piece of aural seduction, really by George from Wham!? Once coaxed past the period black-and-white beach photo cover of *Listen Without Prejudice*, were we prepared to do just that and judge its atmospheric contents on their own virtues? How many of us overlooked that essential nineties album *Older* – with its easy listening tones and cinematic atmospheres – because we were bemused by seeing a superstar performer locked in a seemingly hopeless court case with his record label and wrote off the record as just a rich man's indulgence?

There was also a visual transformation between the George of Wham! and the older George, and it wasn't just the passing of time that did it. The early solo artist was remodelled with designer stubble, shades and a crucifix earring; the brooding George of *Faith* was far more overtly sexual than the fresh-faced young gun of Wham!

But then this was a macho sexuality. Visually associated with photogenically perfect women in the late eighties and early nineties, George Michael's seemingly fluid sexual identity morphed into that of a gay man as the decade wore on. As can be gleaned from the personal testimonies in this book, this was always the true nature of the singer's sexuality, whatever his protestations when he inadvertently 'outed' himself in 1998.

"All the people that I know and care about are perfectly clued in," he'd insisted before the incident, "everybody knows who I am. So for the sake of people that I never speak to, I really don't feel any desire to define myself."

More of a revelation than George's homosexuality was how little difference it made to his public. As a career watershed, the LA outing saw him travel from the point of being a man reticent about his private life to becoming the most overtly 'out' spokesman for gay causes, who at times defined himself almost solely ("speaking as a gay man") in terms of his sexuality. And still the girls that screamed at him in his days as a young gun with Andrew Ridgeley remained in love with their gentle George, whose songs spoke to their emotions whatever his orientation.

In many ways, the career of George Michael is a gauge of changing public attitudes toward personal freedom. Having guarded his sexuality for years and then found it made little difference to his appeal – though the haters, of course, will always hate – George was a lot more candid about his use of soft drugs.

"As far as I'm concerned the album's... a great advert for grass," George would later reflect on *Older*. The album, which wears its many emotions very lightly indeed, is testimony to that; cannabis, the singer-songwriter's drug of choice, seems to have been conducive to his well-being at the time.

Marijuana and its derivatives have been described as like a worn old vinyl record – regular use can get you stuck in the same cracked groove every time. As we will see, George Michael has suffered from two of the saddest bereavements that can mar a person's life. But it has taken him many, many years to get past them, and it may be that the very substance he was using to cope with the emotional pain was returning him to the same dreamily ethereal state of mourning every time, to what he refers to as "my black hole".

You won't find much moralising about George's habits in this book – as far as this writer is concerned, a person's vices are his or her own, as long as they don't impact severely on the life of another person. George's openness about his dope habit also heralded a time when (as an increasing number of US states decriminalised possession) British society had its own echo of the American 'reefer madness' scares of the 1930s – inspired by some genuinely disturbing incidents as well as some exaggeration. Add to this a worsening economic climate when the instinct of those feeling the pinch tells them that the rich and successful are deserving of punishment for *anything* they might do.

But then George's greatest *faux pas* in his middle-aged years are due as much to other substances, and to often comically bad judgement. As his former biographer, Tony Parsons, recently sneered at him, "You were always more Keith Chegwin than Keith Richards" – that is, more like a cheerfully cheesy TV presenter with a booze problem than a chemical-abusing rock star with a superhuman constitution.

George became the tabloids' favourite car wreck – both metaphorically and literally speaking. For a period of between two and three years, he could be relied upon to do something to embarrass himself (or his long-suffering boyfriend) with comical regularity. For British audiences, it somehow served to make him more human – take a look at George sending himself up on *Comic Relief* or on Ricky Gervais' last TV series – although any sense of it being perversely endearing was worn away by the knowledge that someone (whether the performer himself or some innocent bystander) was going to get seriously hurt if things didn't change.

In the kind of harshening, unforgiving climate we're living in today, it's hard for many to accept that the most privileged figures from the entertainment industry have any kind of emotional problems worth considering. In his recent interview with Chris Evans, George conceded that anytime he needed to remind himself how lucky he was, he only had to turn on daytime TV to hear a cross-section of people on society's bottom rung discussing their seemingly intractable problems.

None of which made much difference to his depressed state of mind of mind – until a series of accidents that remained – fortunately, and with little thanks to George – funny rather than tragic finally persuaded him it was time to meet his emotions head on, without being under the chemical cosh. As he has famously remarked, "I'm surprised that I've survived my own dysfunction, really."

The fact that his career survives along with him has been much remarked upon, not least by the artist himself. ("I've spent the last 10 or 15 years trying to derail my own career because it never seems to suffer," he mused half-jokingly in 2007.) In part, it's his often under-praised talent that's the abiding factor: while his work is oft considered to be down the more lightweight end of the scale to more 'serious' songwriters, the songs of George Michael, the solo artist, have an emotional literacy that incorporates all he has been through and all he has felt. As a producer and instrumentalist, he also possesses far more musical creativity than most solo vocalists – as his former manager, Simon Napier-Bell, acknowledges in these pages.

"I'm not what stars are made of," George once claimed back in the 1980s. "I'm not Prince and I'm not Madonna." What he most definitely became later in his career and what he continues to be now is the pop star who puts himself on display in his work. For all his failings and foibles, the singer appears a familiar and accessible figure in the land of his birth, never seeming as remote as, say, his one time role model Elton John.

This impression is largely an illusion, fostered by his many appearances on TV and his willingness to send up his public image. But there is no denying this talented but flawed man's public spiritedness; for years now, it has been acknowledged that the singer has given away a significant part of his vast income to various charities, many of them aiding sick or underprivileged children in London, the city that remains his first home. It's a record which gives the lie to some of his more conservative critics and their claim to lead a 'Christian' life, which for them means little more than mouthing dogma.

And so George Michael, in what is at least the third major stage of his career, continues to benefit from the residues of goodwill he still has stored in British and European pop culture. (The Americans have yet to take him back to their hearts on a similar scale, but it's by no means certain that it won't happen.) He remains the most adored (by the public) and most publicly mocked (by the press) pop performer of the last 30 years.

On a personal note, your author's wife recently told him about an incident in a car park, where she heard a mother reminding her daughter that she was named after George Michael. "Alright, don't tell everyone," joked her dad, a little self-consciously. "How bloody sad are we?" About as sad as we are, acknowledged my wife – between their daughter and ours, that made for one Georgia and one Georgina in the same small area. There are almost certainly a number of boys in their late teens or early twenties named George for a similar reason.

I'd like to say that "it's a London and the Southeast thing – you wouldn't understand." But then I'd be more inclined to believe that there's a similar affection for the singer running throughout most of the British Isles.

Robert Steele
Spring 2011

CHAPTER 1

Round Here

The roads run on endlessly round here, in north London's suburban sprawl. More so than in their polar counterparts south of the river, there are any number of dual carriageways, rows of shops and industrial estates to traverse before the London postcodes expire and you find yourself just outside, in the borderlands of the Home Counties.

This backstreet in the London Borough of Barnet – just a stone's throw from the high street, circumnavigating the choked congestion of the North Circular Road – is only a brisk walk or a straight northward drive from the more urban environs of Highgate, famed for its rambling gothic cemetery. But this particular neighbourhood, East Finchley, could epitomise the cosy anonymity of Greater London's inner suburbs, with its eatery chains and beauty parlours. A parade of aspirational small businesses, it's perhaps apt that this was the constituency of former Prime Minister Margaret Thatcher throughout her years of power.

It wasn't always like this, of course. They've developed the place a lot since the sixties, though its essential unremarkable homeliness remains the same. Back then it was perhaps slightly less salubrious, but it was here, at number 73 Church Lane, that an integral part of modern popular culture came into being.

The family living in the two-bedroom flat above a launderette were themselves a little microcosm of what would become modern Britain. Hard-working people from modest backgrounds, with no academic education to speak of, the parents were a mixed-race couple back in the days when it wasn't so commonplace, when it might still be deemed worth remarking upon.

Their children − neither overindulged nor spoilt, nor in any way deprived − would grow up steeped in the pop culture that, back in those black-and-white TV days, was growing at an imperceptibly fast rate all around them. In this, they would be little different from most children of their era, who learned to consume pop music and soap opera and love songs along with their mother's milk.

But of the three kids it's the son, the boy who will rechristen himself 'George Michael', who will one day become the embodiment of the modern pop era − its joys and absurdities; its creativity and excesses; its modern morality and its cosmopolitan sexuality.

Though his son would later sing of how he 'got here on the gravy train', the newly arrived Kyriacos Panayiotou found that Britain provided anything but an easy meal ticket.

He'd left behind a rural Cypriot town where generations still lived the traditional lives of farmers, fishermen or goatherds. In the more cosmopolitan era of the forties and fifties in which he grew up, Kyriacos (or Jack Panos, to grant him his anglicised adopted name) and his kinfolk had the additional option of working as waiters or seamsters, hoping to work their way up in the restaurant and tailoring trades that they serviced.

But here too, opportunities for advancement were limited and money was in short supply. The lifestyle of Patriki − their small town to the northeast of the island, just outside the city of Famagusta − had survived Nazi occupation and the Germans' expulsion by Allied forces. The now declining British Empire had retained the island state it first annexed in World War One, with its divided Greek and Turkish ethnic communities.

And still things stayed much the same.

The climate was hospitably warm, with balmy sea breezes blowing in toward the coastal villages. The traditional support network of large families sustained many through years of low-paid employment – ensuring survival, even if affluence remained a distant dream to most. To the majority, the family was both the purpose and the defining limit of their lives. They were ruled by strict old patriarchs like Kyriacos' father who, whatever his status in life, insisted at home that his word was law. "You were taught to fear and respect your father in the Greek tradition of things," Kyriacos' own son commented much later. "I never met my grandfather because he died even before my parents met, but everything I have heard points to the fact that he was loved and respected but feared."

By the mid-fifties, the consumer boom that had started in America began to inspire many of the peoples of Europe with a dream of something more. For many, the dream was so vague as to be indefinable; to the more traditionally minded, who neither longed for nor imagined anything other than what they'd known all their lives, it seemed ridiculous.

But to a cocksure young Jack, then in his late teens, and his cousin and best friend, Dimitrios Georgiou, it seemed worth following their dream of better things across the sea. It may not have been, strictly speaking, a gravy train, but the boat journey they took from the Mediterranean to the English Channel ferried them to an England where a more hopeful, hedonistic youth culture was about to be born from the years of grey post-war austerity.

For a short time, the two cousins – who arrived with less than one pound sterling each in their pockets – would enjoy the innocent hedonism of the fifties. But that may not have been their main incentive for emigrating.

"Our fathers came off the banana boat together," Andros Georgiou, second cousin of young Georgios, would observe of how Dimitirious and Jack made it to the UK. "Though they don't admit it, part of the reason they came was to flee National Service."

Back home, they'd had neither the inclination to be called up to defend British colonialism nor to join the Greek Cypriot movement EOKA – which would explode into terrorist violence in 1956, installing Archbishop Makarios III as leader of a newly independent Cyprus by 1960.

The boys from Patriki were not interested in any of that. They'd just heard that there was a better life out there for the taking and they wanted a little of it. And part of that new way of life was rock 'n' roll.

Newly arrived as emigrants to London, Jack worked as a waiter north of the Thames while Dimitrios found employment with a tailor's firm in south London. They also found a new world of teenagers' milk bars and Saturday-night dancehalls. In the Highgate/Holloway area of north London, Jack would strut his stuff like the exotic new Mediterranean arrival that he was.

"My parents were rock'n'roll dancers," Jack's son Georgios would recall at the tail end of the eighties. "They met at a dance and my father used to throw my mother all over the show." Jack's dancing partner was a cute young brunette from Lulot Street, in the Archway neighbourhood that crossed Highgate and Holloway. As befitting the time and the place, Lesley Angold Harrison was a nice girl from a respectable working-class family. She was, however, independent-minded enough to cross the racial barriers and go out with a darkly good looking young man from outside her own social group.

"When he met mum, dad looked a bit like George Chakiris," said their son, drawing a comparison with the Greek-American actor-dancer who played the Puerto Rican gang leader in movie musical *West Side Story*. "He had this great haircut, with a real loose quiff." In the autobiography he would publish while still in his twenties, Jack's son included a photo of his dad on north London parkland, dressed in a dark suit with Brylcreemed hair, pointed shoes and shades – himself still only in his late teens.

To complement his own brooding good looks, Jack had found his dark-haired/fair-skinned English rose. In fact, according to the popular magazines of the time, he might easily have attracted a number of girls just like Lesley. "There used to be a magazine called *Reveille*," observed Georgios, "and they used to do a competition called 'Search for a TV Star'. Everybody sent their picture in with a little resumé and my dad got to the final… mum kept the picture. It said underneath, 'JACK PANOS IS CHASED DOWN THE STREET BY GIRLS WHEREVER HE GOES.'"

It was still a little daring for Lesley to hitch herself so closely and so quickly to a foreign boy. As the Greek Cypriots were assimilating and making their home-away-from-home in north London, it's easy to think she would never experience the bigotry faced by white girls who took up with West Indian immigrants. Her son disabuses us of such a notion.

"Well, it's funny," considered Georgios, "most people wouldn't realise, [what with] the Cypriots being one of the countries in the Commonwealth that were being invited to come to the mother country to rebuild the place after the Second World War. There were places that would say, 'No blacks, no Irish, no Greeks, no dogs' kind of thing. So my father was part of that, and my mother's father did not attend their wedding because [my father] was Greek. In those times, he saw that as absolutely the same as marrying someone of a completely different colour."

Britain had some way to go, in order to become the model of racial tolerance she aspires to be today. Lesley Panayiotou – née Angold Harrison – did indeed have a bad start to the game, to borrow her son's words.

Jack and Lesley hung up their winklepickers and dancing shoes and got wed with a small reception in Holloway, before settling down to the hard grind of family life in the late fifties. These may have been the post-war years, but the corresponding economic boom was yet to truly arrive. There wasn't much money in the Panayiotou household, yet Jack still found little bits of cash to send home to his four brothers and two sisters in Cyprus.

He still tried to spread his waiter's wages thinly when their first child, their daughter Yioda, was born to them while they were living at their suburban flat in Finchley, in 1959. The financial pressures got heavier still when they had a second little girl, Melanie, two years later.

By the time of the birth of the girls' little brother, Georgios, on 25 June 1963, Jack had upped his income by becoming assistant manager at the restaurant where he worked. But with the promotion came an almost incessant workload. Like most working couples of that era, Jack and Lesley Panayiotou were too busy keeping the household together to notice when the sixties started to swing.

The little boy's distant memories of his early home summon up an unremarkable upstairs sectioned off into a flat, overlooking an old row of shops on Church Lane itself and a cluttered yard to the back. "Most kids go out to school when their dad's out at work and they see him in the evenings," observed Georgios. "My dad had the afternoons off and then he would have to go back to the restaurant in the early evenings." Jack, as a conscientious provider, also verged on being an absentee father, working seven lunchtimes and evenings a week.

"Mum and dad worked in a fish and chip shop along here," the adult Georgios would later describe to his lifelong friend David, on camera, telling of a time when both parents had to double up their workloads for the family to survive. "My mum said it was the most disgusting period of her life, because you know how clean mum was, and you couldn't get the smell of the fish out of your skin, your hair. Poor cow, she had to come home and look after us and then go and work in my dad's restaurant."

Lesley Panayiotou also worked a part-time office job at a high-rise block called Hyde House in Kingsbury, for part of her son's childhood years. "The bit I remember about a very working-class existence is that she was exhausted, she was working two jobs with three children to look after, had an extremely unreasonable husband who expected her to work every night at the restaurant because otherwise he would never see her, and through all that the house was spotless and whatever. It's just that she was exhausted and angry all the time."

But her frayed temper was rarely expended on the children. For this is the woman her son would describe as the rock of stability throughout his life; her careful upbringing of him and the close companionship of his two elder sisters would make him as comfortable with women and girls as he would be with male company.

Jack Panos took his family on what would also become the classic trajectory for a Greek immigrant: from the northern part of the city, they moved to its leafy suburbs when their young son was still a baby. "I was here from when I was a year old to when I was about 12," the adult Georgios will later tell his fans on a sentimental journey taken for the cameras. It features an insert of the dark-quiffed Jack with his baby boy held in one arm, looking very like a bouffant-wearing version of the young George Michael.

"On this side [right] was a real old cow; on the other side was a family of eight Irish Catholic children, who were lovely actually." Georgios and his friend took a detour around the back of this typical suburban semi, with its dark mock-Tudor panelling. "I used to sit up there waiting for the sun to come up every morning," he remarked of his old bedroom, "so that I could go out." As we will see, the leafy foliage of suburbia and its creepy-crawly inhabitants would exert a great fascination over the boy.

By 1968, young Georgios would begin his primary schooling at Roe Green in Kingsbury, London NW9 – just a mile up the road from the new family home in Burnt Oak, Edgware, which bore a Middlesex postcode. "That's where they still queue up for the lunch hall," the grown man will later point out to his friend David, at the little infants' school where he could still detect traces of the children they once were. "I can remember getting my fucking legs smacked by an old pervert."

David, who was then called Mortimer but would later change his surname, was in the year ahead of Georgios at school, and a nearby neighbour in Redhill Drive, Burnt Oak. He may have been the older boy, but his memories are not so vivid.

"You remember that down there, the quadrangle?" his old friend George asked him. "That was the toilet, and some of the kids would have teachers come with them, wouldn't they, pull their trousers, their pants, down for them?"

"Uh, no," disclaims David. Memory is oft evoked as a major building block of creativity, and George's long-lived memories seemed still strikingly fresh and accurate.

This was the era when the boy's father, Jack, went into partnership on his first co-owned restaurant in Edgware. He would later become sole proprietor of his own Anglo-Greek restaurant, known as Mr Jack's, in the era when kebabs and Greek salad were still exotic fare to the British palate; the restaurant was named the Angus Pride, which summons up roast beef or steak and chips.

"My early life was very working-class and both my parents came from real, genuine poverty," Jack's son has reflected in more recent years. "But I think I absolutely realised in my mid-teens I was the son of an immigrant: I understood the difference in my ambitions and what my work ethic was from the people around me. I understood that was what made me not very English, you know. It's this shameless kind of graft – move up – graft – move up – graft – move up, which was what my father gave me. And I think genetically I have his drive, so I'm very lucky in that. But my mother, you see, was the complete opposite, so the messages were very mixed at home. My mother didn't want us to move out of our working-class neighbourhood, and my father as an immigrant was determined that we were going to be a middle-class family."

With so much of the family discipline administered by his ever-present mum, Georgios had no reason to regard his dad in the same way that Jack had feared his own father. "There was always the threat *I'll tell your dad* from our mum when we were small, and we knew that meant something serious," he conceded, "but I wasn't afraid of him. He's in no way a violent man – he's a very gentle man."

Once he'd achieved the economic stability necessary to give them regular holidays in the early seventies, Jack took the family on the first of several visits to his Cypriot hometown. He had not returned since the age of 18, 15 years earlier, but his occasional money parcels home had made life a little easier for his four brothers and two sisters.

It was eye-opening for the Panayiotou children to witness life back in the old country, where rubble-strewn roads and rural isolation were offset by the light, tangy smell of mimosa and the beauty of the deep red sunset. As for little Georgios, he was fascinated by his father's calm warning about the ethnic divisions on the island, as they stood before the high gated walls that closed off the Turkish sector. "It was very strange to me," the adult George noted. "My father warned me not to go beyond those gates – he said that they could legally shoot me in there…"

Jack Panos himself expressed no ethnic sectarian hatred, having deftly avoided such cultural and political unrest by coming to Britain. But the age-old enmity of the Turks and the Greeks still persisted; stemming from the earliest days of the Turkish Ottoman Empire, much violence had been inflicted on the Greeks as an occupied people – who, when their own circumstances presented the opportunity, had also performed similarly ruthless acts of revenge.

Ironically perhaps, the Turkish Cypriot people would follow the trajectory of Jack and others like him, many of them migrating to run London shops and restaurants just like their Greek peers. In the modern day, many areas north of the Thames (such as Lesley Panayiotou's native Holloway and Green Lanes) which were formerly Greek Cypriot mainstays are now home to thriving Turkish communities. Many Greek families – much like Jack himself – have headed further north, away from the dirty brown streets of Islington and Haringey, to the counties of Middlesex or Hertfordshire.

Back home in the English suburbs, little Georgios only ever knew two occasions when Jack Panos saw fit to lay a hand on him. One of those times was when, by his own admission, "I was whining about a torch; I wouldn't shut up about this torch that I thought I needed."

It's an everyday scenario, even in our child-conscious times: a little kid gets a fixed notion about a particular consumer product, and then drives his parents to distraction over it until the corrective slap. In the case of the little Panayiotou boy, however, the flashlight may have been more than a bratty whim.

"The first thing I was interested in was nature," he later acknowledged, "I really loved collecting lizards and insects." The torch, for him, was an exploratory device that threw light onto an alien world that began in the back garden – the first garden little Georgios had ever known – of the new family home in Burnt Oak. A fascinatingly microscopic world of creeping daddy longlegs, squirming caterpillars and soil-sodden newts, which extended beyond the garden to a small earthy trench below the playground fence of the local primary school he'd just started attending.

In an alternative universe, studious little spectacle-wearer Georgios Panayiotou may have grown up to be an entomologist, engaged in the scientific study of insects (or maybe a newt fancier, like former Mayor of London Ken Livingstone). But by his own account, fate may have provided a more fortuitous swerve.

"What happened was I was about eight years old and I was running for lunch with a thousand other children," he would recall, many years later, in one of his celebrated interviews with chat-show veteran Michael Parkinson. "[I] tripped at the top of the stairs, slipped along the floor, hit this radiator and cracked my head open.

"There are two things I remember about waking up: one was that all the kids had gone; I'm lying there in a pool of blood and everyone's gone off to lunch – apart from this one girl. I had these two girls that fought over me at seven," laughed the adult Georgios. "They used to fight over me and the one who was, let's say, more homely was there when I woke up. I was bleeding really badly and this girl was crying next to me." Even at such a tender age, the gentle, sensitive young boy had learned how to capture the female heart.

"But the strange thing was, about two weeks later, I turned up at home with a violin. I really wish that I'd picked a different instrument, but that was the first one that I passed around. I decided after two weeks that this wasn't the instrument for me, [but] my parents decided, 'You've started so you'll finish!', and so I played it for seven years – very badly, I imagine."

According to his memories of the time, the boy had possessed no creative interest in music at all up to this point. "I'd been obsessed with bugs and insects, and also I'd been ahead of average in both English and maths. What happened was, in six months, I had no interest in the whole nature thing, I was *obsessed* with music and I couldn't do maths."

According to the adult Georgios's revised view of his early history, minor brain damage may have left him neurologically rewired – his observational focus switching to a mode in which sounds and emotions carried far greater meaning for him. "Nobody in my family seemed to notice but I became absolutely obsessed with music and everything changed after that," he insists.

The idea of the brain being divided into left (logic/organisation) and right (imagination/creativity) hemispheres is a much-argued notion. Some neuroscientists claim that it's an oversimplification of how our most complex organ works; others posit head injuries as a catalyst that can completely transform our personalities. But the idea clearly makes sense of his early experiences to the adult George Michael. It remains a bizarre possibility that a blow to the nuclei of the brain's temporal lobes – which is also its centre of emotion – may have released the late 20th/ early 21st century's genius of the love song like a genie from a lamp, all via the hard impact of an old-fashioned school radiator.

It was also at this time that a lady neighbour, hearing Georgios out on his morning round to dig up bugs, heard him singing to himself for the first time. "Doesn't your George have a lovely voice?" she remarked to Lesley.

This was the first time that his mother began to associate music with her young son. The Panayiotous were not a musical family, though Jack had amassed a small collection of Greek national folk music that left his son unmoved – the kind of bouzouki-backed 'ippy-dippy-dippy-da' restaurant music heard in the Cypriot tavernas of Holloway.

As an adult Georgios would observe, "The first real sign of obsession with music was with an old wind-up gramophone that mum had thrown out into the garage." His mum also gave him three 45 singles to play on the old antique deck. It was music of its era. Not the legendary beat groups of the time, like The Beatles or the Stones – that kind of thing had passed his hard-working young mother by – but it was still classic sixties pop: two singles by Motown girl group The Supremes, the black girl trio who rivalled The Beatles for popularity, and one by macho Welsh vocalist Tom Jones.

"I used to come home from school literally every day, go out to the garage, wind this thing up and play them," he recalled with a still palpable excitement. "I was totally obsessed with the *idea* of the records; I loved them as things and just being able to listen to music was incredible. Later they bought me a cassette with a microphone that I used to tape things off the radio – and at that point I became even more obsessive about it."

It's lost in time as to which of The Supremes' sixties hits were on the 45s, but the classic singles of Diana Ross, Mary Wilson and Florence Ballard ranged from light, poppy, showtune-like numbers such as 'The Happening' and 'You Can't Hurry Love' to the ingeniously arranged heartbreak ballad 'You Keep Me Hangin' On', with its Morse-code guitar motif. As Tamla Motown's showcase girl group, The Supremes – as much as Marvin Gaye or the young Stevie Wonder – were label founder Berry Gordy and songwriting team Holland-Dozier-Holland's ambassadors to the wider world of pop music, making black music accessible to all.

Tom Jones was a different kind of vocalist altogether – but his mid-late sixties belters would not have happened without the influence of soul and R&B music. While his biggest hits included a tearful country ballad and working men's club singalongs, early singles like 'It's Not Unusual', with its *big* vocal and brass orchestration, were a distinctly British take on soul music.[*]

The black soul singers who performed with the polish and choreography of Broadway musicals; the Welshman with the powerful voice who owed as much to black funk innovator James Brown as he did to a white boy like Elvis. It was an interracial mix and match that showed the universality of pop music, occasionally producing white vocalists who would later be termed 'blue-eyed soul' singers.

---

[*] This was reinforced in his later career by tunes like 'Sex Bomb' and a cover of Prince's 'Kiss'.

And little Georgios was becoming attentive to these exciting musical hybrids. As part of his newfound obsession, he was drinking it all in, recording it on his handheld cassette player and studying it – every last note of it.

CHAPTER 2

Hello Yellow Brick Road

In 1973, the year of his tenth birthday, keen young music fan Georgios Panayiotou bought his first 45rpm single. It was 'You're So Vain' by Carly Simon, an evergreen radio favourite that stands apart from the young boy's usual tastes. A catchy character-assassination sketch, the object of svelte young songstress Carly's disillusionment was said, for many years, to be Hollywood actor and legendary lady-killer Warren Beatty. It's only in the new millennium that speculation has attached itself to record company boss David Geffen, then the co-director of Asylum Records in California. While listening back then to the top ten, the young George Michael can have had no inkling whatsoever that the song might be linked to a US record producer who, 20 years hence, would play a role in his own career.

And besides – this West Coast singer-songwriter stuff wasn't the kind of thing young Georgios usually went for. The year 1973 saw the tail-end of the glam-rock era – though many of its most popular acts, like Slade and T.Rex, were still in full flight. Less of a musical craze than a fad for dressing up rock/pop in glitter, sequins and theatrical costumes, the gaudiness of glam rejected the pomposity of much post-sixties rock music in favour of a camp showmanship that recalled fifties rock'n'roll.

Added to the tacky trappings was a sexual ambivalence that glam's premiere performers wore like a badge of rebellion. The androgynous David Bowie was the first artiste to nonchalantly confide to the press that he was bisexual, creating an alter ego, Ziggy Stardust, who seemed part-alien creature and part-explosion in a Max Factor factory. There was a dark artiness to Bowie that many younger pop fans found off-putting at the time, and young Georgios's attitude to him was more of respect than outright adulation. That balance would be redressed in later years, as the young man recognised the extraordinariness of what Bowie achieved in the seventies, in terms of both his diverse music and his ever-changing image.

But for young Georgios, as for most pop kids, it had to be about *fun*, and the tacky early-mid seventies provided an abundance of that. First of all there was campy glam band The Sweet, pounding out catchy but meaningless anthems like 'Block Buster!' and looking, as it was said, like tyre-fitters in drag. Rather classier were new arrivals Queen, whose early identity as a kind of glam-pop version of Led Zeppelin was announced in hits like 'Killer Queen' and 'Now I'm Here'. The young George enjoyed their early records – though, like most British pop kids, he probably wouldn't class himself as an outright fan until the epochal release of 'Bohemian Rhapsody', which would top the charts throughout the Christmas/New Year season of 1975.

This young northwest London suburbanite definitely preferred pop (the stuff you heard in the charts, which your mother might hum along to) to rock (which was bombastic, guitar-dominated and supposedly more serious). Of that early seventies period, he was one of the few self-confessed *male* fans of David Cassidy, the flaxen-haired American pretty boy who found fame in *The Partridge Family* TV series. Cassidy would go on to build a solo career on sensitive ballads that would have sounded equally apt with a female vocalist, like a cover of Dusty Springfield's 'How Can I Be Sure?'*

---

* In his early heyday, Cassidy was considered exclusively a 'girls' act' – as Wham! once were – and paid the price for it when scenes echoing Beatlemania ended in a girl

But Georgios Panayiotou's early musical idol was an unlikely figure who hailed from an outer suburb just several short miles from Edgware. Viewers of the 2005 documentary *George Michael: A Different Life* will recall the ebullient child's voice captured on his cassette recorder, la-la-ing the intro of 1972 hit 'Crocodile Rock'. By now in the habit of mimicking or reinterpreting his chart favourites, the boy's prepubescent tones almost evoke the Greek folk music in his dad's record collection. But it was Elton John that he truly loved.

Born plain Reg Dwight in the obscure Middlesex town of Pinner, Elton is the epitome of how a pop singer can reinvent himself. Before becoming a major star back home in the UK, the former pub blues pianist played residences in Los Angeles with songs (taken from early albums like *Tumbleweed Connection* and *Honky Chateau*) suffused with American movie imagery. Then a homely, prematurely balding young man in his twenties, he triumphantly took his homeland by becoming a pantomime caricature of a rock star: his short sight was made into a virtue by adopting ever more absurd outsize specs, his rapidly thinning scalp supplanted by a series of wigs and hair transplants.

In 1973, the year that Georgios truly discovered him, the ever more flamboyant Elton paid tribute to his Hollywood view of the world with the hit albums *Don't Shoot Me, I'm Only The Piano Player* and *Goodbye Yellow Brick Road*, the covers of both evoking the movies. It was as if the self-reinvented star dismissed his own local history and culture as mundane, pop culture providing his only meaningful reference points. In this sense, Elton John was as much a self-created stage character as Ziggy Stardust – albeit one who wouldn't upset his fans' parents when

---

fan's death at London's White City Stadium in 1974. One decade later, during a brief comeback period, he would be interviewed by George Michael for *Ritz* magazine. The identification George feels with David is palpable, and the younger singer takes the opportunity to express how undervalued he feels as a pop songwriter: "I think the problem these days… is that unless the music you put to those lyrics, or whatever you're singing, is blatantly non-commercial, then nobody gives a fuck what you're singing about.' George also paid tribute by singing backing vocals on Cassidy's 1985 UK hit, 'The Last Kiss'.

he slotted comfortably into *The Morecambe & Wise Christmas Show* a couple of years later. Elton was the modern showman you could happily take home to mum; he had also become a hero to 10-year-old Georgios, who only in his wildest dreams could imagine a time when his pop idol might be a friend and mentor.

★★★

Their exposure to pop culture aside, the aspirational Panayiotou family tried to keep Georgios and his two sisters in touch with their Greek Cypriot roots. Visits to the old country would continue in that same year of 1973, after the boy's tenth birthday.

This was also the second and last time he felt the sting of his father's hand. When his young son and the boy's slightly older cousin, Andros, were naughty enough to steal from a local shopkeeper, Jack stopped Georgios' nascent thieving career with a short, sharp smack. It was the last time the little boy would misbehave in that way.

"We completely rifled this shop," he'd later recall. "It was a game a lot of kids play – you steal something and the next day you go back for something bigger. It started off with sweets and progressed to a 32-box carton of toy cars.

"Andros and I were on… one of those beaches where you can go out for literally half a mile and the water is still only between your waist and your knees. Beautiful white sand, perfectly clear water. Suddenly, we saw the manager of the shop approaching our mothers on the beach. And we just tore out to sea!"

It was several hours before the two cousins conceded to come in and take their punishment, by which time the shopkeeper had come to the apartments where both were staying and dumped a big bag full of evidence – empty toy cartons. "But you don't even *like* Dinky toys!" protested Georgios's mother, before his father gave him the only old-style parental thrashing he ever received.

"My dad never used to hit me so it really shocked me, it worked," his son would later admit.

This was also the year before the eruption of the Turkish-Greek civil war. In 1974, a coup by the Greek colonels' military dictatorship deposed Archbishop Makarios and replaced him with a junta. The Turkish government's response to the threat was swift, dispatching an invasion force. For a brief period that year, much blood was spilled and much of the Famagusta region lay in war-torn ruin. The ethnic Turks would now dominate Cyprus.

Jack and Lesley Panayiotou did not take their family back to the island for two or three years after the civil war. When they did eventually return, Georgios was 13 or 14, and his aunts and uncles had been displaced to camps just outside the harbour city of Limassol. "The refugee camps that my father's family lived in after they were turfed out of their village were developed," he'd recall, "and they lived in better conditions than they had in that old peasant village, but they all missed it, they wished they still lived there and it was a shame to have to change so late in their lives."

Further change was afoot when all of his father's siblings gradually migrated to Britain, once again with Jack's financial help. Only one sister chose to emigrate to the Greek mainland instead.

As an adult, Georgios Panayiotou would look back at the simpler days of his father's early life, quietly mourning a way of life that had passed. He would return himself in the eighties, but by then life was changing further still; on the first occasion, in 1983, he and his musical partner had recently delivered Wham!'s first album to their record label; by the time of his second solo visit, he was a bona fide superstar and Cyprus was well on its way to becoming a noisy tourist trap for drunken Brits.

("I remember everyone being so friendly, so real when I was a kid, and all that's changing," the adult George would reflect, "the changes that happen when tourism comes to a community like that are so sudden, so extreme...")

These ethnic roots aside, however, the grown adult would reflect on how "our upbringing wasn't very Greek. It's completely different when you don't have two Greek parents." On holiday in Cyprus, he was intrigued to see a different side of his father – a resurgent echo of a younger man, dancing to traditional folk music and agilely balancing

19

a wine or brandy glass on his forehead. It was good to see Dad enjoy himself like that – but personally, it left him cold.

Georgios would measure his father's ethnic bias only in as far as he was allowed more personal leeway than his sheltered sisters. All three children were also made to attend Saturday lessons in the Greek language, in Willesden, London NW10. "But everyone else in the classroom had two Greek parents and they could speak it already – they just couldn't write or read it." With neither spoken nor written Greek as a starting part, all that the young boy managed to learn in two years of lessons was a few words in parrot fashion.

"I can speak the occasional swear word," he'd concede. "Because my mother used to speak the Greek swear words when we were somewhere in public and she didn't want the people to know… She would say the words in Greek quietly and we knew what she was saying.

"I have never felt any ethnic connection between the Greeks and me other than how hairy I am," George would insist. "Hirsute. That's a good word." Indeed, it's a fitting description of the man who, when he adopted the mid-eighties fashion for designer stubble, was effortlessly able to grow a layer of facial hair all the way up to his cheekbones.

Despite this lack of ethnic identification, he did concede that, "I'm glad that my father is Mediterranean and I'm not just of English stock. I think I would be a different person, I think I would have grown up with less belief, more reservations about what I wanted to do with my life."

It's a peculiar trait of the British that we can be ashamed of our own aspirations – conscious that we're getting above our allotted station, or that our ambitions might overreach our abilities. In this sense, George Michael's mixed ethnic origins may have been an early saving grace. As the watching world is now well aware, this naturally talented man is far from free of personal insecurities or emotional flaws. But perhaps, if he'd been weighed down with English diffidence, his talent might have been strangled at birth.

Which is not to say that his very singular ambitions received total support. Jack Panos may have provided evidence aplenty of what hard work can achieve, but he'd also find his son's personal aims and aspirations difficult to comprehend. "I always saw it through my mother's eyes in terms of what I should be after," an older George would reflect. It was Lesley who would remain the mainstay throughout his life; it would be she who bolstered his confidence with her own belief when the old man was bemused by his son's life choices.

The mid-seventies was also the period when Georgios – who later described himself as "quite a cute little kid, very popular" – began to develop his first pre-adolescent insecurities. It coincided with that time when a boy's hormones start to run amok and, if his bodily frame has the natural inclination to do so, he starts to fill out.

In the September of 1974, Georgios became a first-year pupil of Kingsbury High School in London NW9. It was also at this time that his family were preparing to decamp from north London. Jack, by now the proprietor of a second successful restaurant in Edgware, had invested in a big house in Radlett, in leafy Hertfordshire – which, according to his son, was "a real old shithole" and would take a year to renovate. Jack was fast becoming a self-made millionaire and his increasing prosperity meant he could afford to indulge his family – for example, he'd buy his musically inclined son a full drum kit for Christmas 1975 – and himself, splashing out on a racehorse before the seventies were out.

But for now, the family home in Burnt Oak had been sold to put toward the costs of the new house, so the only place they could stay was in the flat above one of the restaurants where young Georgios was able to indulge the natural appetite of growing young boys. Steak and chips was sent up from the kitchen every night; he could go downstairs for dessert, ice cream or maybe rum baba, "whenever I felt like it – which was often…"

It had the inevitable effect: "In the course of a year I went from being a skinny 11-year-old to a fat 12-year-old. It happened at exactly the same time as puberty. From then on I was quite a tubby kid… I was just kind of *big* all over."

It was an inopportune time to make the transformation, but then the onset of puberty is never easy. Georgios at this time wore wire-framed specs to correct his myopia; his hirsute tendencies manifested in dark frizzy hair and heavy eyebrows that grew close to a monobrow. Georgios was no longer quite the cute little boy that the girls used to fight over at primary school. Not that the onset of adolescent insecurity ever stopped a pubescent boy's sexuality from erupting.

"I was a great masturbator," George would later confide. "A very early masturbator. I heard that a lot of children are very sexual when they are young, and then there is a point around six or seven where they totally blank sexuality out of their minds until puberty – and that is pretty much how I remember it. I remember the old doctors and nurses games when I was very young. *Very* young."

Such occasional hints at his formative sexual experiences would become tantalising over the years, particularly as the press and public engaged in speculation about George Michael's sexuality. George himself has suggested in recent times that he's ready to tell all – including, it seems, of the first childish blooming of his sexual instincts.

In any case, his first high school year was as much of a false start as his early sexual flowering. When his family finally made the shift from Edgware to Hertfordshire, he would have to start all over again, leaving behind the north London suburbs he'd known all his life. The rural Home Counties didn't bode well for him – he may have been far from the centre of town, but he was just starting to realise the benefits of being a London boy. That summer, around the time of his twelfth birthday, he'd been one of a huge 75,000 crowd watching Elton John promote his album of autobiographical songs, *Captain Fantastic And The Brown Dirt Cowboy*, at nearby Wembley Arena. It was Georgios's first live gig and an overwhelming spectacle – with pyrotechnic explosions, outrageous costumes and dry ice. This was no longer Reg from Pinner at the piano stool but a character who, to his congregated fans, was way larger than life.

But still, such flamboyance belonged on a different planet to the young Georgios. His path to success, as decreed by his parents, would be education, and they were determined he should take up the opportunities they never had. At the age of only 11, however, he'd already provided them with a shock.

"When George turned the private school or education down," as Jack Panos would reflect, "it was very hard for me to not 'accept' but [to] give up to him."

"After I refused to go to a private school – which would have killed my parents financially – my dad gave up on me career-wise," George acknowledged. "I didn't want to go to private school because my friends would have called me a sissy. Plus I would have been intimidated by it and I really didn't want to be with those kinds of people."

The Panayiotou family may now have entered the respectable middle classes, but they were still *arrivistes*. As with many young kids from a socially mobile family, their son had a horror of leaving his longstanding friends behind. Added to which may have been a sense that the sons of the snugly established may not have shared his love of pop culture that made his life so worthwhile. For restaurateur Jack Panos's son, a career in finance or law was off the menu.

"I don't remember ever telling them that I was going to be a pop star at any given point," George would later reflect. "They just knew that I was obsessed with music and that's what I wanted to do. The defining moment was telling them I wouldn't go to private school."

Still, on September 9, 1975 he would separate from old schoolmates like David Mortimer to become the new boy at Bushey Meads comprehensive school in Bushey, Herts. His nervousness can't have been helped by squeezing his expanding frame into the school's regulation dark green blazer and light green pullover. So his form teacher tried to put him at ease by designating one of his classmates as a mentor. In Georgios's case, it was a slim-faced boy whose skin had a similar light Mediterranean tone to his own.

"That morning, when I stood up at the front of the class with the teacher and she asked if anyone wanted me to sit next to them," the adult George asked his mentor many years later, "do you remember by any chance what went through your head?"

"Yeah," answered Andrew Ridgeley, as cheeky and brazen as ever. "'New kid. *Give him to me!*' I looked around and…" Andrew mimed the rest of the class dropping their knuckles to the floor, then himself motioning sharply for the new arrival to *come here*. He'd never been entrusted with a new boy before, so this was his big day.

By playtime, Andrew was recruiting the new kid with the Greek name to play 'King of the Wall' with the other boys. It was a local variation on any game in which you had to try to gain a piece of playground territory without the others kicking your backside, in this case by staying on top of the wall without getting pushed off.

"I taunted George. I made him play King of the Wall," Andrew admitted later. "He didn't want to do it – he doesn't like sport. In that sense, he is not very physical." But he was still a burly 12-year-old boy bursting with protein, fed on his dad's Aberdeen Angus steaks, and he kicked his classroom mentor's skinny young arse right off.

"And from then on we made up for each other's deficiencies," Andrew Ridgeley would reflect. It was the beginning of a friendship in which any insecurity young Georgios felt would be soothed by his mate's grinning confidence. For his part, the Ridgeley kid would soon discover that his newfound friend was not just your run-of-the-mill schoolboy.

They also found that they had a few things in common. Most obviously, Andrew – who, having been born in January 1963, was almost exactly five months older than Georgios – was the second son of a mixed parentage, his half-Egyptian Jewish/half-Italian father marrying an English schoolteacher after migrating to Britain. Before meeting his wife, Jennifer, Albert Ridgeley had led a chequered life that included learning six languages, serving in the RAF and possibly a little cloak and dagger in Cold War-era Berlin. Relocation to the UK had meant a more staid life working for a camera manufacturer in Surrey, where Andrew was born.

"Girls really liked him," a young George Michael later observed of his Wham! partner. "People wanted to be like him. Which for someone who was the same colour as a lot of the people they took the piss out of was quite remarkable… People called Andrew a Paki, meaning a

Pakistani… but the prejudice never seemed to occur to him because he was so popular."[*]

The two boys also shared a sense of humour, that kind of confiding private laughter that creates an us-against-the-adult-world camaraderie. To Andrew, life mostly consisted of good-natured jokes; he had the kind of frivolous nature which many adults don't take to, but which would win others over with a brown-eyed smile. He also revelled in how he'd rechristened Georgios, his new friend, amused to hear Yioda and Melanie pronounce their brother's name with a soft 'g'.

"My nickname comes from the fact that Andrew Ridgeley came home with me when I was 13, or 12, he hadn't met my parents yet, and he heard them calling me 'Yorgo'," laughed George. "In Greek, if you're talking to someone you remove the 's', if you're talking about someone you put the 's' back, so they called me 'Yorgo'. So Andrew went back to school and said to everybody, 'Look, they call him "Yoghurt" at home!' So I was 'Yoghurt' for years and then I got abbreviated to 'Yog' – all my closest friends call me 'Yog'."

"I remember the first time that I was invited to his house in Radlett," Andrew later recalled. "What surprised me was how wealthy they seemed to be. I would have thought that George would be a different character coming from a background like that – it was later that I realised his mum and dad had started out on an economic and class level that was very similar to my parents'."

While Andrew became a fixture in the Panayiotou house after school, it took the best part of a year for his more studious new friend to pluck up the courage to introduce him. "I don't think his mother particularly cared for me at first," he understatedly concedes. There was something about this boy, his cocksure attitude and his easy grin, that could make some distrust him. After all, Yog's family were new arrivals to the affluent middle class; while their children were by now relatively

---

[*] In the less culturally sensitive Britain of the seventies, 'Paki' was a term also applied to kids of Indian, Arabic, North African or even Maltese descent. It was an all-purpose label for those whose dark complexioned parents weren't from 'round here'.

privileged, they received nothing that they hadn't worked or performed chores for. The value of hard work and deferred gratification had been instilled into them from an early age, and Georgios had developed the gentle temperament of a boy constantly surrounded by supportive female relatives. One of the only ways he noisily let off steam was with the drum kit that Jack bought him for Christmas.

And now Andrew Ridgeley – this by all accounts intelligent and charmingly laid-back wastrel – looked set to try to entice Lesley's little boy into a life of indolence and messing around. It was a potential horror to Yog's mother: she and her husband had fought inch by inch for everything that they had, without the benefit of college educations. She'd try to ensure that her son – who'd excelled at all his core subjects and was at the very least a potential candidate for university – didn't throw away all his options for the sake of friendship, by barring the boy from the house unless there were adults present if need be.

"Extremely confident," was the elderly Jack Panos's recollection of the young Andrew many years later. "Very, very, *very* confident."

It was this devil-may-care nature that made his new friend's parents wary. With so much time elapsed, however, the old boy would later concede how the Ridgeley boy had been far from a negative influence on his son. "Because they were so close, at the end of the day I thought I have to trust my son's judgment on his friends."

Which is not necessarily the way Andrew remembers his reception at the time. But still, the two boys were now established as firm friends and it would take something drastic to break that early teen alliance.

In the *Different Life* documentary, George is visiting his old friend's West Country home, complete with grand piano in the comfortably light-toned lounge. "I think I'd probably worked out that you were quite a cool person to hang around with," George reflects on the early days of their friendship.

"I didn't think you were that bright actually," ripostes Andy, now middle-aged and balding but still handsome and irrepressibly cheeky.

CHAPTER 3

Feet Will Find Their Rhythm

Cocky young Andrew Ridgeley and his good mate, Yog, were 13 when Elton John had his first number one hit single in the UK.

In fact, 'Don't Go Breaking My Heart', which topped the charts for several weeks in the summer of 1976, wasn't a solo single *per se* by the bespectacled superstar. It was a duet with Kiki Dee, a female vocalist who had sung backing vocals for Dusty Springfield, was briefly the first British signing to Tamla Motown and whose biggest solo hit was the hypnotically romantic 'Amoureuse', in 1973.

In a style befitting his singing partner's track record (with many seventies pop fans assuming, in their naivety, that Kiki was Elton's girlfriend), 'Don't Go Breaking My Heart' was stripped of the pounding-piano-and-chiming-guitar rock trappings that accompanied much of Elton's early music. With a lightweight string arrangement influenced by Motown and the Philly soul sound, this was soul music by and for white people. It was also the kind of thing that connected with the boys from Bushey Meads.

Yog's musical knowledge and keen enthusiasm were catnip to his new best mate. But it was Andrew who first suggested that they should form a band. With both of them still only 13, it must have seemed like a distant dream fed by the Thursday-night TV nirvana of *Top Of The Pops*.

Or at least George saw it that way. Ever since he'd buddied up with Andrew, he recognised that his friend was the outgoing one, the confident one, the boy who would be a superstar. The only catch was, how would the boy from Bushey achieve stardom? "He looked good, he dressed good and he *thought* he was a good footballer," noted his friend of a common fantasy among British schoolboys. As for himself, George may have been taken to watch Arsenal FC at Highbury, but that was more a mark of his parents' north London loyalties.

"He didn't care if it was as a football player or a pop star or whatever – he just wanted to be famous. And as we grew up together, I encouraged him musically… What I got from him were the aspirations to become the type of person I wanted to be seen as. It was a good exchange."

To young Yog, with his insecurities about his appearance and his parents' rigid insistence that he should put his energies and ambitions into his schoolwork, the idea of two young pubescent pups strutting their stuff beneath the sodium lights must have seemed a virtual impossibility.

It was a seductive impossibility though. The key to it all lay in making a career out of fun, which, in their imaginations at least, would be their personal rebellion against the drabness of suburbia. By the time they began their second year at Bushey Meads, in September 1976, the less forthcoming of the Ridgeley-Panayiotou partnership in crime was trying to dress like he meant it.

With Yioda and Melanie's help, he kept his sporadic eruptions of bad skin (particularly applicable to someone raised on a hearty diet of Anglo-Greek food) under control with acne cream; after a few months of trying to discipline his dark frizzy hair, salvation came early in 1977 with the shaggy perms for men popularised by Liverpool FC star Kevin Keegan and imitated by sheepskin-wearing young football fans around the UK. Unwanted frizz was transformed into cultivated curls.

Then there were the glasses. After much resistance from his optician, George got his own way when his mum and dad supported his demand for contact lenses – "The optician kept saying he's too young, he's too young, but I wanted them so badly." They were in favour of anything that lent their son more confidence. This, after all, was the boy who stayed home when his best friend Andrew was strutting like a peacock around the Bushey Meads school disco.

"George never used to go to school discos," confirmed Andy. "I guess it was shyness… it wasn't his gig. Not until later. Not until *Saturday Night Fever.*"

It would still be a wrench for the self-conscious boy to motivate himself onto the floor, and it was rare for him to dance unless coaxed into it. But this was the kind of scenario that was best tackled by Andrew: give him a few weeks of working out little dance routines with his mate at weekends, provided with Dutch courage by Woodpecker cider and a tape of the latest disco hits, and he'd have Yog dancing there alongside him. It was the birth of George and Andrew as a duo proper, and it all took place beneath the red, orange and green disco lights in their school hall.

They synced together to the dance hits of the era: 'Dance, Dance, Dance (Yowsah, Yowsah, Yowsah)', an early hit by Chic which forsook the love lyrics of classic soul in favour of the pure funk inherent in the title; "I Feel Love" by Donna Summer, the German electro-disco single with the black American vocalist which became, to a large extent, the sound of the early eighties; but most of all there was *Saturday Night Fever.*

"[*Saturday Night Fever*] knocked our socks off," Andrew commented later. "It wasn't just the film, it was everything it triggered – which was modern disco, modern club music. Everything comes from there. There was disco before *Saturday Night Fever* but after that it all caught fire. It revolutionised dance music. And us."

Movies had announced the latest wave of youth music fashions before and would do so again, from *Rock Around The Clock* in the fifties to the rap showcase *Krush Groove* in the eighties. Like them, *SNF* exploited a musical form; unlike them, it didn't so much ride on the music's coat tails as mark the exact point that disco – comprising elements of soul, funk and a little instrumental muzak – transformed from a weekend night out for urban US ghetto dwellers into an international phenomenon.

In part it was the way in which new star John Travolta, in the role of macho Brooklynite dancer Tony Manero, carried off a combination of masculine wish fulfilment and realistic angst. Not to mention how he carried himself, both on and off the dance floor. The young George and Andrew were among an entire sub-generation of young men who, with their youthful Mediterranean good looks, could see a little of themselves in the Italianate Travolta as he went walking rhythmically down the street to the Bee Gees' 'Stayin' Alive'.

Even in leafy Hertfordshire, Tony Manero was the prototype for the suburban soul boy. Their fashions may have been a little more UK-centric and less seventies American – no sharp-creased flares, white suits and pompadour hairstyles, more perms, dungarees and cords, although Yog would acquire a bright red disco suit – but *this* was the youth culture of the late seventies, which is more often cited as the golden era of punk rock. It's true that the Sex Pistols and their ilk were making headlines all over the UK, but their music meant little to fun-loving suburbanites like Andrew and George. Meanwhile, the late 1977 release of the movie was prefaced by a whole series of singles from the newly disco-ized Bee Gees, who'd formerly been a sibling band of ballad singers – 'Stayin' Alive', 'Night Fever', 'More Than a Woman' and the slow-dance school disco favourite 'How Deep Is Your Love?'

It was the soundtrack of 1977, to which Georgios Panayiotou first found his feet and bolstered his confidence. "Dancing was a means of self-expression for George," described Andy. "He is a great dancer, he really is, and that was when it began, that was when he began to express his physicality, his sexuality."

"I was a terrible dancer," contradicted George, "but Andrew and I worked out these routines that we could do at school discos... I was the kid with the sense of humour who would muck about and everybody liked but who didn't get thought about when it came to parties because they didn't expect him to get off with anyone... Then one night I got so drunk I burst a blood vessel in my eye. My eye was red for three weeks. That was the night I came home saying, 'I'm so ugly, no girl will ever like me' – but it had less to do with self-doubt than it did with the bottle of Spanish wine I had drunk. I wasn't racked by self-doubt, but I still didn't feel very confident."

By his own admission, the summer of 1977 had been "the time of spin-the-bottle, cider and everybody fucking in the bedrooms... This was the pre-AIDS generation. I don't suppose the current generation of 14- or 15-year-olds are very different." Media moralists may rage at the idea of teen and underage sex, but each generation has its own memories of what took place once the parents were safely out of the house. But still, as George would admit, he was never one of the kids to be invited upstairs. His own first tentative steps toward a boy-girl relationship would be much more innocent.

"Her name was Lesley Bywaters. Isn't that a lovely, romantic name?" he'd recall in an interview many years later. He also candidly acknowledged, "My mother's name is Lesley – she's not the first girl I was ever romantically linked with, unless you include breastfeeding, I suppose."

"She took off my glasses, which I wore at the time, and this is a typical story of my lack of self-esteem as a teenager. She said, 'Haven't you got beautiful eyes?' and I was convinced she was taking the piss out of me, so I just got up and left the party. That was it. I was actually in between her legs at the time, to be honest. But we did go out for a while after that. Her friends came and convinced me that she wasn't joking."

Lesley was a fellow pupil at Bushey Meads, and for about six weeks she and Yog were briefly an item. They would go out dancing at Bogart's Club in Harrow, one of the original suburban soul-boy discos. "The clubs in the suburbs were always more violent than those in the inner city," as Andrew acknowledged, but Bogart's was just a few miles on the bus and the tall, stocky 14-year-old Yog could make it past the doormen there.

The relationship with Lesley was short-lived, and by George's own account it apparently never made it past first base in sexual terms. But it was still a first love, and he celebrated their first full four weeks together by buying her a disco 12" (Chic's 'Dance, Dance, Dance').

(In 1996, when George Michael prefaced a much-heralded live concert for BBC Radio One with an interview by Chris Evans, the DJ urged the singer to dedicate the concert to "the first lady whose legs you were in-between"; at a time when the media was all but bursting to announce the open secret of his sexuality, George would dedicate the concert "entirely to Lesley Bywaters".)

While Yog remained the sexual novice, he was not regarded as the sexually ambiguous one in the Ridgeley-Panayiotou partnership. "He had luminous soul-boy gear – a sky blue, short-sleeved shirt with a shocking pink tie and cerise satin trousers," George described of Andrew. "And everyone used to say, 'Is he gay?' I used to say, 'No, I promise'... It didn't take much to be shocking in Bushey."

Andrew Ridgeley pushed the boat out a little further by turning up at the Panayiotou house on New Year's Day in a kilt, while the extended family were all present and suitably perturbed. While it was traditional Hogmanay wear, this conservative generation of Cypriots didn't share their ancient Greek ancestors' tolerance of men in skirts – or, indeed, of boy-on-boy love.

(Over the years that followed, gender-bender icon Boy George would look back and claim, "I always thought George was in love with Andrew, it's pretty obvious really." George would laughingly refute the rumour about his straight musical partner. "I can't think of anything less likely than Andrew and I sleeping together. Apart from anything, he's not my type – Andrew is *not* my type, way too pretty.")

As the era of *Saturday Night Fever* slipped into the late seventies, Yog and Andrew were faced with the traditional looming menace of mock O-levels (a trial run for the comprehensive school exams of their day). They were not unduly fazed. In fact, they were so little concerned that they opted for the other traditional schoolboy activity of bunking off instead.

"At school I don't think he did an awful lot of work and I did next to nothing," Andrew would admit. "Neither of us were interested in school beyond the social sense, as a meeting place." When they found out about where the Ridgeley boy had been leading their Georgios, Jack and Lesley were beside themselves with worry. "George was always a quiet boy. He wasn't the kind of boy to go wild," Jack Panos, by now a benign bearded bear of a man resembling Greek singer Demis Roussos, much later recalled. "And I think Andrew was the leader."

Instead of expending their energies on their studies, the two incorrigible boys were spending time up in Georgios's bedroom making parody tapes of the still relatively new and novel commercial radio stations; talk slots, jingles and ads were recorded and parodied, overlaid with an amateur soundtrack produced with Andrew's guitar and Yog's drums.*

Their corresponding comedy skits aside, music was by now becoming Yog and Andy's *raison d'etre*. Andrew, however, was not the most proficient musician that Georgios had regular contact with. That distinction belonged to his old friend David, whom he'd known since his earliest days at primary school in Kingsbury. A skilled guitarist, David was as much a child of seventies popular culture as his old schoolfriend – going as far as to change his surname from 'Mortimer', because it reminded him of Meg Mortimer (proprietor of the eponymous motel in cheesy UK soap opera *Crossroads*), to 'Austin' (redolent of Steve Austin in US TV show *The Six Million Dollar Man*). Together they would make their first forays into public performance.

"I would pretend that I was going to school but I would go to David's house and then we would go to London," explained George of his subterfuge as a 15-year-old. "David would bring his 12-string guitar. There was a really good pitch in Green Park tube station – it was good because the police didn't often move you on from there but you had to get there early." Halfway between Piccadilly and Trafalgar Square, Yog and David made their debut as musical buskers, away from the traditionally busier (and more jealously fought-over) pitches at Tottenham Court Road station.

---

* One of their favourite spoofs was of the *Saturday Night Fever* scene where Tony Manero is getting sexy with a girl who turns out to be a boy in the back of a car.

"We used to do David Bowie numbers and some Elton John songs. We had written a few things and we did those too. And Beatles things. I loved it, I loved busking. I loved the way it sounded – the way the voice and guitar would reverberate down the tube station. And I loved it that we were good and that we were getting paid for it." Their tube station performances gave a first airing to Georgios's earliest songs, as well as providing some pocket money for discos. It also allowed the new songs' composer to break through the embarrassment barrier, showcasing the singing talent that his father had disparaged.

"I think my father was in shock for the first couple of years of my career, because he really genuinely didn't believe that I was talented," George would much later concede. "And I hadn't really shown any particularly prodigious talent at 15, 16, I really hadn't. I listened to pop music incessantly, but there was no real outlet for that. I'd been chucked out of the choir for talking all the time, so there wasn't any real way of knowing that I had these abilities really."

"I always told him that he couldn't sing," Jack would confess years later, motioning toward his eyes. "Blinkered."

"He just thought, what chance was there that this kid was going to be some kind of millionaire pop star?" the adult George tried to empathise with his father. "I suppose that's what most parents would think, but certainly a parent who doesn't have a musical bone in their body…" His words drifted off, still apparently coming to terms with how his dad couldn't provide encouragement when he most felt he needed it. "He just thought I was a dreamer."

CHAPTER 4

Executive Business

In 1979, the era of The Specials and The Jam, music fell like rain to the streets. Or so George Michael would later have us believe in his song 'Round Here'.

In truth, his early musical stirrings at that time had to be forced out of him by his best mate. By this time Andrew had left Bushey Meads high school to attend local Cassio College in West Hertfordshire. "Suddenly, he was a serious fashion victim," George would recall. "He was wearing really outrageous clothes that looked absolutely terrible. And taking drugs and stuff." Such rock'n'roll indulgences were then a long way from Yog's own lifestyle in suburban Bushey – where he'd opted to stay on in the sixth form, studying English literature and art for 'A' levels.

"We were anyway at the time when people normally drift apart – and I think that would have happened to us if we hadn't had the band. And it was on the day he left school that he told me we should form a band."

"We had talked about doing it for such a long time," Andrew recollected for his friend's early nineties autobiography. "George said after the 'O' levels. He wanted to get his 'O' levels because his mum, his parents, were expecting it… Then he said after the 'A' levels. And I just said, 'No, George, it's *tonight*.'"

Not for the first or last time, Andrew Ridgeley had succeeded in breaking through his friend's innate cautiousness. Which was just as well, as the band he was intent on putting together would need someone with the aptitude to string a few lines together – as well as to sing the songs. The other members would be Andrew himself on rhythm guitar, David Austin on lead guitar, Andrew Leaver on bass and elder brother Paul Ridgeley on drums. They called themselves The Executive, and they played their first gig at a Methodist hall in Bushey on Guy Fawkes Night 1979 – going down a storm in front of a crowd of local friends, by all accounts.

George would remember their debut in song as "two little Hitlers in an old church hall", which refers to the clash of musical wills between him and the almost equally dominant David (rather than laid-back Andrew). Surprisingly, perhaps, their chosen musical genre was neither soul nor the soft rock that George had been steeped in throughout his youth, but the musical flavour of the day: ska.

Originally a jagged form of danceable rhythm and blues that rocked the dancehalls and shebeens of Jamaica, ska developed into the more laidback bluebeat, rocksteady and, later, bass-heavy reggae. It had now been revived in the UK as a post-punk musical craze, headed by the 2 Tone record label and leading bands The Specials, a mixed-race group from Coventry, and music hall-tinged white boys Madness, from the heart of north London. Both had released their debut singles over the last few months; if nothing else, The Executive were catching the tail-end of a wave.

The Executive would have been a classic teenage garage band – except that they rehearsed in their families' living rooms. David Austin reputedly received a bad electric shock round George's place. They had to slim down to a quartet and switch to a one-guitar/bass format when the second Andrew left, which was how they cut their first demo in a 16-track studio. It featured signature tune 'Rude Boy', a ska cover of the sixties Andy Williams tune 'Can't Get Used To Losing You' (also being played live by 2 Tone band The Beat, who didn't release it as a single until 1983) and, most quirkily, a ska arrangement of Beethoven's

'*Fur Elise*' (in tune with what Madness were doing with Tchaikovsky's 'Theme from *Swan Lake*'). The Executive scored zero out of ten for originality, but they were certainly of their time.

Most importantly, perhaps, The Executive was the vehicle that towed young Georgios Panayiotou right out of his shell. "Looking back on it, the confidence I had there for a short period of time is amazing," George would confess. "Because I still looked absolutely horrendous, I was way overweight, not really attractive at all, and yet I had more confidence when I was 16 than I have ever had. I looked gross, but when I looked in the mirror I felt great."

Cousin Andros, whom George then hadn't seen for some time but who'd remain close to him throughout most of his life, acknowledged the change in the boy's personal style: "He got off the bus and – he was a completely changed person. He had long hair, a beard – he was always real hairy – and he was wearing this ska suit, a second-hand old man's suit. I thought, 'What a wanker.'"

There was no uniform for the 2 Tone craze, but the initial look was two-toned tonic suits, narrow Sta-Prest trousers, loafers and white socks – just one manic bounce away from sixties mod fashion, with a razored suedehead haircut to go with it. Still, George was far from being the only longhaired/hirsute ska fiend in suburbia, as the craze briefly became a national phenomenon. As Andros remembers, however, his core musical tastes lay far away from the rough-cut Prince Buster 45s which inspired the movement: "He was still into his music – listening to the latest Elton John album, *concentrating* when *Top Of The Pops* came on. He didn't watch that show the way everyone else does – he *concentrated*."

As astute as he clearly was in assessing new trends, for George it was still his old favourites who carried the day. Little wonder, then, that when he and the ever-irrepressible Andrew started making the rounds of record company A&R (artists and repertoire) departments, they were treated as nothing more than just another band of teenage bandwagon jumpers. Andrew was always more optimistic, and therefore more deeply disappointed, when the suits behind the desk didn't see the potential in these amiable, well-spoken young men singing about being a 'rude boy', the Jamaican term for a delinquent, the original rude boys being the fashion template for their white counterparts, the skinheads.

Andrew found it harder to throw in the towel, but George, while disappointed, must have known that, at heart, they and their bandmates were as much rude boys as porkpie-hatted Neville Staple of The Specials was a suburban smoothie. For George was by now a dyed-in-the-wool soul boy – and Andrew would soon be a dole boy.

Undeterred, Andrew felt he'd made an important music industry contact when he sent their tape to Mark Dean – a young A&R man who lived just up the road from him in Chiltern Avenue, Bushey. Just three years older than Andrew and George, he was an old Bushey Meads boy who wore flash suits and flashed the cash in a popular local pub, the Three Crowns. He'd worked for The Jam's music publishers and had been instrumental in signing the leading band of the short-lived mod revival, Secret Affair, who had a chart hit with 'Time For Action'. For all that, Dean didn't fancy the chances of this local bunch of wannabe rude boys either, when his mother passed him the tape after much pestering from Andrew Ridgeley.

It was another knockback – but still, at least a music industry contact had been made. Dean would eventually work with both Andrew and George, although all three would come to regard the experience as a lesson harshly learned.

The final straw came when David Austin told the band he'd got them a booking at Harrow College, where he was studying, supporting a lower-league punk band called The Vibrators who were still playing the circuit. When the social secretary protested to George that he had no record of the booking, the whole thing fell apart in a welter of recrimination. After the inevitable explosive arguments, David upped sticks to the Far East to play with a band in Thailand, and Paul Ridgeley joined a jazz-funk group. As for George and Andrew – well, what kind of group would it be if there were only two of them? They would try to recruit other local musicians, though they had great trouble finding anyone who mirrored their own level of commitment. All the same, the musical train was on the track now and it would start to slowly pick up steam.

For all its brevity, the fizzled-out firework that was The Executive had a boosting effect on young George's confidence that was soon noticeable. "He had been going out to London clubs, to Le Beat Route, and he said you have to come," Andros Georgiou told George's official biographer. "So I went with him and I was outraged at what was going on around me. I never knew these things were going on out there!" This was the early eighties, when the kids they were calling New Romantics were bringing a peacock exuberance to Soho clubs like Le Beat Route and the more outrageous Blitz. Eschewing the grey gloominess of much post-punk music, their music was a mix of Bowie, Roxy Music, electro-disco and funk; their fashion style was a hybrid of high couture on the cheap and transsexual outrageousness. Luminaries on the scene included new chart band Spandau Ballet and the then young and svelte Boy George; to pull a girl at a club only to get her home and find that she was, in fact, a boy was not unknown.

"Just walking around London at 11 o'clock at night was outrageous to me," Andros admitted. "But he had been doing this for a while so he was used to it, he was very cool about it." Indeed, this was the nightlife world where the West End's demi-monde would embrace the newly emerging style media; it was a world the young George already felt himself becoming a part of, though for now it was just the place where he spent pocket money earned from busking and babysitting.

The world that his family wanted him to embrace was that of academia, however, and it was one which he wanted no part of. While mum and dad still pegged their hopes on him entering university after his 'A' levels, he held no such aspirations. Where his hopes lay was indicated in the present he requested for his 17th birthday – a portastudio, to make demo tapes of the songs he was now writing. Jack Panos was having none of it, buying his son a pair of antique guns for £5k that he claimed would increase in value over time.

George would tell in his 1990 autobiography of an argument with his father in the car, when he was playing the tape of a song, co-written with the recently returned David Austin, and receiving the usual discouragement. "I said, 'You have been rubbing this shit into my face for the last five years.' I told him, 'There is no way I am not going to try to do this so the least you could do is give me some moral support.'"

His disgusted father merely sounded the opinion that all 17 year olds want to be pop stars, and that for most it's a hopeless aspiration. To which George gave the classic retort: "All 12 year olds want to be pop stars." He'd nurtured the dream since he was younger than that and now, on the cusp of manhood, it was still his consuming obsession.

When George did eventually leave school after gaining respectable grades in English literature and art, in the summer of 1981, the UK was not flushed with optimism. Rising youth unemployment under the Conservative government of Margaret Thatcher was leading to a kind of entrenched despair among many of the young; instinctive racism and dubious SUS (suspicious person) laws led the police forces of many inner cities to make enemies of black and white, the merely alienated and the criminally inclined alike. The tension resulted in a number of flashpoint riots all over the country, from Brixton to Merseyside, as England seemed to be going up in flames. The seeming hopelessness was recorded in, of all places, one of that summer's number one records, the danceably despairing 'Ghost Town' by The Specials.

And George and Andrew? They were enjoying what George would later call "probably the happiest year I have ever had."

In our own time of rising unemployment and austerity measures, it's often forgotten that there was once an upside to being on the dole for the aspiring dreamer. The Tory government's monetarist policy measured everything from human potential to public utilities in terms of cost and value-for-money; with only scant regard for the impact on human lives, the monetarists accepted that there had to be a pool of unemployment in order to keep the employment market competitive.

With the British economy making a painful enforced transition from manufacturing to services (i.e. from making to selling things – which would result in increasingly fewer workforce skills outside of IT), the government of the time seemed to accept that a life on pretty minimal state benefits would be the fate of a sizeable minority.

It sorted the boys from Bushey down to the ground. While Andrew was, in George's words, "a lazy bastard" and was quite happy to accept unemployment as a lifestyle, his friend and musical partner happily adapted to the casual work culture. Unlike Andrew's more lenient parents, the Panayiotous would never have permitted their boy not to work; instead, he took on two jobs at a time and was paid cash-in-hand whenever possible, earning what he thought was the princely sum of £70 per week. After giving £25 to his parents for housekeeping, the remainder was his to spend on being "a club man or a pub man".

"I was 18 and I felt that the way the media were representing kids my age was completely negative," George later reflected. "There were things going wrong in terms of unemployment and riots but the media were giving the impression that everything was hopeless and you shouldn't even *try* to do anything."

Instead, George used his various jobs as support for his apprenticeship as a songwriter – while Andrew made musical contributions, gave constructive criticism and pondered the practicalities of actually getting a musical career underway in the comfort of his bedroom. George worked on a building site for three days, until reaching the conclusion that work was one thing but hard physical labour was out of the question. From there, his time was divided between a day job as a cinema usher and the most unlikely deejaying gig – at the Bel Air restaurant in down-home Bushey.

"Being a DJ is one thing but being a DJ in a restaurant is horrible," he opined in his autobiography, with a touch of self-deprecating humour, "because you are standing there and everybody's talking, the knives are going, the glasses are rattling and there's a bit of background music and everyone's well into their evening when suddenly the music stops and you say – 'GOOD EVENING, LADIES AND GENTLEMEN, I HOPE YOU ENJOYED YOUR MEAL HERE AT THE BEL AIR

RESTAURANT.' And the whole place stops while everyone looks for where the noise came from." It evokes *The Muppet Show*'s 'Veterinarian's Hospital', where the characters look under sheets and gurneys to find where the announcer's voice is coming from.

While George was commuting to and from his usher's job and the cheesiest DJ slot around, by bus and train, he was mentally preoccupied with what would become his first ever professionally recorded songs. Snatches of lyrics, tunes, instrumental motifs, all would be duly jotted down in notebooks, rewritten and revised. Andrew, meanwhile, was going through some significant events of his own.

In January 1981, on the night before his 18th birthday, the celebrating Andy had met a girl at the Three Crowns. Shirlie Holliman had been in the year above the boys at Bushey Meads, but had never made social contact with them before. She was a striking natural blonde, effortlessly feminine. The young Ridgeley made a move on her straight away. "We just got chatting, it was so instant," Shirlie later recalled. "He started telling me about his band and their singer – and I kept saying, 'Oh no, I want to sing, you have to get rid of your singer.' Not knowing it was George."

Shirlie Holliman had never made a move towards her own dream of a musical career; in fact, she was training to be a horse-riding instructor at the time. But she soon became as intrigued by Andrew Ridgeley, his best friend and their little world as he obviously was by her. She would become a fixture in their lives, running them around their favourite venues in her car (conveniently for them, as neither boy held a driving licence). They would go swimming together at Watford pool, where David Austin was now working as a lifeguard, spin out the hours at McDonald's by making coffee and milkshakes last interminably – or, demonstrating how far she'd entered the boys' private world, they would all make spoof radio tapes together.

It was the beginning of a relationship with Andrew that would last two years – while her association with both the boys would go on for much longer. Indeed, it would become emblematic of the time when they suddenly exploded into popular culture. "The first time I met the boys together, they were such great friends," Shirley later recollected. "The humour, the music, it was all there, and that was the foundation for Wham! And also George needed Andrew because he was the outgoing one, he was the funny one, the charming one. And so he'd almost say, "You go first, I'll be behind you.""

Shirlie, who claimed she "was never a *Saturday Night Fever* victim", was enamoured of punk rock in its first scabrous phase; with her short blonde hair she'd certainly have made a good punkette, without the peroxide. But, with Andrew and George, she became part of a private pop trio who rehearsed all their moves at home. "We used to practise the dance routines in his bedroom before we went out. None of us were working and we just used to dance round in George's bedroom all the time." As she later confessed, "I think Andrew's grandmother thought it was like a love triangle thing with the three of us." But it was less a *ménage à trois* than the final flowering of childhood – or the first bloom of a unique career.

Shirlie's favourite dancing partner was not her boyfriend, but his best buddy: "I always felt far better dancing with George, his rhythm and everything… Andrew was too bony and hard and George was far softer – he just suited me to dance with." Not for the first – and certainly not the last – time, the more sensitive, introspective George was the object of a girl's platonic affection.

By the summer of 1981, Andrew was ready to try to fly the family nest. He and Shirlie briefly set up home in Peckham, inner southeast London, at her aunt's basement flat. It was not the most salubrious of environments for the suburban couple. The London Borough of Southwark was a far cry from Hertfordshire and Peckham was the scene of one of the lesser 1981 riots. Today, the area has been partially redeveloped; in the early eighties, it largely deserved its reputation as a no-go area for non-locals. Added to which, neither Andrew nor Shirlie were enamoured of the old-fashioned outside toilet.

It was also one hell of a series of connecting train and bus rides in order for George, the third component in the triangular partnership, to visit them. The only advantage was that he would use all his commuting time to write and revise songs – while Andrew, the less productive of the pair, would ensure that his best mate kept at it, making him sing and present the lyrics for his approval. What he lacked in creativity was compensated for in drive and ambition; stripped of his popularity at school, the now adult Andrew felt the need to attain similar star status in the wider world.

It was this period that produced the now famous three-track demo tape of songs credited to Georgios Panayiotou and Andrew Ridgeley. If the songwriting credits would not be divided up the same way in future, it was because George would no longer need his partner's impetus to make him create. "I had this belief in the songs and in my own ability," he'd later reflect, "but Andrew had the belief in the songs and in himself."

The first to be completed was entitled 'Careless Whisper' – or 'Tuneless Whisper', according to George's uncharitable sister. "When I first heard 'Careless Whisper' it was just a small demo tape that Andrew had played me," Shirlie reflected later, begging to differ. "I don't know if I'd even met George at that point, but I had a huge feeling that the person singing this song was going to be a massive star."

In George's celebrated 1996 radio interview with Chris Evans, he'd explain its origins: "I remember having a conversation with Andy, because we didn't know what we were doing at the time and we weren't sure whether we wanted to have a band or whether to have just the two of us. We wrote 'Careless Whisper' together and we made this crappy little demo that cost us 30 quid to make. Literally, we were in Andrew's front room whilst his mum was out and he had like a broom with a microphone tied to it and one of those little four-track portastudios that had just come out at the end of the seventies. I remember saying to Andrew one day, 'I don't care what anybody says, whether or not either of us are going to make it, or whether I can be a singer or whatever, someone is going to want to make money out of this.' Because I knew, in my own head, it sounded like a number one song, even though I'd never made a record."

'Careless Whisper' has been the subject of much conjecture. Its narrator's regretful story of romantic temptation, betrayal and regret on the dance floor leads to the enduring lyrical image of 'guilty feet' that 'have got no rhythm' – which, as we all know, plays much better as a song than it does on paper. Some have pondered on whether, in George's days deejaying at the Bel Air, the scenario of man betrays partner/lover with another and is crippled with guilt played out before his eyes.

George himself described in detail, in his 1990 autobiography, how it was inspired by a blonde girl called Jane he'd had an unrequited crush on since first seeing her at Queensway ice rink in west London, aged 12; when he was playing with The Executive four years later, she'd decided that she fancied the singer and the early fan became a girlfriend – even though he was already seeing a girl called Helen. The memory of dancing with Helen and wondering whether she'd find out she was being two-timed apparently inspired the lyric.

In a sense, this is rather like reducing one of the most evocative love songs of the last 30 years to a school disco drama on late seventies kids' show *Grange Hill*, or an overheard lovers' tiff at the local Harvester.

"It was about nothing to me really," George disarmingly told Chris Evans. "I worked at the cinema at the time and I just kind of put [in] lots of bits and pieces, influences, all kinds of romantic imagery that was just totally clichéd."

Having virtually dismissed his own song – which listeners to London's Capital Radio have consistently voted for as "the greatest single of all time" – the composer told of how its structure and hookline came to him as he rode the 142 bus that runs from the fringes of north London to Hertfordshire.

"I remember hearing the melody for it – which is obviously my most famous melody, it's the one you hear in the lifts all of the time – as I walked onto the bus and was handing the guy the change. I remember getting the melody and going up and sitting at the back of the bus, putting words to it and everything. And I used to do just a little bit every day, on my way between working at the cinema and working as a DJ. I used to just kind of work on it every day in my head."

Further embellishment came in the form of the Spanish guitar trills that Andrew added (which would earn his co-writer's credit on the first solo George Michael record). Then of course there was that haunting saxophone motif, now often heard as elevator muzak at Brent Cross shopping centre on the 142 bus route; it came from a boy who had never played the sax, but whose day job ensured he regularly heard the smoothly produced soundtracks of American films. The song is the sound of suburbia, but the musical imagination behind it was cinematic.[*]

Complementing 'Careless Whisper' were two entirely dissimilar numbers in embryo form: 'Wham Rap!' celebrated life on the dole as if queuing for your government giro cheque was as exciting as attending the hottest new dance club ('I said D-H-S-S!' rapped the boys, this being the acronym of the Department of Health and Social Security); its title would become more resonant to the eighties pop scene than anyone, even George, could then have imagined. Then there was 'Club Tropicana' – a piece of pure escapism equally upbeat in tone, but this time celebrating sun-kissed holidays and cocktails. Not bad work for two 18-year-olds either in casual jobs or on social security.

Not that George's employment would last a lot longer. After nine months of deejaying at the Bel Air, with the manager scolding him for bad timekeeping and persistently replacing the restaurant's playlist with his own, George quit.

"But the very last night I ever worked as a DJ I played the demo of 'Careless Whisper'... the floor filled. I remember thinking, 'That's a good sign.'"

---

[*] It's the contention of this writer that the soundtrack to the 1981 film *Body Heat* may have insinuated its way into the young George's imagination. Composed by the legendary John Barry, who died in early 2011, it uses bursts of saxophone to suggest sexual tension and crimes of passion.

It wasn't strictly the last night he would work as a DJ; following the Bel Air there was another short-lived stint, this time at a squash club. But by now, things were getting tense at home. Jack Panos saw his son's life going absolutely nowhere and finally laid down his ultimatum.

His attitude at the time can be summed up in a shouted phrase that soon became familiar: "Get yourself a job or get out of this house!" Except, in his son Georgios's case, the ultimate demand was to get himself a recording contract within six months, or else forget all this music nonsense.

CHAPTER 5

Wham!

It didn't take long for local music impresario Mark Dean to be offered another option on the boys from Wham! – as George and Andrew were calling themselves now, after the dole-celebrating 'Wham Rap!'.

In the interim, Dean, young mover-shaker of the zoot-suited early eighties, had really made his mark on the music business. Discarding mohair-suited mods and rude boys, he'd got a handle on what was loosely described as the 'new romantic' scene. Licensing *The Some Bizarre Album* from the small independent label of that name for Phonogram, he was instrumental in making pop stars of electro duo Soft Cell – whose charismatically camp singer, elfin-faced Marc Almond, took the spelling of his name from late glam superstar Marc Bolan and his band's big number one single, 'Tainted Love', from Bolan's girlfriend, soul singer Gloria Jones.

Less sexually ambiguous than Almond but just as camp in his performance was vocalist Martin Fry, besuited frontman of Dean's other signing, ABC. ABC brought the big pop sound of soul-inspired ballads back into the charts; heavily orchestrated and dramatic, their heyday was short-lived but produced big chart hits like 'The Look Of Love',

'Poison Arrow' and 'All Of My Heart'. Clearly, in a record industry still hawking black vinyl and helmed mostly by men in early middle age, the young Mark Dean, still only 21, was deemed to be in the know in a sense that was simply beyond them.

It wasn't long before the big labels came calling. First of all it was Warner Bros Records which tried to recruit Dean to its operation; he played it cool, but when an even bigger US musical conglomerate, CBS, offered him his own record label within its corporate structure, he signed on the dotted line. All that Innervision, Dean's new record company, needed now was some stars of its own.

"What actually happened was that Andrew gave a tape to someone that we both knew, just literally from knowing them at the pub," George told DJ Chris Evans over a decade later. "And that was our first break, and however shitty a break it was – in terms of it left us in a very bad contractual position, where if we didn't sign it we weren't going to get the rest of the money to finish our demos – it was still an incredibly important day and an incredibly positive thing that we signed it. Otherwise, I wouldn't be here," he reflected philosophically. "I would be somewhere else."

But before the disillusionment came the elation. Innervision Records was very briefly the UK record industry's new arriviste of the time, based on the top floor of 64 South Molton Street, the swanky pedestrianised shopping district at the posh Mayfair end of London's Oxford Street. George and Andrew were continuing to push the cheap demo tape that contained the original unfinished recording of 'Careless Whisper'. In search of record labels or music publishers who would pay for demos to be recorded professionally, the boys had done the rounds, blagging their way in on the back of their sheer confidence. Recorded without a full band line-up or a drummer, the demo tape wouldn't last more than 15 seconds before the drum machine intro of 'Wham Rap!' convinced the A&R men that this was just one more cheap and cheerful electro duo. It was also a big handicap that the labels couldn't come along to check out Wham! playing live, as at this stage they were a bedroom disco operation rather than a traditional group line-up –

although, for one brief moment, there was an attempt to turn them into a full band.

Then Mark Dean came along. It was a gradual process at first, as initially he didn't have any greater hopes of another demo from Andrew Ridgeley than he'd had for the Executive tape. On listening, however, he found something altogether different – a pop act who were no longer just copying the flavour of the month but were defining the times they lived in, with a sense of rhythm and a whole load of playfulness.

Most importantly from the boys' point of view, Dean seemed prepared to put his money where his mouth was and fund new demo sessions in a studio. For all George's later reservations and regrets about the deal they would sign, he'd admit in his 1990 biography that, "One of the most incredible moments of my life was hearing 'Careless Whisper' demo'ed properly, with a band and a sax and everything. It was ironic that we signed the contract with Mark that day, the day I finally believed that we had number-one material. The same day we signed it all away."

George and Andrew recorded the new demos at the Halligan Band Centre in Holloway, London N7, close to his mother's old neighbourhood, with a full complement of musician friends to complete a band line-up. "We'd recorded a demo of 'Careless Whisper', 'Club Tropicana' and 'Wham Rap!', and on the last day that we were there," their young composer later recalled, "the head of the record company, Innervision, turns up with these contracts and says, 'Look, come round the corner with me,' to this greasy spoon café four or five doors up the road, and he said, 'If you don't sign this now, the deal's going away and you won't have finished demos to take away, you won't own them and we won't finish them.' So it was a total threat basically, a complete and utter threat. And we were on our own, we had nobody with us, and we signed."

Despite the absence of legal representatives acting for either side, on March 25, 1982 the two 18/19-year-olds signed a contract which carried Innervision's mock-comic strip letterhead, featuring its logo of a quiffed hipster with hypnotic eyes. (George's legal adviser at the time, Robert Allan, was reputedly appalled by their recklessness.)

"I don't think either of us had any idea that we'd have any kind of chemistry for pop music," George would reflect, with perhaps a little false modesty, in a late eighties interview. "In the few weeks after we signed they were still scrambling to put a band around us. So Wham! could have been some awful six-piece band to begin with."

That following autumn, the contract would be supplemented by the following addendum:

To Messrs:

1. David Mortimer   5. Shirley Holliman [*sic*]
2 Paul Ridgeley   6. D. C. Lee
3. Roger Rudix   [*girls' names pencilled in by hand*]
4. Kevin Robinson

Dear Sirs,

With reference to the agreement between Georgios Panayiotou and Andrew Ridgeley p.k.a. [*sic*] Wham and us dated 25th March 1982 (hereinafter referred to as "the agreement") and a letter dated 13th October 1982 (hereinafter referred to as the letter) sent by us to David Mortimer, Paul Ridgeley, Roger Rudix and Kevin Robinson (hereinafter referred to as the new members). We hereby agree to release the new members ...

The demo's instrumentalists (including David Austin, referred to above under his birth name, and the sax player who first played the haunting motif of 'Careless Whisper') wisely opted out of a contract that George and his advisers would later refer to as "punitive". David had already ostensibly bailed out of Wham!, leaving to play a Thai residency with his other band. By the time of his return to the UK, he found his best friend and rival George had a recording contract.

"I always knew that if I worked with David we would fall out," George later reflected. "We argued all the time anyway and it would have been horrible to have had something serious to argue about, like business. No way would Wham! have lasted more than a year if it had been David and me." But still, in the years to come the friendship between the two would, on occasion, bear musical fruit.

More surprising, perhaps, is the fact that the two girls who, even in those early days, had already become an integral part of Wham!, had also jumped ship. Shirlie Holliman was spending virtually all of her free time rehearsing frenetically syncopated dance routines with George and Andrew. To round out the ranks, she'd recruited a young friend from Bushey – 16-year-old Amanda Washburn, who didn't last long before she was replaced by 20-year-old Diane Sealey (or Dee C. Lee, as she styled herself), an attractive black girl from Deptford in south London, not far from where Andrew and Shirlie once shared a flat.

Maybe the girls too had serious qualms about just what they'd be letting themselves in for, if they were tied to Innervision's conditions. For their own part, at the time of signing, George and Andrew embraced them totally. For an advance of £500 each, to be paid back out of future royalties, their five-year contract stipulated royalties of eight percent of cover price for each record sold in the UK (at a time when an artist's income was largely dependent on vinyl sales), with only six percent for albums and four percent for singles throughout the rest of the world.

As for 12″ singles – which had been a huge craze since the late seventies disco days and now provided an alternative format for almost every single that was released – they were deemed to be promotional items and would therefore attract no royalties at all. Wham! were also obligated to produce an album a year for five years – although, if sales justified it, Innervision was granted the right to up the ante to two per year (a rate of productivity that George's idol Elton John maintained in his seventies heyday but which was beyond the capability of most artists). The album advances too sounded less than generous when stacked up one after the other: £2,000 for the first album; £5,000 for the second; £2,500 increments up to £20,000 for the seventh; then £5,000 increments up to £35,000 for the tenth album.

If it seems incredible now that young pop musicians could be signed under terms verging on pure exploitation, it should be borne in mind that the music business has always been what's inelegantly termed a 'fuck industry'. Exploitative the terms may have been, but the young George and Andrew were far from alone in signing up for them. After all, ran the reasoning of the labels, we're the ones taking the financial risk in putting the product out there; if our young artistes want us to make their dreams of fame come true, they can't expect us to run the operation like a charity.

It's perhaps more surprising that the terms didn't originate from one of the numerous tiny independent labels that proliferated at the time, but from the subsidiary of a major. However, as Andrew (and possibly George) would later tacitly accept, Mark Dean was just as tied down by the terms of his deal with CBS as they were in their contract with him.

"I thought it was good that we had a lousy contract because it was so bad that, from the day we signed it, we were probably going to get out of it," George would later claim, but that may be a rationalisation. As we will see, as a songwriter who often tells a narrative tale, he has a natural tendency to view his past actions in terms of where his mind is at right now.

At the time, the mood was one of elation. George even celebrated by paying for one of the more daring eighties male fashion trademarks, a double-ear piercing. From now on, he would also wear earrings in both ears.

In April, the month following the signing, the boys from Wham! signed a music publishing deal with two industry veterans. They were led to Morrison-Leahy by Dean, who'd formerly worked for Bryan Morrison – one-time manager of The Pretty Things, a group of sixties bad boys regarded as dirtier, more outrageous counterparts of The Rolling Stones. He and his partner Dick Leahy – the tanned, sophisticated old hand who'd once owned GTO Records, which issued Donna Summer's disco classic 'I Feel Love' – now had a very different proposition at hand. Leahy, for one, saw Wham! as "very much a duo that came to see me. It wasn't George Michael with Andrew Ridgeley just sitting there. They walked into the office and almost without hearing the songs you knew that they were going to make it. There was something very, very special about them."

With so many years of promotional work under his belt, Leahy recognised that the best vehicle for the boys would be the club scene. In the more showbizzy first half of the sixties, club appearances – sometimes live, sometimes miming for the cameras – had been a standard way of promoting the artist. The scene had yet to come full circle, but with the increasing importance of the promotional video as a marketing tool and a spurt of electronica-based pop acts, the traditional vocals/guitar/bass/ drums band line-up no longer held full sway. Wham! were absolutely right for these times and, with the aid of CBS Club Promotions, they would take on the early eighties nightlife of southern England like a party in motion.

"I was just so glad that I'd got this break and I knew I was going to be able to officially go home to mum and dad and say, 'I'm going to get a record contract!'" George later recalled about his earliest breakthrough. "It was just overwhelming for me that I just thought for three or four weeks I would go into meetings and talk to people and make it perfectly clear to them I was totally prepared to do anything they wanted if they could make me a pop star, right. It lasted for about three or four weeks, and then I realised that people didn't know how to do it. They literally didn't have a clue how to do it! And the realisation was such a shock that I think my immediate reaction was, 'Right, if they don't know how to do it I'm not going to do *anything* they want me to do. I'm going to lay it down exactly.'"

At their earliest live appearances, Wham! came into being as an all-singing, all-dancing boy and girl band, a disco dance-floor act. Appearances always took place on Friday and Saturday nights, the traditional après-work (or giro-fuelled, to the workless) night out. As many as six personal appearances in one night could be scheduled, an experience George described as "like being strippers – and we got exactly the same reaction". Their debut appearance was at Level One in Neasden, close in both proximity and style to George's old stamping ground at Bogart's in Harrow. In front of 600 people, the foursome came in for some typical weekend revelry when, as he described it, "all the drunks [were] coming up and *joining in!* And the drunks would go up behind the girls; it was an absolute nightmare…"

By the time they made the West End, George accidentally kicked off a shoe during their routine at Stringfellow's, quickly redressing the balance by purposely shedding the other one. He was learning quickly, becoming more of a late-teen trouper with every personal appearance. What was now required was to shed what he'd jokingly refer to as his "snappy pop title" of Georgios Panayiotou.

"I knew I was going to have to change it but they started pressing 'Wham Rap!' and I still hadn't chosen a name." The first 20,000 pressings would carry the credit 'Panayiotou/Ridgeley'.

After a period of pondering, the quiet revelation came in David Austin's living room. "George" was a given — Georgios had long since had his name truncated to 'George' by his friends, when he wasn't Yog that is. For his surname he would emulate Elton John, in effectively having two first names — in his case it would be "Michael", an echo of David's father's name, as well as George's paternal uncle and a Greek boy at school, so that he "didn't have to give up the Greekness entirely".

And so George Michael was effectively born with the release of 'Wham Rap! (Enjoy What You Do)' in June 1982. The song's falsetto refrain – "Wham! Bam! I am a man!" – had its origin in him and Andrew dancing in syncopated style at Le Beat Route.

"It was very much based on Andrew's lifestyle," a middle-aged George would fondly reflect. "You know, living off the state whereas your mother's actually a teacher and your father's working at Canon. You've got a perfectly healthy life at home and they're not making you put anything towards the housekeeping; you just go off and get your money every week, he loved it. So that's what we wrote about. The idea of kids trying to do that now is just ludicrous," he said in an era when the dole seems less of a career choice and even more of a dead end. ("Yes, I don't think a moving tribute to the DSS would do that well now," camp chat-show host Graham Norton understatedly quipped.)

In fact, it initially didn't do very well at the time – peaking at a virtually invisible number 105. Even so, the record's release gained George and Andrew a full black and white cover on the then incredibly hip *New Musical Express*. With their slim-cut blue denim jackets, 'wedges' (side partings) and quiffs cut into their thick dark hair, they looked like the coolest mixed-race soul boys.

Guitar rock, even punk, had been deemed terminally unhip in this club-dominated age, and there to fill the gap were two young smiling hedonists dedicated to dance music. "The only real important thing about Wham! in terms of moving away from what was happening at the time was that most of the recent music had been really 'down'," George later observed. To the *NME* of the time, it must have seemed positively subversive for white boys to celebrate unemployment in rap – a black musical genre so new that Brit teens often misspelled The Sugarhill Gang's epochal 1980 hit as '*Raper*'s Delight', only just then going radical and hard-edged with Grandmaster Flash & The Furious Five's classic 'The Message'.

Even so, if their next record didn't cut it then Wham! would become that most transient of phenomena – the inky music press's latest-but-one cult band, all but forgotten by the time the next big thing came along.

The second single, 'Young Guns (Go For It!)', followed pretty sharply in October 1982. This was the moment in which the girls became fully integrated into the Wham! sound – and when the boys inadvertently created what would become the sound of *Top Of The Pops* for the rest of the eighties. But at first, it looked like they weren't even going to make the UK's favourite Thursday night TV show.

The sassy cut-and-thrust/call-and-response rap parodied the Andrew & Shirlie relationship. He's the embarrassed young funkster who meets his old partner in crime George (named as such on the track) and has to suffer his feisty blonde girlfriend dissing his old mate – "Tell that boy to take a hike… wasting time on some creepy guy," etc – before all four regroup to chant the title line. It was good-humoured and it was tongue-in-cheek – but 'Young Guns' was also an acknowledgement that the good times often drew to a close with the early onset of adulthood and responsibility.

Love it or hate it, this latest white-boy rap would entrench itself in the nation's psyche. But for a while, it too looked like going the way of the first release of 'Wham Rap!' "'Wham Rap!' had come out and flopped and that didn't seem *so* bad at the time," George reflected a few years later. "It wasn't unusual for a first single to flop. Then 'Young Guns' came out and *that* looked as if it was going to flop too." Added to this, according to the singer, was a bout of rejection from a girl he particularly fancied. For a while, the pop dream looked to be just that – a dream, and a hollow one at that.

Enter Dick Leahy. Having promoted the big pop sound of The Walker Brothers and Dusty Springfield on the Philips label in the sixties, and George's early favourite David Cassidy at Bell Records in the seventies, he had an instinct for what might make the teenage heart leap. He went into overdrive, making a series of hounding phone calls, calling in favours, doing anything he could to make the then influential pop media look at Wham! again.

"George Michael was too good not to have happened but if 'Young Guns' had not happened I think it would have seriously affected Wham!" Leahy acknowledged in George's 1990 autobiography. "But fortunately the next week the record went up and then we got *Top Of The Pops*. They did *Top Of The Pops* on the Thursday when the record was at 42 and on the Monday morning at CBS distribution centre there were over 30,000 orders.

"It was outrageous for a band who were only at 42 to get *Top Of The Pops*, but the producer of the show had seen us do a Saturday morning children's show, *Saturday Superstore*, and because it was so different, with Shirlie and Dee and everything, they decided to stick us on *Top Of The Pops* even though we were not in the top 40."

This was the point at which Wham! graduated from being a Saturday night disco novelty or an *NME* band of the week. In a short space of time, the word Wham! – so redolent of comic-book sound effects – would summon up a number of visual images: of two 'white cool cats' with tufted dark hair; of a black and a white chick, with the bitchy blonde being the one you didn't want to mess with; but most of all, of the four of them dancing in jagged-shouldered syncopation. The Tweedledee/Tweedledum nature of the boys in their biker jackets and the integral element of the girls as dancers/backing singers was established immediately.

"I remember being in my bedroom and thinking it's such a shame," George later told Chris Evans, "because basically, no matter how good I am as a musician, I'm never going to be that famous, right, because I don't have that way of pushing myself forward visually, and physically I'm not interesting enough to people. So I was determined to be noticed for what I did. What I didn't realise was going to happen was that whole Wham! thing, obviously Andrew started it off and everything... I didn't realise I was going to be selling my physical persona."

He also claimed that his very first performance on *TOTP* – in front of eight technicians in rehearsal – had filled him with terror. But the on-camera performance was very different.

"I remember the first time on *Top Of The Pops*," David Austin would recall, "first performance of 'Young Guns (Go For It)', George turned round to me, and said – I'll never forget this for as long as I live – 'Right, this is it, this is the rest of my life.'"

CHAPTER 6

Bad Boys Stick Together

The first bright lights of success, for George Michael, were almost swallowed up in an alcoholic blur. Having left the hostile environment of pubs behind (where Andrew still qualified for the status of most shaggable/most punchable patron, depending on one's gender), George threw himself head-on into the clubbing and late-night cocktails culture of the eighties.

"I was still living with my parents but I think my life was about as far from normal as it could possibly have been at that point," he admitted in his early autobiography. "Because I was either working or drunk in clubs and there was nothing in between."

Favourite venues were the Wag and Le Beat Route, as ever, as well as the notoriously boozy and debauched north London nightspot the Camden Palace, where George could be found in various states of semi-inebriation on Tuesday and Thursday nights. As he was a bona fide pop star now, he also carried the full sexual licence that went with it. Not that it was without its emotional drawbacks for a particularly sensitive 20-year-old.

"George couldn't bear the thought that someone was sleeping with him because of who and what he was," Andrew would candidly observe of his friend and partner. "And if George felt that he was being used, what was he doing there anyway? It's a two-way thing. At the end of the day – they get what they want and you get what you want. I don't think you can go around whining, 'She doesn't see me for what I am!' What do you see *her* for?"

In fact, the social scene that George was beginning to inhabit was increasingly separate from that of his partner-in-crime. As the times passed into what would truly constitute the eighties (the beginning of each decade being basically just an outgrowth of the previous one), the young performer placed himself at the centre of London's nightclub and style scene.

One of his contemporaries of the time, journalist Fiona Russell Powell, was herself just beginning to write for eighties style bible *The Face*. She recalls her first meeting with George Michael – at a New Year's special of *Whatever You Want*, the Channel 4 youth culture show hosted by comedian/actor Keith Allen – and the social scene that they both inhabited:

"It was New Year '82, going into '83, and I think it was down at the Fridge actually, it was at a studio in Brixton. They did it so it was like a big, long table where everyone was sitting around having a pretend meal, chatting and everything, and then Keith Allen would come along and pick people out for an interview. He got me and George, so we were interviewed and I teased George, because I'd seen him around at all the same clubs. The Camden Palace, Heaven – he was always at Heaven, it was one of the few decent clubs but very few boys I knew who went there weren't gay.

"He was wearing these jeans which were quite low and he had this fluff in his tummy button; so I was picking it out and joking about his candlewick bedspread. Because I was a bit cheeky, which I haven't really lost, we made friends there and then. Afterwards, when it was over, we went off together clubbing. That's how I met him – we had mutual friends.

"If you look at this part of my generation, nearly everybody I knew became successful in some way or another at some point. A few are dead

now, but many of them aren't. And yet so many of them — me included, I know what my story is — fucked up quite spectacularly. We were all misfits in one way or another, either at home or at school or whatever, a lot of us were runaways or we'd come from somewhere [else] to come to London. And we all found each other — it was the first time I felt I was with people who understood me and what have you, but we all had unresolved issues, we all had things going on which, when you're young, you don't realise it but when you're older it comes out.

"Fat Tony, a kid from Battersea, south London, was young and fat and gay, openly so; he was about 15, 16 and he had come on the scene through Philip Salon — the one who started the Mud Club and was instrumental with Rusty Egan and Steve Strange — aka Steve Syringe — in Blitz and Hell.*

"Marilyn [Boy George's transgender friend] knew George Michael because they came from a similar area; Marilyn was joking and they used to argue, 'I saw you cottaging at blah-de-blah, don't go there, you'll spoil my spot!' because they always used to go to the same places."

For many of Ms Russell Powell's generation, a detour into hard drugs became an almost inevitable hazard — leading, in her case, to eventual detoxification and rehab, a process she has written about incisively. In George's case, however, she suggests that it was the tension of leading a double life and having to suppress his true sexual nature in public that would erupt later.

For a while, George seemed to live the classic swinging bachelor lifestyle. Among his more regular female companions was Pat Fernandez, a voluptuous young black woman often photographed on his arm at public events. One of the hat-and-headdress covered dancers for the

---

* In the small hours of the evening spanning April 2-3 2011, an ageing Philip Salon was subjected to a vicious homophobic attack at Piccadilly Circus which left him hospitalised with severe head injuries. In the words of his old friend Boy George, "In the early eighties there was this sense that things were changing, and becoming more open-minded. But we don't have that sort of gorgeous youth culture any more…"

video to Malcolm McLaren's novelty hip-hop single, 'Buffalo Girls', she reputedly sang backing vocals for Culture Club, the hit band fronted by the 'other George'. In fact, Boy George was one of Ms Fernandez's many gay male friends and she apparently delighted in being called a 'fag hag'.

Fiona Russell Powell, then something of a fag hag herself, has her own take on the relationship:

"The Pat thing was ridiculous, it was like rent-a-beard with her with the whole circle, it was just a joke. That whole thing was just a complete and utter arrangement. They made up the thing about her being a backing singer or an assistant, things like that. And why they chose her – because her other nickname [after 'Black Pat'] was 'Fat Pat' – I could never quite understand that, but I thought, 'Well, actually, they've killed two birds with one stone because they've got a girl and she's black. So really the credential's there.' Pat seemed to divide her time between George Michael and that whole thing and us lot, because she was really good friends with Fat Tony."

Ms Fernandez had also been a semi-permanent fixture at the tiny St John's Wood mews flat of Boy George, where she'd doubled as a cleaner. In the words of the man who would shortly become Wham!'s manager, and whose commentary also informs this book:

"Shortly afterwards, still struggling to prove he wasn't gay, George Michael announced to the press that he'd been living with a girl and she'd 'broken his heart'.

Boy George knew the girl well. She was a bit of a fag hag and had shared a flat with him too. 'Broke your heart, did she?' he sneered… 'She lived with me for three years and all she managed to break was my Hoover.'"

But for now the pretence had to continue. For all (Boy) George O'Dowd's later talk about the 'gorgeous youth culture' of the early eighties, not even this flamboyantly queenish pop star would feel secure enough to admit he was gay until partway through the decade (which begs the question of who exactly Boy George imagines regarded him as 'straight').

Andrew Ridgeley, meanwhile, was living an old-fashioned 'birds & booze' lifestyle, throwing himself into it with such gusto that tabloid reporters came to know him affectionately as 'the vomit fountain'. Life was one big party and, still at the onset of his twenties, the partying didn't stop long enough for the hangover to set in. All that was missing from the equation in his case was the music.

"I never regretted stepping back from the songwriting," he'd candidly admit. "Number one, he didn't need the help. And number two, he didn't want it." The days of George Michael/Andrew Ridgeley co-credits would not outlive those first three early demoed songs. Nor would Andrew's voice be heard too much in the songs from hereon, though he was always a presence on lead guitar. "On occasions I did feel that I would have liked to have got a bit more involved. But they were rare!" he endearingly confessed.

"Andrew Ridgeley was never on the scene with us lot," recalls Fiona Russell Powell. "I always got the impression that he thought, 'That's George's weird, crazy, freaky friends.' I think Andrew was very straight in every sense of the word and I don't think he really wanted anything to do with any of that."

Shirlie, the third original member of Wham!, was feeling altogether less secure in her role. "When they did their first photo session in Corfu I remember they went without me and that was the first time I had this pang. I felt that I was about to experience a huge loss. I knew they were going to be taken away from me. I didn't care about the career. It was our friendship… they *were* my life."

Decked in black leather skirts, the girls were still a sexily fetishised major element of the 'Bad Boys' video – which came three months after the remixed version (suggested by Dick Leahy) of 'Wham Rap!' finally hit the top ten in February 1983, with an accompanying video in which the boys danced in black leather jackets. Wham!'s third chart hit, 'Bad

Boys' was already sailing perilously close to self-parody. Bedecked in their leather motorbike jackets, the lads still looked as if they'd just got out of a taxi at the Camden Palace. "Cigarettes and love bites!" chanted the girls approvingly, while dangerous George warned mum and dad, "I'm big enough to break down the door!" if they didn't let him go out clubbing.

It was if George was trying to be the well-spoken suburban version of leather-clad rockers like Eddie Cochran or Sid Vicious; although you knew that he'd never *really* give his mum any cheek. The four Wham! members danced in their usual group formation, but the bare chests and leather jackets lent the single's video an overheated gay quality. Some critics even compared it to *Scorpio Rising*, the legendary art film which features about 15 minutes of homoerotic biker scenes soundtracked by late fifties/early sixties girl groups. "We look such a pair of wankers in it," admitted George. "We lost a lot of ground with that video." It marked the end of the brief period of Wham! marketing themselves as bad boys.

Macho George was not an altogether convincing spectacle, but he was already grabbing the spotlight from his fun-loving partner. "Our roles reversed very quickly because the singer always becomes the focal point," he acknowledged. "And by that time he was enjoying the fruits of it all and getting very lazy, I suppose. But as long as things are good, Andrew's just fine. He has a capacity to take life as it comes, which I don't. I just don't have that."

To the world's teenage girls, however, the two dark-haired boys were still a conjoined entity. Via the videos, there was an awareness of the records all over Western Europe, in the Far East and as far away as Australia. Wham! were becoming a global commodity and still (the paternal advice of publisher Dick Leahy aside) they had no one to manage them and help feed the global demand.

Not that George ever felt that he needed his own personal Svengali. "I think that somehow, that same force field that came down and said, 'I'm not going to private school!' when I was 11," he'd later boast to camera, "it came down and I said, 'Okay, you have to ignore just about everything they want you to do.'"

"To this day, I've never seen him go up to any outside person and say, 'Okay, what do I do about this situation?'" seconded the older Shirlie Kemp (née Holliman).

Clearly, George was not going to be moved around the board like anybody's little pop-star pawn. But still, in order for Wham! to move forward onto a new international level, industry experience was fast becoming an essential requirement. Management would have to be sought. Via the contacts of Morrison-Leahy, the boys sought out Andy Stephens at CBS International, a consummately calm, gentlemanly figure who nonetheless turned them down.* Stateside, they did manage to elicit the services of Ron Weisner and Freddie DeMann, the stellar management team who represented Michael Jackson and, a couple of years hence, would do likewise for Madonna. Within a matter of months, Wham! had gone from the discos of Brent and Harrow to become embryonic superstars in the making.

With no management representation in the UK, however, their day-to-day affairs were temporarily handled by their legal adviser, Robert Allan. But he could do little to stem the animosity that was festering between the boys and their record label – or, more specifically, between George and Innervision.

The young singer/songwriter was becoming painfully aware of just how far he'd gone in a very short time, and how Wham!, complete with its exclamation mark, was now a household name. And still they had to beg Mark Dean for spare change if they wanted to go to a nightclub or a restaurant. A visit to their label boss's South Molton Street office persuaded him to at least look at the prospect of renegotiating their terms; it was nixed by parent company CBS, which reminded Dean of the tight remit under which he ran Innervision. It was granting him no leeway, and in turn he was transferring the restrictions to his label's chart-topping act. It was no deal.

It was at this point that relations between George Michael and Mark Dean went beyond what a divorce court might term irreconcilable

---

* In due course, he would play a major role in George's solo career.

differences. Any run-ins at the clubs of Soho or Camden would result in screamed recriminations, with a well-lubricated George howling out his disgust and Dean shouting back in return. This was at the time of the recording of the first Wham! album and, the music's sunny demeanour aside, its creator was becoming obsessed by the idea that he was being deeply wronged by Innervision Records. Drinking heavily and brooding, the formerly clean-living boy from a non-smoking household was also getting through a pack of 20 cigarettes a day.

At first, George made a point of never conceding to business discussions with Mark Dean, only ever communicating with him through an intermediary. Then, as his frustrations boiled over, he carried out an act of what nearly became self-sabotage.

"I took the master tapes of the first album and hid them at home," he later recalled in amusement. "Mark said he was going to send the police round to get them. I said, 'What do I have to do? Get my mother to stand in front of them?'" Which, in all likelihood, the loyal Lesley might well have done.

But George was never going to take it over the brink and condemn his first long-player to oblivion. Besides, as Dick Leahy had advised him, "If you are going to have a legal fight, then fight with a number-one album" – a position it would effortlessly reach. And in terms of handling the music industry and all its iniquities, the rather jaded cavalry was about to arrive.

Long-haired rock band manager and ex-army band player Jazz Summers had been after Wham! for some time, ever since hearing their first professionally recorded demos. He'd formerly handled comedy folk singer Richard Digance and lower-league punk band The Stukas. When he'd first approached Morrison-Leahy about their new charges, he'd been told by Bryan Morrison, "You're not big enough, Jazz," and had been forced to concede the music publisher was spot on.

Lately, he'd experienced a bit more success. One of his bands, Blue Zoo, had made the top 20 with an overwrought piece of eighties pop called 'Cry Boy Cry'. Summers fancied his chances of cracking the charts again, but this time with some already established teen idols.

All the same, he'd taken Morrison's words to heart and knew that he couldn't hope to get Wham! on his books without someone with a longer showbiz pedigree in tow.

Enter his new partner: swinging sixties survivor and openly gay *bon viveur* Simon Napier-Bell. Well into his forties but blond and boyish, former jazz musician Napier-Bell was famous for co-writing the lyric to Dusty Springfield's classic 'You Don't Have to Say You Love Me' in the back of a cab with the singer's gay lover, Vickie Wickham. (In jest, the two friends sometimes suggested they should marry and become the pop industry's premier gay/lesbian couple.)

In the period immediately after, he went on to manage The Yardbirds with Jeff Beck on guitar, Marc Bolan (as a solo artist) and John's Children (featuring Bolan). With an eye for manufactured media scandal, he'd encouraged John's Children to have fights on stage and bogusly claimed another of his acts, Fresh, had come straight out of borstal.

In the late seventies/early eighties he'd managed Japan, who had made the transition from a Johnny-come-lately glam act to a Euro-sophisticate electro-disco band. Their blond singer, David Sylvian, with his Bryan Ferry-ish warble, was marketed by Napier-Bell as "the most beautiful man in the world". But at the height of their success, with the hauntingly introspective 1982 single 'Ghosts', Japan promptly split up.

"When I started managing Wham!, a lot of people said, 'How could you do that after Japan?' But George was a great songwriter and they had a good act," Napier-Bell later reflected. Before taking over the managerial reins, however, he and his new partner Jazz (working together as Nomis Management) had two highly regarded young men to impress.

Napier-Bell let Summers do the legwork in chasing Wham! After three abortive no-shows at meetings, however, the aspiring manager left a deeply peeved and pissed-off message on George's answerphone. That, thought Napier-Bell, was the end of that. But somehow it did the trick and the main boy from Wham! phoned back the next day. Simon Napier-Bell describes the subsequent meeting at his luxurious home in

Bryanston Square, near Marble Arch and Hyde Park, in his memoir of managing Wham!, *I'm Coming To Take You To Lunch*:

> *On Top Of The Pops, George and Andrew had come across as lookalikes – two fun-loving teenagers – a matching pair. In person, they seemed complete opposites. Andrew chose the longest settee in my sitting-room and draped himself along it lengthways. 'Nice pad,' he said, throwing his eyes around the room. 'Great for pulling.'*
>
> *George chose an armchair and sat on the edge of it, eager to get down to business. 'Who've you managed before?' he asked brusquely.*
>
> *Andrew remained stretched out. From the coffee-table he picked up a book – something I'd written about the music business in the sixties – and started browsing through it.*
>
> *George remained suspicious. 'We won't want you looking after our money,' he said. 'We'll be appointing accountants.'*
>
> *'Fantastic, man,' Andrew commented a couple of times from his reclined position, then turned to George, 'Seems like Simon spent most of the sixties either drunk or having sex. He sounds just the right person for us.'*
>
> *George ignored him. 'What guarantees can you give us? We won't want to give you a contract unless we have guarantees.'*
>
> *Their different personalities complemented each other well; more important, though, was the quality of the three records they'd released – 'Wham Rap', 'Young Guns' and 'Bad Boys' – all with extraordinary vitality and super-sharp lyrics. If I was going to go back to managing a pop group, at least these two guys were talented and well-spoken. And they had a wonderful image – pure Hollywood – Butch Cassidy and the Sundance Kid – two regular guys, closer than lovers.*

It was an abiding impression of the young men who would be his new clients. Napier-Bell would always find Andrew relaxed, confident and affable, though there was no doubting who ran the show. Beneath his quiet manner and soft speech, he noted the steely resolve in George from the off.

The Michael–Ridgeley partnership (as opposed to Shirlie Holliman and Dee C. Lee, now firmly relegated to the status of backing singers) signed a contract at the upmarket Bombay Brasserie in Kensington, to be clients of Nomis Management at a specified 12 percent of earnings for all territories apart from the USA – where Weisner-DeMann had added them to their exclusive clientele. With their first album now produced and mixed, a frayed and slightly bad-tempered George took time off from what had become a permanent promotional treadmill, taking a summer holiday 'back home' in Cyprus.

Fantastic, Wham!'s immodestly titled 1983 debut album, already played like a greatest hits LP. Rather than the earlier pick-up band consisting of friends like David Austin, the record was performed by a nucleus of musicians including session player Robert Ahwai on guitar, former ABC orchestrator (and later Art of Noise member) Anne Dudley on keyboards and brass arrangements and American bassist Deon Estus. The album was helmed by former Elton John producer Steve Brown, working alongside George – who would always be involved in a production capacity on his musical output from now on.

It featured the first three singles and the forgettably lightweight 'Come On!', a cover of The Miracles' disco hit 'Love Machine', which a whole generation recalls them performing in shorts and sportswear on Channel 4's *The Tube* (when they were reputedly too hard-up to afford any other stage clothes), and two new Michael originals: the funk-happy 'A Ray of Sunshine' and 'Nothing Looks The Same In The Light', a typical eighties soul production about watching a lover sleep. It also showcased the new single, the last of the songs dating back to the very first demo tape – 'Club Tropicana'. Released in 1983 and shooting straight to number one, *Fantastic* would remain in the UK album charts for 116 weeks, more than two whole years.

(For all that it epitomised the fizz and sparkle of mainstream eighties pop, there was a downside to the album. Beneath the Wham! logo of its two component parts dancing in silhouette ran a dedication to two old school-friends, Andrew Leaver and Paul Atkins – both of the same age group as George and Andrew, now both sadly deceased. 'The other Andrew' had been a member of The Executive and had died of cancer at the tragically young age of 20. Paul Atkins was killed several months later in a car crash. "It was just so strange," said George of 1982's darkest days, "because nearly everyone at both of those funerals was still a teenager… what was really horrible about it was that we came back to these funerals as little pop stars." From the moment that stardom became a reality, George had started to feel the pressures of being in what his publishers termed a "scream band".)

'Club Tropicana' quickly gave the lie to the contrived Wham! 'bad boys' image. This was happy, trumpet-blaring soft funk for the British holidaymaker – whether late teens or early twentysomethings, like George and Andrew's friends, heading off for Ibiza in the Balearics (already the established holiday island, yet to become the world capital of acid house), or their parents, overdoing it at happy hour in Benidorm.

Andrew Ridgeley is of the opinion that, while one of Wham!'s weaker songs, the phenomenal success of 'Club Tropicana' (which would go on to sell 400,000 vinyl copies) is due to the fact that the record is a mini-holiday. It's remarkable to think that, in 1983, when youth unemployment was at its highest ever recorded level and social tension was in the air, *this* would become the sound of the eighties. It's often easy to overstate the effects of the medium, but in this case the record's success may have been equally due to the promotional video: full of tanning skin, Ray-bans, cocktails and swimming pools, all taking you to a place where the entrance fee is a smiling face.

As Napier-Bell later recorded in an email posted on his website:

Many people thought Wham! were getting glitzy and beyond their key audience, rushing off to film a video in Ibiza. In fact, the song came to George in the days when he and Andrew were skint and went out on the town once a week with little more than a couple of quid between them. They used to go to a very tacky club in Greek Street called the Beat Route – it had mouldy carpet, stank of damp, etc – if you'd ever seen it with the lights on you'd be sick at the thought you'd been there – that sort of place.

But it had good music and it was all they could afford. So every time he went there, as he was going in the door, George would force himself into a fantasy and imagine he was going into the most beautiful club in the world – Club Tropicana.

When it came time to make the video, CBS Records behaved in the worst way possible. Wham! had already had three Top Ten singles but CBS wouldn't come up with a decent budget for it. They offered just £10,000 – the cheapest we could do a video [for] in Ibiza was £30,000. Jazz Summers and I had just taken over their management and George just said, 'OK, you're our manager, you sort it out.' Then he went off to Cyprus for a summer holiday, refusing to come back until we'd sorted it out. So we went off searching for money from other sources – Wham!'s publishers came up with some, and a few other people. When the video was finished, I was at CBS one day when the managing director, Paul Russell, was showing it to a visiting American and boasting how well CBS looked after its top artists, paying for really classy videos, etc.

The video was shot in Pikes Hotel in the hills in Ibiza. It's a hotel which often gets visiting film and pop stars. They'd booked one suite each for George and Andrew, and a further suite for the two girls to share – Shirlie and Dee. But when they were checking in George insisted, 'No, we'll all stay together in the same suite.' Which set tongues wagging round the hotel.

The director was Duncan Giddings who later died in his own swimming pool in Hollywood. His house had caught fire and he rushed back inside to rescue his cat which was caught inside and howling. Duncan was terribly burned. He rushed out a few minutes later and threw himself in the pool, where he died since he had insufficient skin left on his body to keep himself warm. (There was a terrible picture of him in the papers at the time, in the pool, the firemen trying to comfort him.) It seemed ironic really, since I'd only ever known him through making a happy swimming-pool video in Ibiza.

Less happy around the swimming pool were the Wham! girls, now surplus to any requirements bar looking pretty. "There was no dancing in that video," complained Shirlie. "Just posing." There wasn't any singing either, the smooth closing chant of '*cooooo-ooooo!*' being George's multi-tracked voice. It was the last straw for Dee C. Lee, who left Wham! to join The Style Council, the new soul/funk/jazz-inflected outfit formed by ex-Jam leader Paul Weller, then denouncing rock music and extolling the virtues of socialism. (In time Dee would become Mrs Weller, as well as a solo artist in her own right.) Her replacement would be another good-looking black girl, Shirlie's friend Pepsi DeMacque.

Something sexual was also stirring around the time of the 'Club Tropicana' shoot – though not of the kind inferred by Wham!'s manager in his reference to hotel arrangements.

"In the sixties I often made fancying artists one of the criteria for choosing them," says Napier-Bell. "This certainly applied to John's Children, and also to Marc Bolan. But as time moved on I became much more objective and accepted that the most important thing was that other people fancied them – like Wham!, neither of whom I fancied in the slightest even though they were screamed at by girls in their millions."

It seems their manager was also unsure as to whether George might share his sexual orientation at this point, though later he'd be in no doubt. Claiming to have had his precocious fill of the female fleshpots of London, the young singer was, in private at least, about to make the first personal acknowledgement that he was gay.

"Shirlie and I were at this hotel where we were making the video for 'Club Tropicana', before Andrew got there," George recollected many years later. "The three of us were still very close, and I said to Shirlie – even though they were no longer a couple – 'Look, don't tell him,' even though she told him straight away. So incapable of keeping that quiet!" he laughed.

"I do remember having this quite intense conversation with him in Ibiza and he looked quite concerned, he had this big, doe-eyed 'help me' [look]," confirmed the former Ms Holliman. "I think because we were so young and took it so lightly, we just said, 'Don't worry about it, forget it!'"

"But I was quite confused I guess, because there were girls attracted to him and he still liked girls. So I thought, 'He's just had an experience, he's gone off and done this and he needs to talk about it.' So I didn't take it that it was that big a conversation actually."

"I do remember us saying it was a particularly bad idea to inform your father," the now middle-aged Andrew laughed, in conversation with his old bandmate.

"What I was saying is that I thought it was time that I told my mum and dad," George retrospectively clarified his point. "Because if I'd told my mum and dad the whole situation would have been different, I wouldn't have been able to stay 'in' professionally if I'd told my mum and dad."

But in the closet he would remain, for many years. As Fiona Russell Powell recalls: "When he got famous, everybody just thought it was a hoot that he was putting forward this kind of – well, we say a 'heterosexual image', but even then, we'd look at the videos like 'Club Tropicana' and laugh – because they were so camp, with the little white shorts and everything!"

★★★

Simon Napier-Bell recently wrote his anecdotal recollection of an incident in the eighties that compares the relatively *louche* personality of Andrew Ridgeley to the fastidiousness of George Michael, at that time:

When I was managing Wham!, I was drinking a lot, and I still am. (I think it very important not to drink too little alcohol.) One night I went out with Andrew. After dinner and half a dozen clubs my brain was floating pleasantly in and out of focus and during an in-focus period I heard Andrew mention that his father came from Egypt.

'There's an Egyptian nightclub in Queensway,' I told him. 'Drinks and belly-dancers till 4am. Let's go!'

Once there, we drank another bottle of champagne, our sixth of the evening, and ordered a seventh, but realising we'd now drunk enough Andrew picked up the bottle and poured it over our heads..

We were then confronted with the difficulty of getting home. Too drunk to wave for a cab, and probably too dishevelled to be accepted by one, I thought perhaps we should sleep in my Bentley, but as soon as we got in it, the engine somehow started and it moved off.

'You're drunk,' Andrew told me. 'You'd better drive on the pavement. It'll be safer.'

It sounded logical; there would certainly be less traffic.

Surprisingly, it was only after we'd reached Marble Arch and I was negotiating a zebra crossing, trying to reach the pavement on the other side, that sirens wailed and blue lights appeared. Andrew opened the front passenger door and fled. I sank deep into the front seat ...

I'd been blind drunk and I'd got off, so I asked my lawyer: 'If I'd been found guilty what would the penalty have been?'

He told me £200 and a two-year ban, so I went straight home, donated £200 to Oxfam and vowed not to drive again for two years. I phoned a garage and told them to fetch the car from the police station and sell it.

A week later I had to fly with George and Andrew to Norway, where Wham! were doing a TV show. Late in the evening we found ourselves in the rooftop restaurant of Oslo's top hotel, accompanied by the head of the record company and some of his staff. Andrew related the story of our night out and George asked what had happened in court. When I explained how I'd got off he was scandalised.

'It's immoral!' 'What is?'

'That you got off.'

'But I didn't lie. I admitted I did it.'

'But you used a lawyer who got you off. Why did you do that? You should have pleaded guilty and taken the punishment.'

George on a moral crusade was very unforgiving.

'Look, I paid £200 to Oxfam and vowed not to drive for two years.'

'That's not the point; you escaped punishment for doing something against the law. That's wrong.'

'And what if it had been a silly law – like something to do with apartheid in South Africa, then would I have been wrong to break it?'

George sighed, agitated by the puerile nature of my argument. 'Of course not. You must use your own judgment on these things. But you know perfectly well you shouldn't drive when you're drunk. It's a public danger. You should have let yourself be found guilty and suffered for it.'

I turned to Andrew for support but he was already floating in too-many-cocktails-land and hadn't heard a word we said. I was on my own.

And George, of course, was right. He could be very annoying like that.

George himself has said, "It's almost impossible to remember what happened at the beginning of Wham!, because, when I look back on it, it was happening at such an outrageous speed." As suddenly famous (but certainly not rich) 20-year-olds, he and Andrew Ridgeley also spent a good deal of their time anaesthetised to the pressures of fame by booze. It's perhaps fortunate for George that he didn't own a driver's licence at this point – his father had stopped paying for his driving lessons, reputedly, when he got drunk and lost his last deejaying job at a squash club.

But, as his former manager acknowledges, he has always shown contrition when his behaviour has been revealed as not quite equal to his moral code. It would be many years though before he would have reason to feel truly contrite.

CHAPTER 7

I Gave You My Heart

In the summer of 1983, a soul boy from north London flew to the southern USA to meet one of the godfathers of soul. George Michael first liaised with Jerry Wexler at his home in Texas, before flying over to his legendary Muscle Shoals Studios in Alabama.

Wexler was already 66 at this point, a Jew from New York City who, having moved from music journalism to record production, had been instrumental in the careers of R&B/soul greats Ray Charles and Aretha Franklin. He'd also proven the crossover potential of black music by producing Dusty Springfield's classic 1968 *Dusty In Memphis* album, on which the north London Irish girl sang 'Son Of A Preacher Man'. He therefore seemed the natural choice to produce the first solo recordings of a young white soul boy.

The principal song in question was 'Careless Whisper', which George regarded as an unrecorded vintage work by now. "That's the thing that people would point at me about and say, 'That's his greatest moment,'" he reflected several years later, "which is a bit scary... to me it's a precocious piece of work, drawing in a lot of different influences. To me it doesn't sound like a song that was written by a 17-year-old, but I don't know why not as I didn't know anything about life and I certainly didn't know anything serious about romance."

What he *did* know about was the sound and feel of classic soul music, which he expected to be inherent in the work of the producer who co-founded Atlantic Records and even coined the term "rhythm and blues" (R&B) back in the fifties. But, while he'd describe Jerry Wexler as "a wonderful man", he was disappointed with the outcome. "I'd gone to Alabama and literally been so overwhelmed by his track record that I felt that I should just sit back and allow things to happen," he said. "Which really was a mistake, because however good it was, it wasn't actually going to be the record that I initially had in my head."

The original Wexler cut of 'Careless Whisper' can be found online today: it moves along to the kind of soft R&B rhythm that would be termed 'swing' in the late eighties/early nineites; the instrumentation is sometimes sharper and more dramatic than the later version, although the blaring saxophone has a smoother texture. But the vocal is less characteristic of the George Michael who'd emerge as a solo artist, and it is definitely *not* the tune that would have lonesome hearts consoling each other on the disco dance floor the following year.

Although Wexler gave George sound advice that he appears to follow to this day – warning against the histrionic shift up one key at the end of a song that modern R&B vocalists like Whitney Houston made into a cliché – the young singer was unsure enough of the song's original cut to shelve it when he returned to London. In part, this was because his publisher, Dick Leahy, persuaded him that the definitive take of the song was yet to be recorded. But another huge factor was that both his publishers and his management were concerned that the track might become the property of Innervision, against whom they were about to join forces to fight on Wham!'s behalf.

According to Jazz Summers, then of Nomis Management, a mutually acceptable compromise which handed the boys back their careers – while still leaving Innervision with an investor's stake – was briefly a possibility. All they needed to do was take the matter to CBS, the parent company, and have them redraw terms for its hottest new act which would be in everyone's favour. But then it all fell down.

"Later I said to him, 'Look, don't be an idiot,'" recalled Summers of his negotiations with Mark Dean. "What you should do is come hand-in-hand with us to CBS and we'll say, 'Look, this guy wants a million pounds to run his record company. These guys want a million pounds or half a million pounds because they are broke.' And then everyone would have been happy. No lawyers' fees. We could have been off and going. But no. 'Don't be ridiculous,' Mark says. 'I've got a contract.'"

In October 1983, Wham!, Nomis and Morrison-Leahy all ganged up and got litigious on Innervision. They enlisted the specialist services of Tony Russell, a music business lawyer who'd prove critical in later battles fought by George Michael as a solo artist. But for now, Russell's opening salvo was a 24-page legal letter which stressed the incongruity and indignity of CBS's best-selling new artists living on a record company allowance of £40 a week.

With a court hearing set for November, co-manager Simon Napier-Bell formulated a plan to raise revenue that foreshadowed what would happen when the record industry collapsed in the next century: if little money could be made from records, then it was time to get the show back on the road, with an extensive 31-date tour of the UK. He secured a £50,000 sponsorship deal with Fila, the sportswear manufacturer, which would clad George and Andrew in its clothing for the next tour. It was a goodbye to the mock-bad boys of the early days, but it was also timely in the sense that this was the era of 'the casual' – the soul boy or football fan who rejected the outrage of other recent youth fashions in favour of expensive designer clothes.*

For the boys from Wham!, it was another chance to ratchet up the fun element. With their hair growing long (and, in George's case, with blond highlights applied by sisters Melanie and Yioda), pictures of the

---

* Rumour has it that Fila came to regret the Wham! deal when it realised that many casuals didn't acquire the clothes over the counter, but by shoplifting.

time show them sporting a softer, Duran Duran-ish, pretty-boy look. Bopping rhythmically about the stage, they ended a mock game of badminton by stuffing the shuttlecocks down the crotches of their white Fila shorts. The music critics baulked at their antics; the teenage girls in the audience loved it. Guess whose opinion carried the day?

Meanwhile, with no new material that he could legally promote till the court case was resolved, Mark Dean of Innervision remixed and repackaged three tracks from *Fantastic* under the title 'Club Fantastic Megamix'. It left only one track on the album which hadn't been issued as a single. But the real cause for concern came with his scheduled intent to issue the original Wexler cut of 'Careless Whisper'.

Dick Leahy went into overdrive. First of all, he persuaded George that he could and should do better, pencilling in a new recording of his oldest song for the near future. Secondly, he prohibited Innervision from issuing the original cut. "Because a publisher has one great weapon," Leahy explained. "He has the right to grant the first licence of the recording of a tune of which he controls the copyright."

In the first round of Innervision Limited vs. George Panayiotou and Andrew Ridgeley, an injunction was placed on Wham! to stop them signing with another record label. But, as 1983 melted into 1984, music biz veteran Simon Napier-Bell came into his element and took off the gloves, ready for a dirty battle of wits. "I provoked Mark Dean into doing something," Napier-Bell happily admitted. "I had a phone conversation in which I was rude to him and then he wrote me a threatening letter... It was delivered to my front door by bike and I put it in a safe and when we went to court there it was ready to pull out and show what sort of person Mark Dean was. It's a tough game," he genially acknowledged.

Those in the Wham! camp knew that Dean actually had little choice as to whether he'd let Wham! go by that stage. If he did throw up his hands and allow them to sign elsewhere, he'd become the subject of litigation by CBS in turn. But in Napier-Bell, who George could never really bring himself to either trust or admire, they had the perfect fighter in their corner – a man who could conduct a battle of words very pugnaciously indeed.

As Innervision ran up legal costs of £80,000, CBS executives decided to switch sides in favour of the group. "They were going to put in the receivers unless I agreed a deal," complained a chastened Dean. "There was too much power play going on, too many egos, too many reputations to be scored, and not enough peacemakers." The young wannabe Svengali had discovered that he was punching above his weight.

In March 1984, the Royal Courts of Justice announced their judgement, releasing Wham! from their contract with Innervision. It was effectively the end of Dean's personal empire, though he'd find employment with the music industry in the US. The boys were now free to sign with a major CBS subsidiary, Epic, for a deal which vastly upped the ante in terms of advances and royalties.

"Mark Dean told Dick Leahy that it took him a long time not to want to smash the radio every time he heard a record by Wham! or me," George has remarked. "Most people's mistakes don't follow them around so loudly, do they?" Drawing breath in spring 1984, the songwriter would soon reveal how he'd made use of the creative hiatus.

And the man who made their legal victory possible? In his book about managing Wham!, *I'm Coming To Take You To Lunch*, Simon Napier-Bell makes the following comment about their new deal with Epic which he extends slightly here:

Was it a good deal? Not at all. It was the same old stuff in a more attractive wrapping.

(I meant: all contracts with major record companies are on a par – they're full of deceptive clauses designed simply to cheat artists of royalties and rights. In financial terms, Wham!'s new contract was vastly better than their previous one. In moral terms, no different.)

In the music business you don't get out of an unfair record contract to get into a fair one; you get out of an unfair contract with bad financial terms to get into another unfair contract with slightly better financial terms. As you climb the pop hierarchy you get better contractual conditions as you go, moving from a bottom rung where you are ripped off by every technique a record company knows, to a higher-rung deal where you're ripped off with greater subtlety.

For all that there was little love lost between the vocalist/songwriter of Wham! and his canny co-manager, these were sentiments that George Michael would find himself echoing in his next major legal battle, one decade hence.

In May 1984, Wham! came bopping back in poppy triumph with 'Wake Me Up Before You Go Go'. From the opening call of "Jitterbug... jitterbug!" to the title's "go-go" refrain, redolent of sixties disco dancing and the go-go music that briefly predated house in the States, this was mid-eighties Day-Glo pop in its essence. With the girls relegated further to the status of dancers, with just to the odd "yeah yeah" to sing, in the video George wore a black-on-white 'Choose Life' T-shirt – cheekily cribbing the look from the 'Frankie Says' T-shirts and slogans popularised by their main chart rivals of the time, Frankie Goes To Hollywood – and swayed rhythmically to and fro in front of legions of adoring fans.

It was Wham!'s first number one in Britain and it heralded a march on the charts that would see out the end of the year. The happy-go-lucky, near-nonsense lyric was inspired by a message that a sleepy (and probably two-parts drunk) Andrew left for his parents, absent-mindedly writing "go" twice before hitting the Land of Nod. The incongruous phrase struck George and transformed itself into a joyous celebration of... well, nothing in particular, but if 'Club Tropicana' demanded a smiling face then this one wore a big cheesy grin.

"I think 'Go Go' is undoubtedly the most remembered Wham! song – because it is that much more *stupid* than anything else!" George later conceded. "Because what I was then and what I am now – one of them has to be a fake! I just hope people realise that the old one was the fake." They would, but they'd have to learn to listen without prejudice first.

This was the beginning of Wham! as a national press phenomenon. Every nightclub performance, every half-heard drunken comment and romantic rumour was deemed worthy of report in the tabloids. George's wavy, blond-highlighted bouffant hairstyle of the time became instantly recognisable, like a male counterpart of that other suburbanite, blonde-highted sensation, Princess Di.

Rumours of sexual flings; Andrew drunk in nightclubs; rumours of adultery with aristocratic women; Andrew drunk with glamour models. It was the kind of behaviour that had made former girlfriend Shirlie Holliman and the other half of Wham! into just good friends a year previously. "Andrew could be very childish," said Shirlie of her ex-boyfriend. "But I don't think George was ever young... he has always seemed too mature for his age. I can't imagine what he will be like at 40." As she would later find, life still had at least a few surprises left in store.

And if George was the more sober part of the equation, that didn't stop journalistic eyes from prying into his private life and fuelling the slowly growing speculation. In the years that followed he would speak of the intense pressure of living his life under newspaper scrutiny, of the arrogant press demanding to know that which they had no right to. On the other hand, his contemporary Fiona Russell Powell opines that the British press (which is notoriously predatory) showed some restraint in their treatment of the young George Michael, and that if he'd been a less respected figure his private life would have become public knowledge much earlier. As she recounts: "I remember, and it's hysterical, [but] George would only dance to his own records sometimes! [laughs] I mean, please! Fancy doing that in front of everybody! Fat Tony used to deejay at the Wag Club, and he would get on the microphone and make all these bitchy, camp comments about George's sexuality. That's what [Boy] George O'Dowd did, and the reason is that *everybody* knew George Michael was gay, but he was hiding it. Well, a lot of people in the music industry knew. But it was all kept quiet because he was bringing in the money. He was just one of those people who you accepted that, when you went out, you were going to see him – but then he got *famous*, when Wham! took off ...

"I don't know about all this because I can see both sides. A lot of our mutual gay friends didn't like the fact, which was one of the reasons why George O'Dowd used to bitch and snipe at him and so did Fat Tony. But the thing is, Fat Tony was good friends with George Michael as well as Boy George, because he deejayed at loads of George's private parties. I can understand the point of view. Patrick Lilley – who used to run loads of gay pubs, he started Queer Nation – was part of that whole crowd as well. He was a real militant, out-there gay: everyone who's gay who hides it should be outed. But I used to say, 'Well no, I think it's a personal thing and no one else has a right to do that.' In those days, back in the eighties, it was still very difficult to be young and realise that your feelings were a bit different to how they were supposed to be, there weren't all these helplines, you couldn't go on the computer and Google it if you were a young gay man."

One of the first steps in the new masterplan would be the re-recording of 'Careless Whisper', which would finally introduce the world to George Michael as a solo artist. Simon Napier-Bell, always as in thrall to the singer's talent as he was nonplussed by his aloofness, recalls the painstaking perfectionism that made the final cut what it was:

Elusive qualities are elusive, which is why it's impossible to pin them down. I couldn't hear it. Nor could the two sax players we got in (and one was David Sanborn, for heaven's sake). Nor could Jerry Wexler, probably the world's most experienced record producer. But George could. George felt there was something in the way the sax had been played on the demo that wasn't coming out of David Sanborn's sax, nor from the sax of the second player we got in. Eventually George got the same guy to play on the track as had played on the demo – an amateur musician from north London. The secret seems to have been that he hadn't been properly trained and therefore fingered the instrument wrongly, which produced a fractionally different texture on a couple of notes. Inaudible to me, but not to George. And since it was the biggest selling record he ever made he was almost certainly right. Although no one else could hear the difference, there must have been a subliminal quality that seduced the world into loving the record. And buying it.

'Careless Whisper' was the sound of summer 1984 in continental Europe. But it also hit the number one slot in places as far afield as the US (where it was billed as by 'Wham! featuring George Michael'), Brazil and Australia. Its shared songwriting credit of Michael/Ridgeley, dating back to the bedroom sessions of 1981, would help ensure the latter could take a leisurely early retirement. It also carried a dedication to George's parents: "Five minutes in return for 21 years."

Released in July, the song was accompanied by a video in which a dark-haired George clenched his fists in anguish, playing the role of a star-crossed cheating lover as he mimed the words. Napier-Bell recalls the video shoot:

The 'Careless Whisper' video was originally intended to be shot on location in Miami. And was. But after it was edited it looked a bit too lightweight so we thought a bit of gravitas would be added if George were to re-sing the song onstage in a theatre (no audience – lonely, after-hours stuff) and intercut it with the location material. Which is what we did. I don't know how anyone ever got hold of the original edit for YouTube. But these days it seems everyone digs out their darkest video secrets and displays them to the world.

The video overshot its £30,000 budget by £17,000 when George's hair went frizzy in the heat and he stopped the shoot, flying sister Melanie in for an urgent re-style. Although in retrospect it's a rather corny and over-literal US soap opera-style actualisation of a great song, which shows George making out with and two-timing two generically sexy models, the video neither hindered nor was responsible for its huge success.

Later that summer, George and Andrew would alight to the south of France for the recording of their second album at Chateau Minerval, the Provence home of jazz musician Jacques Loussier. This was the time and place when George finally came face to face with his childhood idol. Elton John was holidaying in the region with his wife of the time, Renate Blauel, a German recording engineer he'd married in February of that year. Though there would be much unkind speculation as to whether Ms Blaeul was a 'beard' (i.e. a platonic female friend helping a gay man mask his sexuality), the self-professedly bisexual piano player would continue to support his former bride when their three-year marriage ended.

It was here that the bespectacled superstar first got acquainted with his young admirer – the performer who, over time, would variously be his duettist, his good friend and, eventually, his verbal sparring partner.

And Andrew? For him, it was business as usual. "Andrew just couldn't give a toss," George would blithely admit of his partner's perpetual booze bender. "Not only did it get to the stage where he became a kind of laughing stock, but people were very jealous of him. He seemed to be getting too much for doing nothing."

On their return to London, Wham! made a brief detour into politics when they got involved in the most significant British sociopolitical clash of the decade. Members of the National Union of Mineworkers had been on strike for several months, opposing the scheduled closure of the UK's coalmines by the Thatcher government.

"They personified the whole Thatcherite dream, didn't they?" argues Fiona Russell Powell of Wham! "The aspirational nonsense, because [George] always struck me as a prototype Jay Kay [of Jamiroquai] type. I do think they represented an era, completely. I don't think the nineties could have produced them – because it was all about aspirational ideals, wasn't it?"

Despite all such appearances, however, George especially would make his liberal-left leanings increasingly clear over the years. To his political conscience, it was only appropriate that two such privileged entertainers should contribute to a benefit for the families of the strikers, who were undergoing increasing hardship.

That was the theory anyway, and it may have looked good on paper. On September 7, 1984, Wham! joined the bill of the miners' families benefit at the Royal Festival Hall organised by Red Wedge – the socialist musicians' collective that broadly supported the aims of what was then a more traditionally left-wing Labour Party. As George and Andrew had both voted Labour in the general election the previous year (when the party leader, old-school socialist Michael Foot, was trounced at the polls), they felt it was time to stand up and be counted. On a bill with radical soulsters The Style Council and radical comedian Alexei Sayle (then a Marxist – more recently the voiceover on ads for financial services), Wham! were on a hiding to nothing when they turned up to mime four tracks instead of performing live. When their backing tapes went out of sync, the audience let the boys feel the full force of their derision. Humiliated, George apologised and personally offered a refund to anyone who'd bought tickets because they believed Wham! were playing live. The one-time cover boys of *NME* were showered with ridicule by the music press for weeks to come.

On a far happier note, the second single from the new album was released that same month. Sales of 'Freedom' would eclipse 'Wake Me Up Before You Go-Go', with its energetic Motown-poppy tribute to the joys of monogamy and the tribulations of being with a two-timing girl. On *Top Of The Pops*, George and Andrew mimed the 'doo-doo-doo, doo-doo, doo-doo' lines like the cats who'd lapped up a whole dairy.

Their penguin-suited band were led by bearded veteran keyboard player Tommy Eyre, the boys' new live musical director, who'd played on Gerry Rafferty's 'Baker Street' (which features the second most famous sax motif after 'Careless Whisper'); he too looked like he'd been transported to bubblegum pop heaven, as did the rest of the backing band – Hugh Burns on guitar, old faithful Deon Estus on bass, Trevor

Morais on drums and trumpeters Paul Spong, Colin Graham and David Baptiste.

The album itself, with the *fait accompli* title of *Make It Big*, followed the next month with a launch at the Xenon nightclub. Guests included such names of the eighties as Duran Duran, Spandau Ballet, Bob Geldof, Nick Heyward – and Sandie Shaw, the sixties songstress then undergoing a resurgence by singing with The Smiths. Other veterans present included David Cassidy, Lulu, comedian Frankie Howerd and actor John (*The Elephant Man*) Hurt.

With a cover picture featuring the smouldering, longer-haired George and Andrew, like its predecessor it was very much a singles album. Complementing the last three 45s (including 'Careless Whisper') were 'Like A Baby', a gently ethereal, guitar-led ballad that anticipated some of the George Michael solo output, 'Heartbeat', a beautifully produced epic pop song pitched between early girl groups like The Ronettes and early Springsteen, a cover version of The Isley Brothers' 'If You Were There', and 'Everything She Wants' – the most serious song in the duo's repertoire, a piece of tense white-boy funk that lamented a materialistic girl driving her overworked boyfriend to distraction. This was the way George wanted to go as a songwriter.

"I had decided that I was going to write without any restraints in terms of the band," he later reflected. "So I thought, 'What do I want to do? Do I want to write in a much more personal sense and throw off the band image, or do I want to go with the band image and write for the band?' And I didn't think that either were necessary; I believed that I could do both and live with the results for a while and make up for it later, which was basically the plan. So it was a big decision to make, and at times I was thinking, 'I'm never going to get out of this, I'm never going to be seen as a writer, I'm never going to get my credibility back.'"

Given the level of his success, his worries appeared to verge on neurotic. But it would be some time before the critics would learn to listen to George Michael without prejudice. In retrospect, even he has been unduly harsh on himself. "If you think about it, the second album doesn't have any kind of cohesive identity," he claims. "It's only the image that was consistently naff!!

In fact, the second album is much like the first – a successful collection of pure pop songs. But then, maybe that was becoming a problem. "We didn't think we could take the concept that was Wham! into adulthood. We were right," said an older Andrew. According to him, even at that point he knew that George's future as a songwriter/performer would take place without him.

Make It Big made it predictably colossal on both sides of the Atlantic, hitting the number one slots for several weeks before staying on the charts for well over a year. At the end of the year, the only thing that kept Wham!'s seasonal hit, 'Last Christmas', from the top of the charts was the Bob Geldof-Midge Ure-penned Band Aid single, 'Do They Know It's Christmas?', an act of glitzy showbiz charity to aid the starving in Ethiopia and the Sudan. And of course, the all-star eighties pop line-up – Sting, Bono, Simon Le Bon of Duran Duran and pop music's über-queen, Boy George – wouldn't have been complete without George taking a prominent vocal line. (Andrew was notable by his absence, sleeping off the night before. "I didn't even know that I was supposed to be going," he later said.)

Behind the apparent camaraderie of the famous video showing all the singers turning up that morning, looking a bit dishevelled, George was feeling uncomfortable. "I was very aware of the prejudice against Wham! in there," he would admit. "Everybody in there had said things about everyone else in the press and, to a lot of people, Wham! were the laughing stock of the year. Some of it was jealousy and some of it was a genuine lack of respect."

The disrespect came to a head when Paul Weller tried to take George to task for speaking out against Arthur Scargill, the National Union of Mineworkers leader, his resentment building up ever since the Festival Hall debacle. The boy from Wham! stuck to his guns – he'd wanted to aid the miners in their plight, but opined that their leader was "a wanker" for his communist sympathies and insistence that the Soviet Union was a free country.

Even at the number two slot, 'Last Christmas' sold an incredible one and a half million copies; George and Andrew turned over all their royalties from the single to Band Aid, raising a further quarter of a million pounds for the cause. It's Wham!'s most saccharine hit, its tinkly little melody and wounded love lyric ("I gave you my heart, but the very next day you gave it away") are still the cue that Christmas is coming round again at every chain pub or restaurant in Britain. "It was just nice to see someone coming up who had an ideal grasp of how to write a song," Elton John, George's spiritual godfather, later acclaimed. "'Last Christmas' being a classic example."

The young songwriter himself was rather more sensitive as to how his craft was perceived. "They were so turned off by the image that they couldn't hear what this 20-year-old kid was doing," he'd later complain of the press and the critics. "I was producer and arranger, and I knew how to make these records and make them jump out of the radio. The idea that just because I was wearing ridiculous shorts and curtain rings in my ears would actually stop people from noticing that, when I look back I still think it's kind of stunning."

At home in London in March 1985, George received some of the recognition he sought when he became the youngest composer to win the Ivor Novello Award for Songwriter of the Year. He also accepted a second award for 'Careless Whisper' as Most Performed Work. The main award was presented to him by his new friend, Elton John, who introduced him as "the Paul McCartney of his generation". For the first and only time in public the boy from Wham! lost his composure, with tears welling up in his eyes and interrupting his acceptance speech.

It was a public coming of age for George Michael, still only 21. Now a self-made millionaire who could stand toe-to-toe with his similarly driven father, it was time to leave his family's suburban nest. He rented an expensive flat in the upmarket central London district of Knightsbridge, where his modest furnishings were nonetheless remarked upon by the few journalists who visited. For the time being, and for many years to come, he would live alone.

CHAPTER 8

The Mighty Wei Ming

As Wham! had now also hit the top of the US charts, the view was that they were not making the anticipated big leap across the Atlantic. "Weisner-DeMann was not convincing CBS that Wham! was a huge band," said Jazz Summers. "Because if you go into CBS and they tell you that you're not going to get Michael Jackson treatment with this act, then you've *got* to get Michael Jackson treatment with this act."

As there was no binding long-term agreement with the American management team, Summers and Napier-Bell convinced George and Andrew that they should step in and fill the gap. "Andrew and I didn't make a particularly great effort to break the States," George has said. "I don't remember being in a particular hurry to make it happen." But still, the management would put them through their paces in spring 1985, on lightning tours of Japan, Australia and the US.

By all accounts, the first US tour saw George indulge in the traditional rock'n'roll lifestyle on a similar scale to Andrew. According to his cousin Andros, "There was a point where George was fucking everything that moved." Or at least, as far as the official version had it, he was having as many women as were prepared to throw themselves at him. As to whether he was indulging the full extent of his sexuality is a moot point, even today, though perhaps there's some indication in his jaded comment of several years later: "Now I'm so aware of the fact that I'm a catch. The women are not the catch. *I am the catch*. It's not a very attractive feeling for me."

Erotic indulgence aside, the presence of his Wham! partner and less serious other half meant that George could partake of some silliness and old-fashioned fun. In Japan, Wham! were promoted by a cheesy TV ad in pastel video tones, in which they performed a limp version of 'Freedom'.

"Oh that advert," George laughed in his 2005 biographical documentary. "We shouldn't really take the piss out of the Japanese by letting them know. Basically, we started off with a very bad impersonation of Simon Le Bon's version of the moonwalk, and then we finished it with a version of 'Freedom', it was about a relationship with an overweight girl: 'Doesn't matter that you're slightly porky, ever since that day we met in Torquay... People think you're chubby, baby, you're the fish-face I adore!' They asked us what fish-face meant and we said it was a term of endearment. And they showed it!"

The Japanese, with their love of western pop culture filtered through a slightly askew oriental lens, were an obvious target audience. More compelling to co-manager Simon Napier-Bell was the question of how to turn Wham! from an internationally touring pop band into a global phenomenon. The answer that he hit on also lay in the Far East, but beyond the technophile shores of Japan – both geographically and culturally. As he later explained in an interview for the BBC TV show *Hardtalk*:

I and my partner Jazz Summers made a plan with them of how to make them the biggest group in the world, without having to go through the enormous palaver of touring America endlessly and having to do 6,000 radio interviews. And over dinner at the Bombay Brasserie and a bottle of wine, we suddenly hit on the idea of 'Why don't you be the first group to play in Communist China?' And George, who had this marvellous way of knowing a good idea when he heard it, went, 'Yes! Fix it!' So it suddenly went from having this bottle of wine over dinner to having to go to China, meet heads of government and get them to agree that Wham! could be the first group ever to play in China.

I went 17, 18 times eventually – once a month for 18 months before I got approval. It was Deng [Xiaoping, Chairman of the Communist Party] himself who gave approval, no one lower down was going to give approval for that – I met people lower down, it went up and up the chain. Couldn't find a way in to begin with. You went to China and if you wanted to talk to the head of government you didn't just say, 'I'm Simon Napier-Bell, can I talk to the head of government please?' I had this policy: I went every month and I phoned all the people I knew and left messages that I was here and went away again. And by the third month these people had seen these messages appearing on their desk, they must have thought I was quite important because I was coming all the time and it didn't seem to bother me, I left messages to them so they began to think I must be talking to someone else who was more important about something else. Eventually I began to get one or two calls back, so I just found my way to the right department, talked to them, never ever asking a question that they could say yes or no to. That was how I got Wham! into China, by never asking a question.

I just used to say things like, 'You know, it would be marvellous if a pop group came to China, it'd be lovely for you to see our culture.' And then we'd go and have a dinner. And then the next time I'd go I'd say, 'You know that thing I said about a pop group coming? It'd be wonderful if it was Wham!, the group I manage, because they're awfully good.' And then another month would go by and I'd say, 'If one day Wham! came to play in China it'd be wonderful if they could play at the Workers' Stadium, as it's such a nice stadium.' This went on and on and on until finally I'd really said it all. I knew they were consulting other people because during the course of this I'd taken five members of the Politburo to Japan to see Wham!, and paid for the whole thing and had them see the reality of it.

Finally I couldn't stand it any longer. I just said, 'You know, it'd be really wonderful if one day Wham! did play China and it was March the 14th at this place.' There was still no yes or no there, so they didn't say anything. I went back to Singapore and I thought, 'I can get them to do it,' and I announced to the press that they'd said yes. It was on the front of every paper. I knew they'd been discussing it at the highest level, they just couldn't say no. But I still didn't know and I came back to England and we were fixing the tour, it was going to cost nearly a million dollars. We had to get the money from CBS Records and I still wasn't 100 percent sure, because no one had said yes. So I sent a telex to the office I'd been talking to; I said, 'Can you send me a plan of the layout of the Workers' Stadium for March the 14th?', which was the day we said. Three days later it came back, and where there was usually a basketball pitch there was a stage, and on the stage it said 'Wham!'

The publicity coup of taking the West's biggest pop band to Red China is indisputable. Still, the motivation for doing so would always be argued by George, who says he was thinking in terms of innovation, of being the first, rather than the publicity it would generate. There may be only a thin line between the two, but, claimed the mainman of Wham!, "Simon always builds his masterplan and then in retrospect writes in what happened as though it were part of the original intention. He's very good at that." Indeed, it's a very human trait to interpret your own past actions in terms of where you are now – a trait shared by George Michael.

The first performance at the 10,000-seater Workers' Stadium in Beijing didn't actually take place until April 7, almost a month after Napier-Bell's suggested provisional date. It was preceded by two much more lucrative gigs at the Coliseum Theatre in Hong Kong, but the fact that the event was taking place at all was truly historic, to be recorded for posterity by veteran British film director Lindsay Anderson. Even the arrival in Beijing was bizarre, with the mighty 'Wei Ming' (as they were billed – literally meaning 'mighty') met not by screams, but by po-faced officials from the Communist Party and the All China Youth Federation.

The boys from Wham! were filmed bemusedly attending functions with the ageing party members who headed the monolithic Chinese state; when not serving as propaganda tools, George and Andrew are seen in the documentary wandering vaguely along the Great Wall of China, around Beijing's Tiananmen Square – which would become the scene of murderous state violence four years later – or in the Forbidden City, home to China's dynastic emperors in its long pre-Communist history.

Anderson had been George's choice – a distinguished if not very commercial filmmaker best known for his surreal black comedy trilogy (*If...* , *O Lucky Man* and *Britannia Hospital*) which satirised the hypocrisy and decline of British institutions. These are presumably the works the young singer knew him for, but in the fifties Anderson was a noted documentarian of such essentially British subjects as funfairs and Covent Garden fruit market. He was also a waspish old queen, with very little tolerance of anyone who wasn't consumed by the filmic process.

"George Michael was totally uninterested in what we were doing," complained Anderson. "He never showed any interest at all in the whole idea of what filmmaking was. He was extremely bright in his own field, but he didn't want to learn."

The filmmaker was scathing about how Wham!'s record label had been talked into investing £1 million in the production, entitled *Foreign Skies* – after costs of at least £400,000 for staging the concerts themselves, with 150 crew members erecting tons of equipment, both George and Andrew's families in tow and the handing over of all door receipts to the Youth Federation in Beijing, or the Ministry of Culture in Canton. It was a very effective way of sinking a large amount of money. In the face of all this, to the semi-impoverished filmmaker Anderson, George just seemed like a "poor little rich girl".

The film director may have detected his own sexual orientation in the younger man, or he may just have been venting his notorious spleen. Napier-Bell, however, was aware of the persecution that gays might face in China, where – despite any blinkered sympathy that sections of the Left might still have held for communism – the totalitarian values of the great workers' state could invade the bedroom:

> *I never once talked to Wham! about how I'd managed to get them into China. Despite George's insistence that he was the ultimate decision maker as to what they did and didn't do, he had very little idea of all the work that was done behind the scenes on his behalf.*
>
> *Whether or not the Chinese authorities knew I was gay is an interesting question. They certainly had a folder on me with personal information, but perhaps they never connected sharing a house with two other guys to anything they would think improper.*
>
> *I'm sure, if someone had told them that George was gay, and made a point of explaining what they meant by it, Wham! would not have been invited to play there, but I'm not sure at that time if George himself knew. Also, you must remember, the Chinese government were very head-in-the-sand about homosexuality. When I asked them what their policy was towards it, they said they didn't need to have a policy because in China there was none.* [*]

(As to the suggestion that George was still unsure of his sexuality, Fiona Russell Powell demurs: "It just makes me laugh, all that, because they both bloody knew! Just look at a lot of the people Simon Napier-Bell has handled – nearly all of them are gay.")

As the documentary film records, Wham! were real showbiz troupers on the two nights that they played. With George in white jacket and no shirt and Andrew in tartan strides, they put on an energetic performance despite being circumscribed in a number of ways. (The volume of their performance was too low; there could be no sexual suggestiveness to their movements; 'Love Machine' could not be performed – although they got away with it afterwards in Canton.) The Minister of Culture in Canton had pre-instructed the

---

[*] As we have seen in the previous chapter, George was by now acknowledging his personal sexuality – though only in private.

audience who attended the show, "Enjoy it but don't learn." Such decadent Western indulgences as dancing were also banned among the audience, the ban being strictly enforced by armed guards. In the Workers' Stadium, a boy was dragged out of the audience and beaten up outside for smoking a cigarette.

According to a bemused Andrew, the major hit of the night was opening act Trevor Duncan, a black breakdancer whose enthusiasm infected audience members who had to be physically restrained from trying to copy him. ("The audience probably thought, 'I don't like those two white guys who came on after Wham!' I wouldn't have blamed them.") But for the most part the audiences were staid and uniformly dressed in Mao suits. The front rows of both concerts were monopolised by party and federation officials.

"To let the kids in town know they were there, we gave loads of cassettes away. But in the end I don't think anyone in China knew Wham! were playing there at all," complained Napier-Bell.

George too was uneasy after the event. At the time he'd mouthed the party line about being cultural ambassadors, making an embarrassing speech to the Youth Federation which included the Neil Armstrong-like phrase,"I think I speak for everyone when I say that this may be a small step for Wham! but a great step for the youth of the world."

On his return to London, he was much more sceptical. As he told *The Face*, "What was basically going on was that the Chinese government was trying to encourage the Western world to accept Chinese product. They were saying, 'Look, we have our arms open, we are going to accept Western music.' That was total bollocks. They used us. We were a propaganda item." As he'd seen with his own eyes, the Chinese youth did indeed want their freedom – but they would only be offered a tantalising glimpse before the state stole it away again.

The true measure of how two young Western pop performers were used as propaganda for a vicious and decrepit regime can perhaps be gauged from the following quote from *Time* magazine, in summer 1985:

"Just five years ago, rock'n'roll was denounced as 'decadent' and said to be a cause of rape, prostitution and drug addiction. But the judgment on Wham!'s music by Zhou Renkai, an official of the All-China Youth Federation, which invited the group, was that it was 'very healthy for the youth'."

Napier-Bell had his own view. In *Black Vinyl, White Powder*, his memoir of the music industry, he writes of returning to the Workers' Stadium in Beijing a month after Wham! had played. This time a mass trial was taking place: "A shifty bunch of officials sat on a podium passing judgement on a succession of hang-dog petty criminals... Most of them received the death penalty. They were then taken outside to a field near the river and given a bullet in the back of the head."

With the passing of time, Simon Napier-Bell would come to regard Wham!'s Red Chinese sojourn as one of the factors that instilled a yearning for freedom among educated youth by osmosis. "Wham!'s music was presented as harmless happy youth culture," he observes, "but was almost certainly one of the many Western influences that leaked into China in the eighties and helped foment what happened in Tiananmen Square." But then, as before, the response would be bullets and bloodshed.

Back at home in the UK, most of the publicity was fixated on the grim distraction of trumpet player Raul D'Oliveira suffering an apparently drug-induced psychotic freakout and harming himself on the flight. ("Trumpeter Whams Himself" read *The Guardian*, outdoing the tabloids at their own game.) For manager Napier-Bell, the real press was coming from elsewhere:

Wham! played China in order to get an entire week of once-an-hour coverage on the three US news channels. It worked, and the resulting flood of publicity was enough to take them from being just another Brit pop act to being a 'stadium' group. Three weeks after they played in Beijing, we were booking up a US tour in 70,000-seater venues.

George Michael made his own return to the US in May 1985, the month following the China gigs. Predating Wham!'s second US tour, he performed at a quarter-century anniversary celebration of the Tamla Motown label, at the Apollo Theatre in Harlem. Paying rapt tribute to the soul-pop fusion music that first thrilled him as a boy, he sang duets with Motown greats Smokey Robinson and Stevie Wonder. It was a landmark along his way to becoming the world's greatest white soul performer, among whose repertoire would be several Stevie Wonder covers.

George would be back in London for July, to participate in the most monumental live event of the decade – Wham! in China notwithstanding. As Simon Napier-Bell recalls:

It was extraordinary. I was going backwards and forwards to China to fix up publicity for my group – totally as a pop manager, nothing else, just thinking of money and publicity. At exactly the same time, Bob Geldof was equally using politics to do something rather more worthwhile, which was Live Aid. And we'd been talking rather a lot about this together, he'd asked me what I thought about it and I'd pointed out various ways where he could make a lot more money than he was contemplating, and of course got George Michael involved in doing it. Coming back from China, which was a triumph in that I'd achieved what I set out to achieve – certainly Wham! had been made enormously famous in America that week when they were in China – I came back to see something really worthwhile, which is what Bob did.

Live Aid was the natural culmination of the Band Aid project and their record 'Do They Know It's Christmas?' It made a national figure of Bob Geldof, formerly remembered only as vocalist of once-popular pop-punk band The Boomtown Rats, now a freely swearing media spokesman on behalf of the starving of Africa. Continuing the theme of pop-music-can-feed-the-world (and as easy as it is to be cynical about grandstanding pop stars and corrupt African regimes, lives certainly were saved), Live Aid collected the stars who'd contributed to the single and their various bands on one stage at Wembley Stadium, while American stars paraded themselves for the cause semi-simultaneously at JFK Stadium in New York.

Besides the eighties pop stars who performed on the single, the old guard were out in force, not least Paul McCartney and The Who. Queen, many years down from being a glam band, took the opportunity to showcase themselves as rousing crowd-pleasers to a satellite-linked international audience. And then there was Elton John, performing his soul-searching 1974 hit 'Don't Let The Sun Go Down On Me' – accompanied by his young friend George, who sang the greater part of the lyric, wearing near-beard designer stubble and shades.

As much as the release of 'Careless Whisper', this was the moment for many pop lovers when George Michael became a solo artist. It almost seemed to be a statement of such – Andrew was conspicuously absent, though he was singing backing vocals at the back of the stage with Elton's sometime duettist, Kiki Dee. While almost visibly nervous before the 70,000-strong crowd, it was a sterling performance by the Wham! frontman, who seems to have both anticipated and slightly resented the hugely positive response he received worldwide.

"It showed that people wanted me – quite unfairly – to do stuff on my own so that they could admit to liking me," George remarked in his 1990 autobiography. "I was out of tune for the first couple of verses. I actually sing a lot better than that on my records and I don't see why everyone should suddenly like me just because I am up there with musicians twice my age and I am taking myself away from my friend."

If his words seemed overly defensive, it may have been because he knew he'd taken an irrevocable step down a different road – one which Andrew Ridgeley, to his credit, had already accepted was inevitable.

With three number-one singles in the US, Wham! remained very much a viable proposition for the immediate future. Nomis Management had already engineered the step to stadium-sized venues via Napier-Bell's king-making strategies in China. While George was reluctant to pursue the traditional grinding tour schedules that came with 'breaking America', co-manager Jazz Summers believed he'd found the perfect ratio of venues per city/per tour by increasing the size of the auditoria. Where once Wham! might have played to US audiences of 5-6,000 in one night, now they could attract crowds of ten times that size. To make that practical leap, he switched from their previous booking agents to the Triad Agency, where an enthusiastic young Californian named Rob Kahane was only too willing to lend his services.

"I had seen them at the Hammersmith Odeon in London and people were going bananas," Kahane later recalled. "And I thought this was the second coming. I thought this was The Beatles."

Kahane spent two full months getting the itinerary together for the second US tour. When the dates were announced, 30,000 tickets sold immediately for the Miami leg of the tour. Then Summers phoned from Nomis in London and disaster seemed about to strike: George didn't want to do the tour; he hadn't wanted to take the traditional rock'n'roll route of slogging around the smaller venues, but he didn't want the strain of touring massive stadiums either.

Summers, desperate, pleaded with Kahane to come over to London and reason with George. The US agent, bemused and deflated, saw it as a desperate last-ditch attempt. If his own managers couldn't talk the performer round, what good could *he*, a total stranger, do?

But after this bombshell it seemed there was very little left to lose, so Rob Kahane made the transatlantic flight. He worked up his spiel and dropped in on the young singer when he was being consulted on the edit of the *Foreign Skies* video.

"I went down there with a map of the United States and George walked out: nice to meet you, da-da-da," Kahane explained, "and I said, 'Look, I have worked on this for a long, hard time, we are only doing these places, we have sold the tickets and we are going to do the business. It's two weeks out of your life.' And he looked at me and *that's* when our relationship started, that's when I felt the power of George Michael. He said, 'I'll do it. I've gotta go, but I'll see you in America.'"

"An artist like George Michael was a dream," David Austin would say of his lifelong friend's relationship with the music industry. "He'd just step up to the front line, make a decision and there was always somebody to blame. But it never went wrong, it just snowballed with Wham!"

In truth, Rob Kahane had achieved his goal of talking George into a reverse decision while letting him feel that he was keeping his professional autonomy. It was a successful dynamic that would continue for over a decade of the artist's career, before coming to an abrupt halt.

As Fiona Russell Powell recalls of the Wham! frontman, prior to the duo's second US tour: "Certainly by '85, George was in another league, he was like a megastar by then. But he would still go down the Wag Club and everybody treated him exactly the same, in fact they took the piss out of him even more. And he used to go into the loos all the time to do the old marching powder. He used to openly do it because everyone would openly do it at the Wag Club. Then he would get completely *off his tits*. Why else do you think he danced to his own records in front of everyone?"

(His youthful nightclub flirtations with cocaine aside, the only drug-taking Ms Russell Powell knew the singer to be regularly indulging in was smoking joints – his later status as 'the poster boy for cannabis' stemming from way back.)

"I think what happened was that George was also partial to partying but he worked very, very hard for a number of years – they really make you earn your money, the record companies. It's very pressurising and also – I only got a teeny-weeny taste of it when I was in ABC [at this time, Ms Russell Powell played the role of cartoonish sex kitten Eden in Martin Fry's former chart-toppers] – when you go on tour it's so *lonely*. It's so boring – you're away from everybody you know and care about, one hotel looks like another, so I totally understand why people go crazy."

The Whamamerica tour began in late August 1985. It worked its anticlockwise trajectory around the United States, beginning at Illinois in the Midwest, heading north across the Canadian border to Toronto, all the way down the West Coast to northern and southern California, southwards over to Texas and back up the eastern seaboard to Philadelphia and Detroit. Though he was still performing pure pop, in image terms the tour saw the birth of George Michael – rock star. His blond bouffant was cut down to a shorter length and a tone closer to his natural dark colour. His designer stubble and gypsyish earrings were complemented by a return to the bad-boy black leather jacket look plus fingerless gloves, speaking to some of S&M. Unbeknownst to all at the time, the tour's final date, at the Detroit Pontiac Silverdome on Tuesday September 10, would be the last ever live US performance by Wham!

Co-manager Simon Napier-Bell remembers the end of the tour as one example of how tightly George himself – the artist who refused to be managed – held both the professional and financial reins:

At the end of the American Wham! tour our backing band had been magnificent. It seemed a good idea to give them a tip to thank them. So my co-manager Jazz Summers went to see George about this tip and George said, 'Give them a T-shirt each.' Jazz didn't think that was a good idea, but George was adamant, so Jazz had to tell the band they were getting a T-shirt each. He ended up in hospital with a busted nose.

Musical director and keyboardist Tommy Eyre had already quit three days before the last date. Despite having previously played for such old blues-rock bruisers as Joe Cocker and Alex Harvey, he was indignant at the poor pay and hotel accommodation that he claimed were foisted upon Wham!'s backing band. As with many professionals in his industry, while George always had an open heart and an open chequebook for a good cause, he seemed at times to be less sentimental in his treatment of musicians for hire.

During the itinerary of the tour, the vocalist received the kind of personal endorsements that lesser performers could only wonder at. On the opening Illinois leg of the tour, his dinner date at the Mayfair Regent Hotel was beautiful American model-actress Brooke Shields, two years his junior; up in Toronto, Wham! were offered a multimillion-dollar deal to promote Pepsi Cola. If both aspects seemed part of the glamorous tapestry of superstardom, neither would be without controversy.

George would confess to Q magazine that he'd basically managed to seduce the Latinate brunette Ms Shields, then known as "the most famous virgin in America", but that when he entered her bedroom, "for what I thought was going to turn into the Real McCoy", he was met by the sight of her bed sealed off by yellow police tape. The grotesque spectacle was completed by Brooke's mother and a security guard, who are alleged to have jumped out and yelled, "Surprise!" After the offended singer told Ms Shields the next day that they wouldn't be seeing each other any more, she is said to have spent the week before she entered college crying in heartache.

That at least was the official version at the time. But by now there were detractors. In the British tabloid press, rumours appeared that George had been spotted sniffing poppers (amyl nitrate) at outrageous gay performer Leigh Bowery's Taboo nightclub. As drug scandals go, it was pretty tame – as noxious a substance as it is, the heart stimulant amyl nitrate was legally available over the counter of sex shops. More pointed was the strong inference that it was a mainstay of the gay club scene, with gay men using its short rush to enhance sexual pleasure.

Boy George of Culture Club, who were Wham!'s pop-chart contemporaries, was also beginning a bitchily entertaining war of words over George's reluctance to publicly come out as gay. Dismissing his fellow vocalist's right to a private life, when he saw George and Brooke Shields together at Grace Jones' birthday party at the Palladium in New

York City, the other George approached Ms Shields and whispered, "He's a poof, he's a poof," in her ear.

It's not known if she recognised the parochial British insult, but she probably got the gist. After all, it was only a year since she was romantically linked with her long-time friend Michael Jackson – a relationship she later described as "platonic". Unsurprisingly, Simon Napier-Bell has his own take on events:

There was a time when we built up a bit of publicity about George Michael and Brooke Shields getting along rather well together. But as far as I remember, the idea was to stop any gossip about being gay and the problem was, anytime any famous person wanted to do that, they always seemed to wheel out Brooke Shields. She was obviously a bit of a fag hag. So it seemed to confirm it rather than contradict it.

So it seemed to confirm it rather than contradict it.

In terms of sexual liaisons on Wham!'s US tour, Fiona Russell Powell gives what seems a far more credible account with hindsight: "This really annoys me actually. I stopped the whole gay rumour spreading. I was in LA with ABC, we were at the 'Riot House' where Led Zeppelin used to throw TV sets out the window, the Hyatt Hotel on Sunset. Yet another one of our crowd, Paul Lonnigan – another gay guy, a stylist who had lived in LA, because I'd never been there before – said, 'Just phone these three numbers and they'll look after you.' Well, it turned out I was immediately in the cream of LA society and everything that was going on. I went to stay at the home of this English guy who had been a contemporary of David Bowie and who looked like him, called Paul Fortune. He had this house up in Laurel Canyon that he'd totally designed. He had a sort of annexe in his house, you went down some stairs and you were in another part. He was renting it out to a photographer called Brad Branson. I had my very first fix of heroin there. I've got photographs of Brad cooking up and sticking it in his arm and everything.

"I'd met him before in New York, in Bianca Jagger's penthouse apartment at her birthday party. I'd done a piece for *Interview* magazine and he'd done some photographs, that's how we knew each other. So I ended up staying in his part of the house, because I didn't want to stay in the hotel. That very night we went out; there used to be a club in the eighties called the Dirt Box, done by a guy called Phil Dirtbox who went out for years with Siobhan Fahey from Bananarama. In LA in those days everyone seemed to go to bed at ten o'clock; for people who did want to go clubbing there really wasn't anywhere to go, so they started the Dirt Box out there and it was very popular. So me and Brad went there, and who should be there but George Michael? I didn't even spot him actually. I was near the bar and Brad started going, 'Oh my God, oh my God, oh Fiona, Fiona, look who's over there!' 'Oh it's George! How funny, he's here at the same time.'

"Brad was being very uncool actually, it was embarrassing: 'Oh you must introduce me, he's so cute, oh my God, oh my God, you must introduce me!' So I did introduce him, and he made it so blatantly obvious. But George, I swear to God, had got the whole poker-face thing down pat. I really didn't think George was interested. We were chatting away and at one point he went off to the loo for quite a long time. While he was gone, Brad was going to me, 'He really fancies me.'

"'No he doesn't.'

"'No, he does.'

"'No he doesn't.' Brad had taken some ecstasy as well as the heroin and he was off his nut. I said, 'Look, I would know if George fancied you.' But the thing is I wandered off quite a lot, because I got bored with it. I wandered off to dance, to talk to other people, whatever, left those two together. But George was really playing it cool, it wasn't like the two of them were just chatting away.

"Anyway, what happened was that George said, 'I'm going,' back to his hotel, he was staying at the Mondrian. I said, 'Okay, 'night.' About a second after he's gone, Brad's going to me, 'I'm going to go back to the hotel, I'm going to follow back to the hotel.'

"I said, 'You can't do that! That's so naff, you can't do that!' He's going, 'He was really giving me the come on, he's really into me,' blah blah.

"I said, 'I don't think he is, Brad! I think you want him to be.' Because he was going on and on about how gorgeous he was, how cute, blah blah blah. I couldn't quite believe it really, but he followed him back in this little battered VW Beetle. I thought I'd see him again half an hour later – well, I didn't see him again for three days [laughs]. I made my way back to Brad's place and the next day he rang me: [whisper] 'Guess where I am?'

"I said, 'I don't know.'

"'I'm in George Michael's suite, he's gone in the bathroom.'

"I'm going, 'Honestly, Brad, I can't believe you, you're outrageous. But you were right!' Brad was going on and on about getting off with him and everything. Basically he just stayed there and then he came back after three days, really full of himself. Not that they were madly in love or anything, but they'd certainly got a friendship going.

"I went to New York after all that – I was part of the hip, happening crowd in New York. The gay crowd were going to me, 'Oh, we've heard all about George Michael and Brad Branson!' I said, 'Oh really?' If you're part of that sort of crowd that's okay, that's cool. But if an outsider starts asking questions you have to be a bit careful. Then when somebody who wasn't part of that crowd was saying to me about it, I knew it'd come back here and end up in all the papers. So basically I just said, 'Oh, I don't know what you're talking about. No, absolutely not.'

"I stopped that rumour dead in New York. Because it would have come over here and it would have gone in the papers and George knew. George knew that I knew about the whole thing with him and Brad Branson; George knew me, he knew I was a journalist. What annoyed me about the whole thing was I'd done him a huge favour, and it'd got back to him. Rick Sky [then of *The Sun*'s 'Bizarre' column] said, 'You did well, Fiona, because it would have been everywhere, it would have been a huge thing.' It would have ruined his career at the time, wouldn't it?

"And it really annoyed me, because he wouldn't ever do an interview with me! We could have done an interview for *The Face*, but some people wouldn't do interviews with me then because they were afraid of what I was going to dig out of them. I don't know why, but they had this idea of me that wasn't true at all really. I could never understand why George wouldn't do an interview with me, because I kept asking him if he would do one and he would always smile enigmatically and make some excuse. I thought it was a bit off, really."

But for all the innuendo and conjecture about the true nature of George Michael's sexuality, the so-called 'cola wars' would briefly become an almost equally delicate point in terms of his career. In fact, he would claim, they played a role in the final dissolution of Wham!

CHAPTER 9

A Different Corner

In the young George Michael's 1990 autobiography, *Bare*, Jazz Summers opines that, "The Pepsi thing was the final nail in the coffin for Wham!"

According to the boys' co-manager, "The money started off at $250,000 and every time we had a bit more success it went up – eventually it was $3.3 million. Everything was signed. Tough negotiations. Huge budget for the commercial. Then George called me up and said, 'Jazz, are you sitting down?' He said, 'I don't want to do the commercial… I want to split Wham! up,' he said. 'And I want to do it now.'"

Thus fell the bombshell that was the demise of Wham! It is, however, a moot point as to whether his rejection of the Pepsi Cola deal was really the factor that made George jump. As we will see, it wouldn't be so very long before he took up a similar offer with their main competitor.

More pertinent to the young singer/songwriter's state of mind was the role that he found himself trapped within. As Simon Napier-Bell insists, "Wham! split because George Michael wanted to be a solo artist. The timing, and the reason for them to split at that particular moment, were compounded by various things." Among which was a business deal struck by the management which George would decry as unethical.

But the central issue for the artist was intensely personal. It lay at the core of his being, and how he felt it conflicted with the image he was compelled to project from the stage. "The thing is, it's not about what you thought when you were 18 is it?" he'd insist to Chris Evans over a decade later. "Everyone feels the same when they're 18, they're entering the business and they're just desperate. And desperation makes you think that you love everything that you're doing.

"I was 18, 19 years old, I wasn't exactly the most desired male at my school and I had only just left school, people forget that; I hadn't had any kind of real adult life before I went into the business. I was thrilled to be the centre of all this attention, absolutely thrilled, and this completely new area of my life opened up that I never expected to. And of course it wasn't until I was a little bit older, a little bit more mature, that I realised how, ultimately, I was on the wrong bus really."

It was a bitter pill for Andrew Ridgeley, Dick Leahy, Bryan Morrison, Napier-Bell and Summers to swallow – although Andrew has said that he'd long seen it coming. But it had been plainly evident all along just who the real boss was in this network of business relationships. As such, the best they could do was rally forces to ensure the whole operation ended on an upbeat note.

The first scene of the final act really set the fan's pulses racing. With the break-up plans as yet unannounced, the rushed November release of 'I'm Your Man' may have seemed like just another Wham! record. But it was quite some record – it had a stomping beat not far removed from northern soul clubs, underlining the emphatic refrain, "If you're gonna do it, do it right!", with an arrangement and a vocal urgency that might have suited those early Motown or Tom Jones records that little Georgios first heard.

The video was a timeless celebration of popular music. It was filmed at London's historic Marquee club in Soho, where acts as crucial to pop music as The Rolling Stones and The Who had played in their early days – and where Wham! were sounding the first chords of their last onslaught on the pop charts. The black-and-white promo showed audience members (albeit paid-up extras) singing along to the backing vocals with Andrew and bassist Deon Estus, while couples took time out to grope and tongue each other's tonsils.

'I'm Your Man' hit the top of the charts, as expected, and was far too upbeat for anyone out of the management loop to take it as a requiem for a band about to become extinct. It makes George's melancholic reflections on that time seem all the more jarring. "I had to get away from the whole up-up-up thing because I felt so *down*," he'd later reflect. "And I didn't know when I was going to feel good again." With the press invariably encamped on the doorstep of his Knightsbridge flat, he reacted to the intrusion by isolating himself, promptly withdrawing into his domestic shell – with or without the aid of alcohol or drugs. This pattern, occasional at first, would become a more entrenched habit as he became an older man.

If ever a performer had inhabited a role, it was the young George Michael. But he'd played it so well, so effusively, that the cocky optimism he communicated to his audience became, for them, vibrantly real. Now there would be an outpouring of joyful pop music and live performance that, while it chimed with the chords of apparent spontaneity, was as well-planned as any military campaign.

First there would be an interim solo single by George, his second, which would indicate one of the directions he would follow post-Wham! There would be a final Wham! EP, George having neither the time nor the inclination to compose a whole album's worth of new material in the allotted period. Then there would be a grand finale performance too, intended to underline the end of an era.

In the meantime, in early 1986, the boys from Wham! would finally head off into their separate lifestyles. Hit by a £600,000 tax bill, the free-spending, free-living Andrew would decamp with his current girlfriend, model Donna Fiorentino, to the tax haven of Monaco, where he hoped to follow his dream of becoming a Formula Three racing driver.

George would spend an increasing amount of time in Los Angeles, the city that would soon become a second home to him. Having spent the earliest part of the year there after crossing the Pacific from Australia, with Andrew and two other buddies he'd been holidaying with, he opted to stay on awhile. He'd spend his time relaxing, swimming and writing new material – both for himself and for his terminating partnership with Andrew.

On his return home to London, the performer lapsed into a recurring depression which seemed to be partly chemical, emotional and situational in origin. "I can honestly say that I never lost my temper until I was 22 years old. And then for a period of about six or eight months before the end of Wham!, I really lost it," he'd confess.

The tabloids ran a photo story about George losing his rag to a photographer, as he left Stringfellow's in Covent Garden; the look of rage on his face as he turned was a portrait of celebrity at the end of its tether. The same venue was the scene for a blow-up between him and David Austin.

"It was probably the most embarrassing thing I have ever done. Half of the club was out on the street watching us roll around all over this car trying to hit each other. Thank Christ that for just *once* there were no cameras outside." According to George, the eruption came after Austin accused his bisexual friend of lusting after his girlfriend. (Veteran club owner Peter Stringfellow claimed to have witnessed the unthinkable, George turning on Andrew: "Suddenly they were rolling on the floor fighting. They always used to horseplay but this was serious... At one stage, George had Andy pinned to the floor and was letting him have it. We had to split them up." But this seems to have been a mistaken sighting of the Michael-Austin spat.) In any case, the singer would never patronise the laddish Stringfellow's again.

Drama of a less trivial kind erupted when Nomis Management tried to capitalise on their success with Wham! by floating themselves as a public company. Jazz Summers did a deal with Harvey Goldsmith, the famed live music promoter who helped Bob Geldof organise Live Aid, and his business partner. Given Goldsmith's respectable credentials, Summers quickly accepted his suggested buyout by parent company Kunick Leisure.

It was only during negotiations that he found out one of the co-directors was South African entrepreneur Sol Kerzner – owner of the notorious Sun City, a massive gambling casino and show venue set in the middle of an impoverished black township during the apartheid era. Only the previous year, the venue was made the target of a protest record, 'I Ain't Gonna Play Sun City' – a harder-edged version of the multi-star Band Aid-style statement, featuring the talents of hip-hop producer Arthur Baker and jazz musician Miles Davis, as well as white songwriters like Bruce Springsteen and Lou Reed. To a conscientious liberal like George, to be seen as giving even tacit approval of Sun City was intolerable. As was the way he first found out about it, a headline in an entertainment paper.

When US agent Rob Kahane showed him the oversimplified *Hollywood Reporter* headline that read, 'Wham! Sold To Sun City', George reputedly went ballistic. "This was the first time I saw George Michael lose it," Kahane later testified, "because he is pretty together. He was so angry and pissed off and he kept saying, 'How could they do this? How could they sell me to something they know I don't believe in?'"

Back in London a month later, Wham! were due to appear at the British Phonographic Industry (BPI) Awards to be presented with an award for Outstanding Contribution to British Music, in recognition of their being the first pop act to play Red China. (Elton John was up for a similar award, in belated recognition of his pioneering performances in the Soviet Union in 1979.) There was some droll merriment among the crowd at the expense of the award's unlikely presenter, Conservative Party chairman Norman Tebbit – a stalwart member of the Thatcher government which denounced Nelson Mandela as a terrorist.

Napier-Bell and Summers were summoned to appear on the same podium as George – wearing a full-grown beard and Stetson hat – but otherwise ne'er the twain met between the boys from Wham! and their two managers. In fact, they were told on the night that, if they wanted to speak to George in future, they should go via publisher Dick Leahy or lawyer Tony Russell. Eleven days later, a press release was issued on George's behalf stating that he had cancelled all business relations with his former management.

As Andrew hadn't reacted so reflexively and was yet to sever his own connections, Napier-Bell was quick to counter-attack. He put out his own press statement that Nomis would continue to manage Andrew Ridgeley; the implication was obvious – that Wham! were no longer a cohesive unit and had effectively split. It sounded far less amicable than it actually was, but it served Nomis's purposes of making Wham! – rather than their own business dealings – the focus of the news stories.

It was becoming the end of an era in more ways than one. Nomis, which had been formed specifically to look after Wham!'s interests, was quickly dissolved, with Simon Napier-Bell and Jazz Summers going their separate ways. Publicist Connie Filippello was retained to look after the boys and Nomis's former office administrator Siobhan Bailey became George's personal assistant. The Kunick deal fell through and Harvey Goldsmith would decide to extricate himself from any link with Kerzner's enterprise.

For Napier-Bell, the legacy of the glittering heyday of Wham! would be bankruptcy. As he explains:

I lived in Paris. As a foreign resident you were allowed 90 days in the year and I'd come to London on Tuesday and go on Friday, but when I started managing Wham! the authorities said I was here more than that and I probably was. So they gave me a tax demand for £5 million for four years, which was actually more than Wham!'s gross earnings.

After several years of sleeping on friends' couches, the irrepressible bon viveur would bounce back, both as a pop manager and a pop writer. In the shorter term, his former protégé would continue to make bigger waves of his own.

By the time that 'A Different Corner', the second George Michael solo single, was released in April 1986, it was known by the public that Wham! were a very finite entity. If the singer couldn't begin again from point zero, he could at least showcase how he intended to produce a new body of work that would face the full range of his emotions – whether ebullient or weepy or all those confused points in between.

Performing the song on *Top Of The Pops*, still then the UK's gauge of mainstream musical popularity, George looked not unlike Bono, the vocalist of U2 – although he was fuller in the face at that time – with a two-tier mullet hairstyle and a tasselled leather motorbike jacket. The subtly jangling electronic backing was delicate in tone though, as were the emotionally insecure lyrics. "It was the first time I used my own experience and emotions for a song," George later confessed. "It was totally therapeutic, I completely exorcised that little part of my life."

The specifics of the emotional trauma behind 'A Different Corner' remain one of the songwriter's guarded secrets – something the man himself may be ready to reveal to us in due course. Suffice to say that suffering rejection from someone he regarded as "the one", a person who felt disinclined to be an appendage to a superstar's life, produced his most wounded yet warm performance to date. For the last several years of his young life, while he had fought hard to gain what he wanted, it had been granted to him in spades. Now, with this crushing personal disappointment and the return to an earlier, less secure state of mind, he had become 'one of us' again. The crucial difference was that he had the musical vocabulary and the performer's gift to articulate all those tear-flecked, bittersweet emotions that seep from time to time into the lives of everyone who isn't emotionally numb.

In this sense, it was the true birth of George Michael as a singer/songwriter.

"The thing that fucked me up was the idea that it was made impossible by my circumstances," George would say. "I had everything I wanted, this was the first time I had ever really fallen in love and it seemed that it couldn't work because of everything I already had. It was like someone saying, 'You don't think that you can have it all, do you?'"

For all his retrospective self-analysis, he has always been too gentlemanly (or too guarded, or both) to identify the object of his affections, the person who spurned him. The lyric contains nothing resembling a chorus, proceeding delicately from verse to vulnerable verse, confessing the singer's paranoia about the shallowness of his relationships and "this fear of being used"; opting defensively for the sad certainty of loneliness and confusion. The monochrome promo video – with George reaching dejectedly in a white room for a white phone which doesn't appear to ring – is as far from the black-and-white sixties pop aesthetic of 'I'm Your Man' as it is from 'Club Tropicana'. It shows a life lived in luxury but devoid of all emotional warmth, which has been bleached from the fabric of existence as surely as the colours have.

The love focus of 'A Different Corner' has never been definitively identified as male or female – though, in the context of the day, its composer spoke about 'girlfriends' in relation to the song. On the grander scale of human emotion it works either way, with gender being largely irrelevant to a truly great love song.

At home in London in June, George went through one of the standard procedures of young manhood that his extraordinary life had so far precluded. He passed his driving test on the first attempt and celebrated by buying himself a Mercedes. It was a new freedom for him, outside the parameters of being ferried around by management or chauffeur-driven. (His driving skills would, of course, later provide some of the more controversial moments of his life, in early middle age.)

Around this time he also gave a celebrated interview to Julie Burchill for the *Sunday Times*. As he remarked to Fleet Street's doyenne of the bitchy barb, "I'm not what stars are made of. I'm not Prince and I'm not Madonna." In other words, he was no larger-than-life fantasy figure, as both of those single brand names were. As he would later concede, however, "'George Michael' was in part a constructed character, one that Georgios Panayiotou had learned to play very well."

His interviewer, Ms Burchill, is renowned as a pop-culture pundit who treats celebrity trivia and world affairs in the same wittily off-the-cuff manner. She often takes political sides in international conflicts as if cheering on her favourite teeny-pop group, while writing about self-indulgent rock stars as if they were war criminals. But she clearly adored George Michael.

Years later, he would remind her of the interview at his west London flat, claiming that it was one of his tentative attempts to come out as gay in the eighties: "I asked him what it was I 'hadn't noticed' and he said, 'Do you remember that I stood there with one hand on my hip? And when the tea arrived I said, 'Shall I be mother?' Did you not think that added up to something?

"I thought he was just being friendly. He said he was camping around and I was totally oblivious."

Whether or not his actions were as overt and as intentional as George retrospectively paints them, estranged manager Simon Napier-Bell was notably tolerant of his former client staying in the closet. As he later wrote for gay magazine *Attitude*:

Many people have suggested he should have come out when he was still in Wham!, but that's certainly not my opinion. The image of Wham! was the classic Hollywood image of male friendship – Starsky and Hutch, or Butch Cassidy and the Sundance Kid – two straight guys whose friendship with each other transcends all other things. These leading roles had to be played as straight as a die, which was how George played his part in Wham! It was just play-acting – he knew one day he would have to emerge and become his real self. But at that moment, the image expected of Wham! was a heterosexual one and that's how he played it.

Back in the rehearsal and recording studios, George continued to channel his energies into Wham!'s final *pièces de résistance*. For all his subsequent revelations of depression, back then he could turn the cocksure, ebullient Wham! persona on like a lightbulb in a darkened room. It was June 1986 that would see the glorious long last bows, with 'The Edge Of Heaven' released early in its second week. It sounds less like the work of a depressed man than a tribute to the most upbeat works of Holland-Dozier-Holland, songsmiths of the Motown hit factory.

"Yeah-yeah-yeah!" goes the traditional hookline, bouncing along on the brass backing. But listen a little closer and you'll hear some dark stirrings within the libido of Wham!'s songwriter. "About a week before

'I'm You're Man', I had wildly good sex – for about a week!" proffered George by way of explanation. "I think that everything before that was in a strange way kind of asexual... 'Edge Of Heaven' was deliberately and overtly sexual, especially the first verse... 'You know I wouldn't hurt you – unless you wanted me to.'"

Knowing what we do now of the range of George Michael's sexual tastes, it's quite likely that the "wildly good sex" had an emphasis on the "wildly". As for the S&M overtones to the lyrics, it seems certain that if George hadn't been to those extremes then his imagination certainly had.

The video continued the celebratory nostalgia feel of 'I'm Your Man', once again in monochrome, with old mate David Austin sharing the old-school rock guitar heroics with Andrew. But this time there's an almost eerie feeling as shots are inserted from the 'Hotel Tropicana' and 'Careless Whisper' promos in black and white, making them seem as if they were a lifetime ago instead of just a couple of years. While there's nothing maudlin about the performance, the words 'Goodbye' and 'Thank You' also run across the bottom and top of the screen like a tickertape at the end.

Filling out the EP were three more tracks: a re-recording of 'Wham Rap!', a cover of 'Where Did Your Heart Go?' by literate funksters Was Not Was (by far the dirtiest sounding Wham! cut, with the sleaziest saxophone sound) and a new Michael original, 'Battlestations' ("We spend more time now in battle than we do in bed"), which used elements of early house/drum & bass music. If this had been the 1986 debut of a new band, they'd have seemed like musical radicals in the making. As it was, the departing vocalist/composer was the one to watch.

The Final, as Wham!'s *au revoir* was entitled, was naturally held at Wembley Stadium. It took place three days after George's 23rd birthday, on June 28, prefaced by a couple of warm-up dates at Brixton Academy. Its timing prevented Andrew (who wouldn't have been able to get insured by the promoters) from taking part in F3 events that summer – "So that royally fucked the racing," as he laconically put it.

It was one of the most memorable musical events ever to take place at that gigantic, atmosphere-free venue. On the hottest day of the year, 72,000 people (out of more than ten times as many ticket applicants) were crammed in to enjoy a carnivalesque atmosphere. "It was just sparkly, everything was sparkly," as backing vocalist Pepsi DeMacque remembers it. "It was sunny, it was warm, the crowd had made an effort, everyone had dressed up. It stopped at a good time, it stopped on a high. So that's what people remember: just good-time music, basically."

The numerous secondary stars who provided back-up were either contemporaries of George and Andrew, or else were big during their seventies boyhoods. Gary Glitter, that sequined old pantomime rocker, was the warm-up man. (And let us not forget: his unmasking and downfall put all George Michael's subsequent misadventures into proportion. Glitter is a vile pervert; George is merely very naughty, but nice.) Good old Uncle Elton was there to entertain the boys and their tens of thousands of chums, dressed up in a theatrical giant pink quiff that evoked Sigue Sigue Sputnik (a pseudo-punk band who were briefly big that year) and presenting the headliners with a three-wheeler car with 175,000 miles on the clock as a gift. Lots of fun was had by all.

Except, perhaps, by the boys themselves. As George wrote in his personal section of the programme notes, "Of course, dreams are not always what they're cracked up to be."

"I didn't enjoy it as much as other shows, I have to say," an older Andrew would admit to George two decades hence. "That whole period leading up to that was a difficult one for me. I kept thinking when the encore's over, when everything's done, that's it! And that was a really, really difficult concept to get to grips with."

"I can barely remember," replied George, "it was just so overly important."

For the final number of The Final, George duetted with panto-outfitted Elton on 'I'm Your Man'. The girls, Pepsi and Shirlie, looking very sexy in black leather skirts, motorbike jackets and shades, synced the final line with their main man: "If you're gonna do it, do it right!" And then it stopped dead. Over.

George was interviewed for TV that day, in a dark get-up and shades that made him look as much like Roy Orbison as the young boy of four years previously. He offered "a huge thank-you to everyone, not only for today but for the last four years". After the final number was finished, Andrew too turned to the audience and said, "Thank you to everybody." Then he modestly turned to his partner. "And thank you, George." He was rewarded with a massive emotional hug.

The boys from Wham! then headed down to the Hippodrome with their entourage, for the last time, to get drunk. It would become something of a recurring theme over the weeks and months to come.

"He was tired of having potshots taken at him as the lucky guy who coasted along on George Michael," his friend and partner later said of Andrew, "and he was so much more than that." Indeed, he was the man who effectively forced his friend to become George Michael. But the Butch to his Sundance was acutely aware that, wherever he was going, his old partner could not tag along for the ride.

As his contemporary, Fiona Russell Powell, sees it, "I just think he had enough power, when he ditched Andrew – because in a way it was almost like Andrew could do all the hetero stuff for him, do you know what I mean? He could do all that and there wouldn't be so much of a focus on George. But when George was on his own [and he was] mega, there was the Chinese girl model."

"If I was going to go to the place that I believed I was about to go to," explained George, "there was no way we could hang out in the way that we'd always done. There was just no way, it would have been too difficult for Andrew. So I understood that our relationship was going to have to reach some different kind of level. And that was tough, you know, that was tough. And I had no idea how much I was going to miss that kind of support, or how close to lunacy I would feel without that support."

If George can be likened to any of his historic Mediterranean forebears, then it's not too much of an exaggeration to say that, on that day, he was left like Alexander the Great, crying in his twenties because he had no new worlds left to conquer. George, who had only just turned 23, had sold 40 million records, performed at two of the biggest concerts in British history and yet somehow found it all wanting. And like Alexander, at least for the time being, he would turn to the grape for consolation.

The young singer was also in a certain degree of physical pain, as well as emotional uncertainty. Towards the end of the show he had torn a tendon in his leg; it added to the occasional discomfort he was already suffering with his back, which had first gripped him in pain two years earlier on Wham!'s first American tour. It was the price to pay for a formerly non-athletic youth who had become such a physically demonstrative performer, later described by a US TV anchorwoman as "the human swivelstick".

It was after the break-up of Wham! that George Michael first met Kathy Jeung, in Los Angeles. She was a striking Chinese-American model and make-up artist, who at first seemed singularly unimpressed by the fact that she'd met a pop superstar. Given George's insecurity about people desiring his media persona rather than the person behind it, she couldn't have given him a greater come-on. As they took time to get to know each other better, they would spend time around the pool or at LA's cooler nightspots. For the singer, it was a brief chilling-out period before the maelstrom of activity that awaited him. She had the personal independence to pursue her own lifestyle and the confidence not to seek to be anyone other than herself. In theory, this too is the privilege of the showbiz superstar – indeed, it's the reason why many people dream of a career in the industry. But George had been finding his own self-constructed persona to be a straitjacket for some time now, and he drew strength from Kathy's sense of self-actualisation.

Ms Jeung's delicately chiselled features, her experimental stylisations with facial cosmetics and hair colour, could verge on androgyny but at the same time were purely, almost paradoxically feminine. The overused cliché "stunning beauty" is appropriate in her case, and anyone with a strong sense of aesthetics – man or woman, straight or gay – might find her particularly attractive. But she was far from a permanent fixture in his life and he continued to live much of it privately, in the shadows, whenever he could.

At first, taking a little R&R to improve his irritable nervous state and to self-medicate his aching body was no bad thing. "I spent a lot of time going backwards and forwards to see Kathy in LA and she would come here," he explained about the woman who would briefly become his artistic muse, "or we would go to Portugal or France or wherever. I travelled about a lot but I did the same thing everywhere."

"The same thing", in this case, always amounted to drinking. For many, this would simply be among the perks of the job, and George certainly had enough money not to indulge in any old rotgut. LA, New York, Miami and St Tropez became the venues for his extended lost weekend. "For a time I really didn't want to get back into the music business when we finished Wham!" he'd confess. "The problem was just that I had developed a character for the outside world that wasn't me, and I was having to deal with people all the time who thought I was."

And as very many people know, the comfort of booze is that it allows you to live with those parts of yourself you don't really like in a kind of cynical, inebriated marriage of convenience. Alcohol can be the perfect loner's drug, as George found when Kathy went back to her own life and he was left to his own devices. Sometimes, he would drink to the point of passing out and nurse the hangovers for days at a time until his system felt less dissipated, only to begin the process all over again.

With the additional calorie count of booze, he was piling back on some of the weight that he'd worked and exercised so hard to lose, on his face and his waist. But he could afford to drink like a connoisseur rather than an alcoholic, and so, while he might occasionally tie one on with Jack Daniel's, Southern Comfort or tequila, it was Californian wine that he favoured and that he considered least damaging to his vocal cords. However, as he'd later tell Chris Evans: "The reason I stopped drinking red wine was that I was informed that it was the absolute worst kind of alcohol for a singer. Red wine makes all your sinuses swell and stuff like that, so I stopped, but of course then I started smoking cigarettes; there wasn't much point in changing over, I should have stuck to the red I think."

Like many people who came of age in the eighties, George was also inclined to extend his chemical indulgence to other drugs. "For a while I took ecstasy when it was not very available over here. I took it simply because it made me feel that everything was wonderful," he'd explain matter-of-factly. This was several years before the acid house explosion and the 'Second Summer of Love' in 1988, even predating the end of Wham!, but George would learn a lot of the same lessons as later users.

At first, the drug MDMA would deepen his perception, stimulate his senses and drive him upward into euphoria. But, as with any form of amphetamine, the comedowns would become gradually more intense. The regular boosting of serotonin, the feel-good chemical in the brain which produced the high, would gradually produce a corresponding drop in its natural production. For all the temporary relief the drug gave, the side effects can only have deepened George's depression at the time.

"I'm not the kind of person who can actually escape though anything like that," he'd later admit. "I get a terrible down from that stuff and it hits me at three in the morning. All the things I'm trying to escape from, all the nasty things, suddenly become very clear..." He was clearly no gurning E-casualty, but the need to exercise caution was becoming greater.

As a safer alternative, George was already a regular smoker of cannabis in both its herbal and resin forms. In the eighties, it was mostly seen as no big deal among most worldly people under a certain age. Already solidly established as the UK's favourite illicit drug, the stronger strains of dope could produce a similar hallucinogenic euphoria to ecstasy, but with fewer biological risks aside from bronchial damage. At the time, opponents of its use tended to point to cannabis as a "gateway drug", claiming it often led to harder, more dangerous substances.

It's an equation which didn't really apply to George Michael, who, like many of his contemporaries, had experimented with a harder drug (ecstasy) at around the same time anyway. In fact, the one substance he claimed a pronounced dislike to was the quintessential drug of the yuppie eighties: cocaine. The obvious physical dangers and the user's tendency to become an egocentric bore aside, George had formed a dislike for the culture of the drug that his younger self had used as a stimulant on the club scene.

"There's this whole thing about let's-drive-around-the-block-in-a-limo-and-then-go-back-to-the-club," he complained. "And this sniffing business and making sure you haven't got any on your clothes or nose. I find it disgusting, all that disappearing into toilets."

At the time, it sounded eminently sensible. But the passing of time would add an ironic level of comedy to at least one part of George's sentiment.

CHAPTER 10

White Boy Soul Man

The long, lost weekend finally ended in the autumn of 1986. Perhaps the least likely person to pull George Michael out of a drink–fuelled depression might have been his old partner. But Andrew Ridgeley, who flew in from Monaco to LA to visit for a few days, understood the clear division between indulgence and compulsion. If he was going to get blotto then it had better be *fun*; he saw little point in wasting good booze on some kind of gloomy introspection that deceived you into thinking that, to quote George's stated viewpoint at the time, "everything was a pile of shit".

On the other hand, Andrew was all too willing to crack open a bottle (or two) while George poured out his insecurities. As the latter would say of his own state of mind, "I felt for a long period that my career was running my life and that I didn't. I felt very empty a lot of the time; I felt very empty for a lot of the eighties, definitely." As has been observed many times, the gift of creativity often comes coupled with the stalking black dog of depression.

It was a syndrome that would recur again and again with George Michael. Whether he was falling victim to his personal insecurities and lack of self-belief –which was the case when Andrew was shocked to find him looking puffy and rundown in LA – or to a seemingly malign fate that later seemed to strike at those he loved, he'd be brought up close against his darker side with painful regularity. "I had no idea that he felt so bad emotionally," Ridgeley would later explain. "He was doubting everything and, more than anything, I think he just needed to get all the tears out."

All his fellow former young gun could do was listen in sympathy, get drunk with George and let his friend work up enough defiance to spit in the face of his own melancholia. It was a random method, but it seems to have worked. Crying in his Beaujolais would be, according to him, nothing less than "an exorcism" of his personal demons.

When George woke in the morning to face what should have been another devastating hangover, instead he found his mood and his mind had cleared. His self-doubt and his self-pity had been talked out of his system, with the help of the friend who was willing to listen without becoming judgmental or offering too much advice. "I gave myself a quick kick and said, 'You know there's not really anything else you want to do,'" George later admitted. "I decided to just come back and do it again, but maybe on different terms."

The post-Wham! advent of George Michael as a solo artist seemingly kicked off in early 1987. It was a little bit of a cheat, as his duet with Aretha Franklin, 'I Knew You Were Waiting (For Me)', had been recorded in 1986 in Detroit, motor city birthplace of Tamla Motown, during the final days of Wham! The record would inevitably be a hit, but it's also something of an anomaly in his career. Produced by Narada Michael Walden, the musician and soundtrack composer who would work with late eighties/early nineties divas Whitney Houston and Mariah Carey and composed by country & western songwriter Dennis Morgan, the song bears no resemblance to that genre – being a big production number based around the title line and clichéd metaphors about deep rivers and high mountains.

It's a rousing performance simply by virtue of the two vocalists. Ms Franklin takes an unremarkable lyric and soars around it in her gospel-diva tones, while George pins the melody down like an anchorman

128

and gives her something to work with. (He later said he was trying to avoid the histrionics of 'Sisters Are Doing It For Themselves', Aretha's collaboration with the near-operatic Annie Lennox – though it's fun to hear the sparks fly on that record.)

As a record, it's equal neither to the Queen of Soul's classic sixties cuts like 'I Say A Little Prayer' or 'You Make Me Feel Like A Natural Woman' – truly soul-stirring stuff that brings a near-religious tone to the details of everyday life – nor to the more exceptional moments of George's solo career. In terms of its relevance to that career, however, it was a collaboration engineered between Ms Franklin's management and Rob Kahane – the former booking agent who was now acting as de facto manager for the ex-Wham! singer.

("We were in the ghetto and it was scary," recounted the effusive Kahane of the session for the song. "We pulled up outside this building in the ghetto and George and I looked at each other and said, '*This* is the recording studio?'")

As a man with an eye for the main chance, Kahane had made his move as soon as he saw how Nomis Management's association (albeit indirect) with Sun City would offend George. ("What the fuck are you doing, Jazz?" he'd hollered down the phone at Summers.) It was also his initiative to get George onto the bill at the Motown Returns To The Apollo show, knowing how much it would mean for the singer to perform alongside some of the legends he'd been listening to since childhood.

When Kahane proposed himself as the ground-level member of a US management team, George displayed the characteristic caution and controlling instinct that he brought to all his business dealings. Yes, he'd allow Rob Kahane and his new partner, music business lawyer Michael Lippman, to represent him on a provisional basis.* But he

---

* Lippman's extensive experience at the sharp end of the business began when he represented David Bowie as an attorney in the seventies, before a brief stint as manager when the ultimate seventies star became addicted to cocaine and psychologically unstable.

reserved the right to be ruthless in his business dealings, and if someone he considered more amenable to his interests came along, then Kahane-Lippman would be out.

However, as George would late concede of Rob Kahane, "He's a typical, hyperactive, over-the-top American, and he ended up proving himself incredibly. There's not one thing that could have happened for me in America that didn't eventually happen."

In a manner and on a scale that even he could not yet fully comprehend, the future of George Michael lay in the United States. This was where he wrote the songs for his soon-to-be-recorded first solo album, and where he and his new management would negotiate a new deal with Epic Records – which, as lucrative as it was, also bore the seeds of future discontent.

In the short term, however, George returned to London. On April 1, 1987 – officially designated as 'International AIDS Day' – he performed at The Party at Wembley Arena. It was a benefit gig for the Terrence Higgins Trust, the UK charity set up to combat the AIDS crisis. With his bisexuality still very much under wraps at the time, he was nonetheless happy to make a personal cause of what was still then termed "the gay plague" by many. Sharing the stage with him was a notable line-up of gay (as well as hetero) British performers, including Elton John (then a married man but about to be drawn into litigation with *The Sun*, who defamed him by claiming he'd consorted with rent boys), Boy George, The Communards and Holly Johnson of Frankie Goes to Hollywood. At the event, George reteamed with Andrew for what would be the first of an occasional series of Wham! reformations; they sang 'Everything She Wants' before Andrew exited and George delivered a cover of Len Barry's sixties hit, '1-2-3', plus one of his increasingly regular Stevie Wonder covers.

In June 1987 he bought his first house, a luxurious testament both to modern design and to his north London roots. Situated in Hampstead, London NW3, it was valued at around £2 million. The spacious, five-bedroom mansion house had windows designed to flood its living rooms with light. George furnished it in his characteristically sparse style, with a state-of-the-art sound system taking pride of place and a TV set in every room. The garden ran to three acres and the garage was big enough to accommodate both George's Mercedes and his new Range Rover.

The 24-year-old did not need to take out a mortgage and paid for his new abode in one lump sum. It was the first time he'd been tempted to move from rented accommodation to a home of his own as, despite his affluence, he shared the fear of the finality of that big step common to many new owners. At the same time as he put down roots, however, he was about to embark on one of the single most busily restless periods of his life.

It was in that very same month that the first single from his yet-to-be released debut solo album made headlines. The song – 'I Want Your Sex', a piece of steel-edged eighties funk – took everything back to basics while making use of the clarity of new digital recording techniques. Giving the eighties soul-man shout of *"huur!"*, George made an overt but quietly erotic statement of lust.

It was the essence of pop music reduced down to its vital fluids. Ever since the advent of rock'n'roll (or indeed before it, going back to the 'race records' of early rhythm & blues), the subject of boy-meets-girl has carried the connotation that after they meet, there will be some physical rocking-and-rolling going on in whatever venue presents itself. All 'I Want Your Sex' did was make that statement honestly – without any of the violent misogyny that was coming to the fore in both the US gangsta rap of that era and heavy metal.* It was nothing more than a simple celebration of what the lyric called 'one on one'.

As the lyric opined of this most basic of human activities, "not everybody does it, but everybody should". But to sections of the media,

---

* George later expressed an opinion of those genres that claimed, "I'd rather have no youth culture than a nihilistic youth culture, which is what America is having to deal with."

it was somehow inadvisable to say this – as if human sexuality had to grind to a halt in the age of AIDS. Indeed, you might have thought that George Michael had personally invented sex just to provoke the radio and TV networks. Forced by limited airplay to defend his record, the songwriter explained, "The most attractive form of sex you can promote is the idea of being totally in love with someone but wanting to rip their clothes off. It really wasn't as throwaway or irresponsible as they tried to make it out to be, to the extent that the word 'monogamy' appeared in the video."

The video marks the point at which Kathy Jeung passed from being a girlfriend and companion to becoming a muse. Directed by the collaborative team of Andy Morahan and George himself, the promo features Kathy as a sex object in blonde wig and basque who is subjected to the singer's sexual imagination. He paints the words 'EXPLORE' on her thigh and 'MONOGAMY' on her back. The singer's own naked (and hairless) torso is not his own but that of a body double, one Chris Beedie – less hirsute than the singer and also more toned at the time, as George was reputedly going through one of his seesawing weight periods.

In another brief scene, its image borrowed from the contemporary Mickey Rourke-Kim Basinger movie *Nine And A Half Weeks*, George blindfolds Kathy with a bandana so that her other senses – particularly that of feeling – are enhanced. It's erotically suggestive but – despite the lyric's provocative asking of "What do you consider pornography?" – entirely non-pornographic.

Seen from the vantage point of two decades hence, when a girl singing about kissing other girls hardly raises an eyebrow at the top of the ever-less-important pop charts, it's hard to tell just what all the fuss was about. But, as the UK's radio controllers reeled from the association of popular music with sex, the video became another element in the unlikely controversy. The BBC effectively barred the song from their daytime radio schedules. Radio producer Trevor Dann charmlessly claimed, "You've got to be a tosser not to know that that's going to happen. Write a lyric like that, it's not going to get played on Radio One." It could more readily be heard in an Eddie Murphy movie, *Beverly Hills Cop II* (which had an original soundtrack by 'I Knew You Were Waiting' producer Narada Michael Walden), while Kahane-Lippman were forced to seek out club, bar and café environments where the original promo video could be shown. George himself is reputed to have insisted that no further copies were sent to any BBC stations.

All this is almost certainly why the single's chart performance didn't equal other recent successes – though it hit the number three slot in the UK and number two in the US, which for most artists would be a resounding triumph. As the ensuing months would prove, however, George Michael's new scope for success across the Atlantic was almost without limit.

The proof wasn't long in coming. In October 1987, the title track to the artist's first solo album, *Faith*, was released as a single. Despite George's reinvented self-image as a white soul man, 'Faith' copped its licks from the guitar-twanging end of the fifties, as suggested by music publisher Dick Leahy: "In the fifties all we did was: you go into a guitar lick, you go back into a bridge and into the outro. Two and a half minutes... why not make it a fifties record?'

It seemed at the time like an unlikely move – George Michael as a rock'n'roller? – although the straightforwardness of the lyrics suited the urgency of the guitar-driven beat, harking back to a time when rock'n'roll meant rhythm rather than blaring riffs. "To me, the better the song is, the simpler it should be recorded," explained George, "or the simpler it should be recorded, the better the song it has to be. So [with] something like 'Faith' – which was really, really simple – the arrangement has to be absolutely rock solid, so that with a really, really simple format everyone's still going to get it."

The simple lyric, about the need to have faith in oneself or one's relationships with significant others (a faith that the composer was all too prone to lose), definitely rang a bell with the pop industry. "'Faith' was brilliant," Elton John later acclaimed. "It was like Elvis Presley all over again with all the black leather and shades. The fact that he'd made all these dance records and come out with this kind of rock song was a brilliant move."

While it may not have been quite *that* radically brilliant (Elvis had, after all, appeared seemingly out of nowhere in the mid-fifties, dragging rock'n'roll out into the American mainstream with him), it did strike a resonant enough chord to hit the number two spot in the UK and number one in the US – a taste of things to come. But Elton was quite right in attributing some of the record's success to the image that went with it: black denim jeans and biker boots; black T-shirt and motorcycle jacket; aviator shades; trimmed designer stubble, growing into a short beard. One softening touch might have been the dangling crucifix earring George now regularly wore, but even that was more gypsyish than androgynous. "I never considered it a particularly macho look," he protested, "but I tried to soften it just a bit by having a string of pearls on one of the shoulders of the leather jacket."

"The famous Triumph leather jacket belonged to a guy called Lee Barrett," recalls Fiona Russell Powell. "He was Sade's manager who lived in my flat. He sold that jacket to George and he was on the cover of one of the most famous editions of *The Face*, the 'Hard Times' cover. It brought in ripped jeans as a fashion statement and he was very, very cute looking when he was young; Lee looked like a young James Dean. He also was another person who struggled with his sexuality."

"I've never really understood why he wanted to portray that image," Andrew Ridgeley would remark, "the brooding, macho guy of *Faith*. That's not him. That's not how he is with his friends."

But Andrew's former partner was a smart cookie, to coin an American cliché. With a savvy US management team on his side, he knew that US superstardom was now within his reach. But he was realistic enough to know that if he was ambitious enough to take on America, he had to try to take her on her own terms.

"I deluded myself," George would reflect in the mid-noughties, by which time he'd become more open with the world about who he really is. "I knew I was moving into a more adult period of making music, but I kind of deluded myself that I was not going to attract a whole new generation of young girls with the *Faith* image. If you look at it you're like, 'What do you expect? You're waving your arse at the camera.' It was quite a nice arse though," he joked, perhaps only partly in jest.

Faith, the album, wore its monolithic concepts on its sleeve, with icons representing 'FAITH – MUSIC – MONEY – RELIGION – LOVE'. It was launched at the Savoy Hotel in London's West End, with a party that had a £100,000 catering budget. Among the very mixed bag of variously graded celebrities were Elton John and his wife, Bob Geldof and hip new TV presenter Jonathan Ross, soon to be a neighbour of George's in Hampstead – alongside Bill Wyman's teenage girlfriend Mandy Smith, *EastEnders* star Anita Dobson, ex-*Coronation Street* star and playboy manqué Chris Quentin and former south London brothel madam Cynthia Payne. George may have been reticent about his sexuality at the time, but the camp side of his tastes shone through on the guest list.

Faith would become something of a monolith in its creator's career.

Former club buddy Fiona Russell Powell sees it as a self-fulfilling prophecy: "He was such an arrogant kid and it was almost like, 'Of course I'm going to be rich and famous, because I'm brilliant!' It's like he thought it was his due and I think he still thinks that, because his prophecy for his own brilliant career was fulfilled. He just gave off this air that it was never in doubt.

"Unfortunately, I came across it time and time again whenever I interviewed somebody who was famous and successful, whether they were a musician or an artist or an actor; nearly all of them – and I don't see this in George – have got low self-esteem but a massive ego. And they all talk about this thing that they can't quite believe they've made it, they don't really think they're *that* good and they always talk about how one day they're going to be *found out*. Whereas I never got the feeling that he'd got that."

As George explained of the title, "What *Faith* meant – the album, the campaign, all of it – was that I had faith life was going to deliver, that I was going to get the things I wanted, that my life would bring me the things that are important to me." To which can only be added the old admonition, *Be careful what you wish for.*

It made number one album in the UK for one week after its November 1987 release but it would indicate where George Michael was really going by maintaining that position at the top of the US charts for a full 12 weeks and remaining on the *Billboard* chart for another year. Throughout its lifetime it would sell ten million copies on vinyl and CD, making the former boy from Wham! into the transatlantic superstar of the late eighties.

The musicians this time around included Hugh Burns and Robert Ahwai on guitars, Betsy Cook on keyboards and the familiar Deon Estus on bass. Demonstrating his underrated ability as a multi-instrumentalist, much of the music was played by George himself, who also acted as arranger and producer. The album's other tracks included 'Look At Your Hands', a starkly dramatic, Elton John-influenced number where the narrator chides his ex for getting into an abusive relationship ("You got two fat children and a drunken man"). Its composer was very clear that this was one song *not* taken from his own life.

'Kissing A Fool' is another standout, a piano-backed ballad of wistful regret with a breathy vocal by George. It has a deliciously bittersweet sense of heartbreak, like a melancholy show tune or maybe a classic country ballad like 'Crazy' by Patsy Cline. 'One More Try' would make another US number one – an epic soul ballad with gospel organ tones and a bravura vocal performance by the artist, it's one of a number of songs to reflect George's spiritual yearnings with its line about "looking out for angels".

'Father Figure', a further hit, is simply sublime. A tender love song verging on obsession whose brooding nature manages to make it almost menacing, it laments those lying lovers "who said that they cared and then laughed as you cried". Its smoky video, another co-direction by George and Andy Morahan, is once again in black and white. This time, it lends an air of film noir to proceedings as George plays a cabby in shades who has a sexual relationship with his fare, *Vogue* model Tania Coleridge, which may be real or imaginary – superseding as it does her more likely fling with her photographer. The Arabian airs of the opening and closing motif enhance the mood, as George the cabby is seen in the audience of a fashion show. Is he a stalker, as in the movie *Taxi Driver*? All is ambiguous, and mood is all.

In the UK, there appeared to be a resistance to George Michael going dark and moody; 'Father Figure', his best single to date at that point, only reached 11 in the charts, the lowest position since before Wham! made it big. In the US it made for his latest number one, cementing the boy from Edgware's new status as a major American star.

By now, it was clear that the performer was drawing from his own unique well of white soul. Among the album's other tracks, 'Hard Day', 'Hand To Mouth' and 'Monkey' are all very serviceable pieces of white funk with an electro-tinged production; while they're not the equal of the other tracks, 'Monkey' would make for yet another big US hit as a dance remix by producers Jimmy Jam and Terry Lewis.

Ex-manager Simon Napier-Bell has opined that George may have cribbed his smooth, unfussy vocal style from a 1979 song about two-timing lovers called 'This Is It' by Kenny Loggins: "Like being presented with a new voice in a gift box. But didn't he take it and use it brilliantly!... For George it was something he turned into his trademark singing style." If that's the case, however, then the Anglo-Greek boy would expand his delivery far beyond the semi-whispered emotions of the ex-Loggins & Messina man's track.

It's no small factor in his success that George is in large part responsible for his own arrangements and production, and that he was part of a new wave of soul singers in the eighties who put out some particularly strong material: whether black performers like Terence Trent D'Arby or Seal, or white English girl Alison Moyet. Few have withstood the pace of time and some sadly verge on being forgotten. These are George Michael's true contemporaries – not the Frankie Goes to Hollywoods and Culture Clubs – and if he's the only one to make household name status, it's because he was the best of a mostly excellent bunch.

And it all began with *Faith*. It topped album charts around the world and drew plaudits from critics who wouldn't have granted Wham! anything more than an indulgent smile. It was now official: it was okay to like the grown-up George Michael.

"There you go," the artist himself would reflect at a later stage of his career. "I was off on bad trip number two really. I honestly believed that they had overrated *Faith* – because that's what happens in America when you become the hot thing, I suppose. So many people were writing [good] things that I thought, 'Hold on a minute – I know it's not *that* good!'" As amazing as it may seem to fans and onlookers (or indeed to Fiona Russell Powell), neither critical kudos nor public adulation was enough to overcome the perfectionist's sense of self-doubt.

In America, different ends of the press were unanimous in their praise. "With *Faith*, the pop star grows up," acclaimed *Rolling Stone*, the post-hippie lifestyle journal; "It's arranged with wit, intelligently written and beautifully sung," chimed in *Playboy*; "No one is playing the pop game as cannily as George Michael," praised *Time* magazine.

Kahane-Lippman swiftly set about capitalising on the universal praise, by renegotiating the basis of the new deal with Epic Records. In the interim period since George had signed his latest deal, there had been seismic shifts in the record industry. Ravenous multinationals were snapping up the major labels where they perceived potential crossover profits. Chief among these was the Japanese electronics giant Sony; back in the days when CD albums were recorded in expensive studios and played on expensive audio equipment, the more high-quality CDs there were on the market (so the logic ran), the more hi-tech sound systems Sony would sell.

In early 1988, Sony's acquisition of Columbia Records and its subsidiaries would allow George Michael's management to renegotiate the basis of his deal. Initially, they would be pleased with the lucrative $11 million advance they'd secured for their client, obligating him to deliver only seven albums over the next 15 years. A few years into that deal, however, they'd have little choice but to come round to George's view that he was being kept on the roster by a payment from massive profits that he'd already earned the label.

Back home in Britain, at the end of 1987 the *Sun* tabloid estimated that generous George had given away over £6 million in gifts to friends and family. Included among this was a small fleet of motor vehicles: £14,000 BMWs for his mother and his sister Melanie, a £17,000 Toyota sports car for Kathy Jeung and, giving him most satisfaction, a Rolls-Royce for Dad.

"Because we were up to our third single and my father was saying, 'Save your money, boy, this is not gonna last,'" George later mused. "And I never believed that – from the moment I got my foot in the door I believed it was gonna stay there. I found it quite amusing, actually – it took him a good couple of years before he finally thought, 'Actually, I'm *totally* wrong.'"

All that remained was for the artist to make the traditional tour to promote his album – a glitzy treadmill that would occupy most of the next year of his life. In 1988, after receiving the trophy for Best Male Artist at the BPI Awards in London, George Michael was booked to play almost 170 shows worldwide, beginning at Tokyo's Budokan Theatre in mid-February and ending in Pensacola, Florida, on October 31.

The demands of spending so long on the road were met by the singer's disciplining of his own body to withstand the strains. He engaged a personal fitness trainer to tutor him in workouts that might last as long as four hours each day. His personal chef stabilised his weight by keeping him from fattening foods and sticking to white meat, roasted vegetables and salads. This was not the excess of sex & drugs & rock'n'roll as seen in the seventies, but a well-oiled professional entertainment machine that had to keep its human components in check.

Despite the pampered lifestyle of the superstar on tour, living in a kind of gilded cage (like the prop that lowered George to the stage on the Australian leg of the tour) insulating him or her against the outer world, such a draining itinerary has to make an impact. In George's case, it would affect both his personal sense of well-being and his physical health. This may have begun with the Australian dates early on, when he realised that he couldn't hear himself singing above the screaming and felt like he was back in the days of Wham! It was at that moment, he would later claim, that he realised he had to change his life.

Which is not to say that the shows were anything other than triumphs in themselves. Basing most of the set on the *Faith* track listing, with a smattering of the better Wham! songs, George also paid tribute to the black artists who'd influenced him by covering some familiar soul tunes: Labelle's 'Lady Marmalade', Wild Cherry's 'Play That Funky Music, White Boy' and Stevie Wonder's 'Love's In Need Of Love Today'. When he hit home in the UK in June, Andrew joined him on stage in Birmingham to momentarily reform Wham!, with a rousing 'I'm Your Man'.

On Saturday June 11, George returned to Wembley Stadium to perform at the birthday concert tribute to incarcerated African National Congress leader Nelson Mandela. Instead of making some grand speech against the evils of apartheid in South Africa, he let his performance do the talking, covering three classics by some of his favourite black vocalists: Marvin Gaye's 'Sexual Healing', Stevie Wonder's 'Village Ghetto Land' and Gladys Knight's 'If You Were My Man', with the necessary gender change to 'woman'. It was a warm-up for his own concert that evening at Earls Court, which he would long regard as his single best performance. Of the Mandela concert, however, he was rather more cynical; detecting little of the idealism among the audience that he'd felt at Live Aid, three years earlier, George regarded many of them as being there simply to get drunk at an 'event', while a large proportion were only there to see stadium-rock band Simple Minds. "As it was, a lot of people criticised me and said they were bored and would have preferred to hear 'Father Figure' or 'One More Try'," he complained. "Very few people thought it was a good idea."

Other factors were also starting to overshadow the seemingly endless tour. In the first five months the singer had been forced to consult eight doctors in different countries about the throat pain that was starting to cause concert cancellations. At home in London, George was finally diagnosed by a specialist as having a large cyst in the pit of his throat that demanded operative surgery. A hiatus in the gruelling schedule had become a necessity; the vocalist's mother had already expressed a reluctance to come and watch him sing any more, as she could detect him wincing in pain onstage.

"But the thing that annoyed me was that by the time we got to England everyone thought it was a joke," he would complain. "Bruce Springsteen's manager said to Rob and Michael, 'Apparently George is really great when he shows up.' I was starting to be seen as temperamental or cracking up – and I knew that was nothing like me."

It was not only rumours of capriciousness or a prima donna mentality that the media picked up on. When the European leg of the tour reached the Netherlands, while George recuperated and rested his throat in an Amsterdam hotel, he found himself the subject of AIDS rumours in the British tabloids. At a press conference in Rotterdam, he announced to the throng of journalists, "What I'm not here to do is make a series of denials into speculation about my private life." But when a *Daily Mirror* reporter asked him if he'd been tested for HIV, in the spirit of "you're damned if you do and damned if you don't," his denial was taken as evidence that he was afraid of catching the disease.

The rumours were less symptomatic of the artist's general state of health than they were of the times. While the HIV virus and its attack on the immune system had made inroads into heterosexual life, the terminal disease was still more easily passed by sex between gay men, which had a greater chance of blood-to-blood contact. As George had been vocally supportive of AIDS charities and was the subject of ongoing speculation about his own sex life, the two facts fused in the tabloid imagination and bred a morbid urge to uncover anything potentially scandalous.

George would later describe his fluctuating relationship with the popular press to Chris Evans:

My old famous quote always used to be, 'As long as they don't call me a child molester, they can call me what they like' – and now of course, that's not such a joke any more, is it? There's almost nothing that I can think of that I would respond to. Normally, if they're having a go about money, or sex, or anything like that, I just kind of brush it off. When they make me out to be some kind of real arsehole, that tends to be when I get the most tempted.

The only time I sued The Sun *was over this ridiculous story that said I had gone into the Limelight club and thrown furniture around and said, 'Don't you know who I am?' And then apparently I threw up over some poor girl.*

It was the fact that I hadn't actually entered the club. I hadn't actually done anything other than walk up to the club and seen that there was a private party for, I think, Andrew Lloyd-Webber, and I walked out again. So everything that they actually put in there was fabricated. It's incredible, The Sun *has this way of rephrasing things so that you're not even sure whether you said it or not. You just know that you don't remember sounding as stupid as that. They have 'Sun-speak'.*

Of course, when you first start you welcome them with open arms; it makes me go cold to think I had someone from the Daily Mirror *at my 21st birthday party.*

In the following year, when music journalist Tony Parsons drafted the young star's official autobiography, *Bare*, George would hold forth on the subject of the world AIDS epidemic that the gutter press had sought to link him with: "The number of people screwing around over the last 30 years with lots of different partners has produced so many nasty new viruses that we were bound to come up with something very potent sooner or later. I don't think AIDS is the wrath of God – it's the wrath of nature."

It was a scientifically rational line to take. Despite rejecting the poisonous bigotry of the "AIDS is God's revenge" fundamentalists, however, there was still a moralistic strand to George's thinking that perceived the epidemic as a form of vengeance. "AIDS is nature's way of saying, 'You can't do this for ever when the species has been here for hundreds of thousands of years and then suddenly the whole world changes its sexual patterns,'" he expounded. "I still don't know anyone who has died of AIDS. There will be a period when I'm going to know people… But I think the generation of gay people which follows them is not going to fall in the same way because I don't think they're going to be anything like as promiscuous."

The distance he placed between himself and gay people ('them'/'they') seems quite deliberate now. But a time would come when George Michael no longer held the same moral disdain for promiscuity – as well as a time when his own life would be touched by the terrible epidemic, which would sadly occur much sooner.

★★★

The tour's hiatus was spent in St Tropez. After George's recovery period a further 42 US dates had been scheduled; the greater part of the 1988 world tour and its trappings became suitably grandiose.

"I think the *Faith* period was the only time I thought, 'Ooh, he's being a pop star!'" laughed Shirlie Kemp (née Holliman, since married to ex-Spandau Ballet bassist/actor Martin Kemp). "The ego's there, and he's got the entourage around him.'"

To maintain a semblance of normality within his artificial bubble, George would regularly have his best buddies David Austin, Andrew or cousin Andros flown out to wherever he was performing. As they didn't have to shoulder the same pressures as their friend, they became more enamoured of the trappings of stardom that they experienced at one remove. "It was just a bit surreal actually," Austin would reflect, "because we spent a lot of time in Los Angeles and it was in the superstar league. Jets, women, money – it was a fantastic ride, an amazing ride."

Their experience of what their friend was undergoing was a world away from what was going on inside him. "Even your friends feel that they're not dealing with the same entity that they were at home," George later reflected, "and that really starts to play with your head. That kind of hysteria coming at you four nights a week – and then to come offstage and find that your security have been fighting with your friends because your friends want to take you out on the town."

"I have seen them pushing Yioda, his sister, around, or his mum and dad," Andros complained of the security team. "And I said,

'That's his sister.' And this guy said, 'I don't care who it is.' I said, 'You don't care? You will... *you treat these people with more respect than you treat George*.'"

The singer would admit that the only way to maintain sanity and perspective in such circumstances is to "put your heart on ice". For all his geniality and gentle manner, the calm ruthlessness that George Michael can display in regard to his career was in evidence on the *Faith* tour. Session musicians – in whom he has relatively little faith, believing they lack the cohesiveness and commitment of a band, whether that band is permanent or a pickup – were quietly terrified into working on time, in key and in tempo. One former addict who incapacitated himself with heroin on the night of a New York date found that his transgression was tolerated just the once; the session player didn't screw up again, knowing full well that he'd be out without a murmur the next time.

At the end of the tour, the performer had kept reality at arm's length for most of the ten-month period. He knew full well that his personal relationships on tour were artificial and that there was no one available to "call you a wanker", when the situation might otherwise have demanded it. The upside of this was that he was now a megastar in the USA, a performer with only two or three true peers. At the close of the tour, at the very end of October 1988, *Faith* had become the biggest-selling album in America that year; it had yielded an almost unprecedented six hits in the top five of the *Billboard* chart and had been nominated for a Grammy award for best album, its nomination regarded as a shoo-in. But still, in the midst of all this triumph, satisfaction was *not* guaranteed.

"I was intelligent enough to know that this was the wrong road," George reflected many years later, "in terms of if I was looking for happiness I should not be trying to catch up with Michael Jackson, or Madonna, or whatever. Which was absolutely what I was intent on doing, as a British star. But I don't think there's any way I could have controlled my ego enough to have stopped me checking the possibility of being the biggest-selling artist in the world."

As well as the Grammy nomination for *Faith* as best album, both the album itself and George as best performer had also been nominated in the R&B category. It was a tribute to how he'd assimilated the musical and emotional legacy of the great American soul performers he'd been listening to since he was a boy. But it would not be without controversy, as R&B was the genre that the Grammies traditionally used to honour the black American section of the music industry, now suddenly the province of a white Englishman.

"It's a very intense thing to go through for ten months, which is what effectively I did with *Faith*," George would testify, "and by the end of it I felt like I was going insane, it has to be said. It was like, 'I'm a massive star and I think I might be a poof – what am I going to do? This is not going to end well.'"

These words were spoken almost two decades after the end of the tour. By then, George Michael, older and a little wiser, could afford to laugh at himself. The intervening events of 20 years, as wounding as they would sometimes be, had at least allowed him to come out the other side relatively intact.

At the end of 1988, the young man who'd only recently gone through that experience issued one more single ('Kissing A Fool'), which would be his last release for the best part of two years. He had by now attained a near-record number of American number-one hit singles throughout the eighties – eight, as against Michael Jackson's nine in the same decade.

And yet the elevation to super-megastar status was little consolation to him. As he would remark shortly afterwards: "I wouldn't really have believed that by 24 I would be so desperately unhappy; I wouldn't have believed it would be possible to be that unhappy when you have all that privilege and good fortune."

CHAPTER 11

With Extreme Prejudice

"Won't you gimme a break? Somebody gimme a break now!" This line from 'Crazyman Dance' was first aired two years before the song's release on vinyl. It was featured in a TV ad for Diet Coke that ran to less than a minute and a half. The ad was partly soundtracked by The Gypsy Kings, the flamenco band then enjoying popularity in yuppie bars with their traditional folk sound. Intercut with their world music were shots of an American street lit up with neon signs, as futuristic as *Blade Runner* by comparison. The steel-tipped cowboy boots and studded Triumph biker jacket of the figure walking down the street were revealed to belong to George Michael, seen taking the stage in the final frames.

If this seems like a very elaborate way to promote a cola drink, it's also an unusual step for a man who would soon express reservations about promoting his own musical output. "They realised it had been a great advert for me and a crap advert for Diet Coke," the artist laughed at the corporation's expense. "While they were making it, they had people putting the product in. I kept taking it out. I had complete control."

The reason the Coca-Cola Company had pursued him so vociferously was that the patronage of another US superstar had provoked the so-called 'cola wars'; Madonna, then still making great use of the traditional nun/whore stereotypes applied to women throughout history, was already signed to Pepsi for a series of commercials said to be worth $9 million to her.

According to the official version of events, Pepsi was pursuing Wham! in their dying days as a group (see Chapters Seven and Eight). But in an interview later given by George to the *Sunday Correspondent*, this same scenario plays out in Coke's pursuit of him as a solo artist. "The money just kept getting bigger. I kept saying no... Eventually, on Christmas Day they phoned me up and said, 'We'll give you this much money.' It was a *huge* amount of money. They said, 'Make the advert. If you don't like it you can give it back to us.'

"My managers had been working for six months on this and they said, 'How can you say no?' I had this big argument with all the people around the dinner table at Christmas. Eventually I said yes."

What's intriguing about this account is how closely it follows the description in *Bare*, the 1990 autobiography, of how Pepsi was said to have (unsuccessfully) pursued the star and his partner – right down to the length of time and the figure which, in Coke's case, sealed the deal: $3.3 million.

The ad was shot over two days, one in New York and one in Spain, each day earning the singer over $1.6 million. The director was Stephen Frears, the filmmaker whose long career includes such quintessentially British works as *Prick Up Your Ears* – about outrageous gay playwright Joe Orton, who spent part of his time 'cottaging' in north London toilets – and, later, *The Queen*, about how Elizabeth II publicly handled the tragic death of George's contemporary, Princess Diana. Here though, Frears would earn an easy pay packet by cuing up the audience response to George performing a fraction of an as-yet unreleased song.

The ad became big news in America, first broadcast on January 30, 1989, but was not syndicated to Europe at the time. According to the performer himself, the reason was that it simply didn't work very well – which seems to have been a matter of some relief to him. Apart from one interview, George was reluctant to talk about the affair, regarding it as a rare instance where he lost control of his public persona. In fact, the issue of control may have been important enough for a revised version of the episode to be presented in *Bare* – in which George is offered a fortune by Pepsi but declines, rather than being offered the same amount by Coke and accepting.

After the mass exposure of 1988, George Michael would be, by contrast, almost a phantom figure on the 1989 pop scene. Early in the year, he created a US sanctuary for himself by buying a second home in Santa Barbara, CA. Built by the innovative architectural firm of Hickman Designs, its extensive hexagonal shape stood out from the Santa Ynez hillside, looking rather like the Tracy family's island home in the old kids' TV show *Thunderbirds*.

The Tracy Island effect was completed by George's ability to control every aspect of the house – from the security gates to the huge glass windows – via a push-button 'starship console'. Set on a remote clearing in the foothills of the region's mountains, George's 'vacation/investment' home (at an estimated sterling cost of £3 million) was as far away from the prying eyes of the media and the unwanted attentions of obsessive fans as he needed to be. It was here that he would spend much of 1989, continuing into the following year, to complete songs and demos for his ambitious second solo album – provisionally entitled *Listen Without Prejudice* and now mooted as a double album, as the amount of good releasable material was accumulating steadily.

He was briefly audible (and very visible) on an early 1989 single release co-written for his bass player, Deon Estus, entitled 'Heaven Help Me'. A lightweight soul ballad with some nice muted trumpet, the backing vocals by George were signposted by closing and opening shots of him in his *Faith*-era get-up in the video. It was as if the promo was about to go into a George Michael number but then skipped a track.

This may have been another factor that influenced his decision to withdraw from the whole promo circus. In the interim, however, the year's first controversy presented itself at the American Music Awards – where George (or his LP *Faith*) was nominated for Favourite Male Artist (Rock and Pop), Favourite Album (Soul/R&B) and Favourite Male Artist (Soul/R&B). Staged at LA music venue the Shrine, the trophies would turn into a poisoned chalice when the artist walked off with all three. As flattered as he was by the recognition, he was well aware of the incongruity of a white Englishman winning out in categories intended to honour black American music.

The controversy that briefly blew up was immortalised on vinyl, on the B-side of radical hip-hop band Public Enemy's 'Fight The Power' 12-inch. On 'Help Me Out', black film director Spike Lee's voice is sampled, asking rapper Flavor Flav, "Flav, I was watching the American Music Awards – what is George Michael doing there? How'd he win all the awards? How'd he win the R&B category?"

George weathered the short shit-storm as best he could, trying to be gracious toward the industry that had bestowed the honours while sympathising with those who felt marginalised by them. "I didn't ask to be given those awards," he defended, while still acknowledging, "I'm not going to pretend I wasn't happy to get them. But I do understand the argument that says that this guy is just an acceptable version of black music for white America."

It was a thorny issue. Anyone who claimed that white singers couldn't perform soul music was underrating the emotional power of the music itself, which permeated its way into the consciousness of vocalists like George Michael in their formative years. To uphold these divisions was to insist on a kind of pop-cultural apartheid.

But there was another side to the argument, and the singer himself had the good grace not to challenge the commonsense statement by one of his personal old favourites, Gladys Knight: "If Bobby Brown had across-the-board play and he could compete in the same categories George Michael competes in, that would be a whole 'nother thing. But to get to be Pop Male Vocalist of the year – he's just not going to be considered."

The bitter aftertaste of the awards left the singer feeling more uncomfortable than ever with his status. "That was the turning point for me," he'd later acknowledge. "That was the point at which I had to negotiate some new relationship with celebrity that wasn't going to destroy me."

In Spain that summer, the singer gave several rare 1989 performances in Madrid, Malaga and Barcelona, after celebrating his 26th birthday in Ibiza. Back in London throughout the rest of the summer and autumn, George would lay down the tracks for *Listen Without Prejudice* at Sarm Studios West and the Metropolis Studios. Giving every aspect his customary care and attention, he played the roles of composer/arranger/producer on the work that was shaping up to be his magnum opus. Overdubbing many of the instruments himself, he was augmented by Chris Cameron on keyboards and Estus on bass. By this point, he was planning on putting out two albums – *Listen Without Prejudice Volumes One & Two* – as the tracks were separating themselves so neatly into the funk cuts inspired by black music and a more angst-ridden strain of lyricism. Apart from an inspiring vocal performance on a cover of Stevie Wonder's 'They Won't Go When I Go', all the songs on the mooted double set were new Michael originals.

He would be beaten into the stores by the first (and only) solo recordings of his old partner in crime. In autumn 1989, Andrew Ridgeley had made a minor ripple with his single 'Shake', its chart position falling just outside of the Top 50. "I started writing songs in 1987," explained the other half of Wham! "I realised that there was something lacking in my life, that I wasn't going to make a career in racing, for whatever reasons, and that I couldn't just doss around for ever. It might have been different if I'd had friends to doss around with but my friends were all working. It's really not much fun being the lone playboy," he conceded.

'Shake' was followed in May 1990 by the release of *Son Of Albert*, Andrew's autobiographically titled debut album. Despite it showing another side of the partnership that once set pop music alight – with a concentration on guitar music and a band format, rather than the soul/ funk stylings of Wham! – the world was largely indifferent to what the lone playboy was doing with himself these days. Sadly, *Son Of Albert* very quickly sank from view.

Andrew Ridgeley would ultimately take an early retirement with a new life in Cornwall, on England's western coast, dedicating his time to surfing, golf and drinking real ale.* His life would be derailed in the early nineties, not long after he quit playing music professionally, when he and his brother Paul both caught a strain of e-coli from raw sewage in the ocean. After recovering from the potentially fatal illness, the chirpy one from Wham! snatched victory from disaster by forming the pressure group Surfers Against Sewage (SAS). It was the birth of a committed involvement in aqua-environmentalism in the UK.

Today, Andrew is a partner in a company that manufactures surfing equipment and lives in a 15th-century farmhouse with Keren Woodward, the brunette from the all-girl trio Bananarama. He is, by all accounts, a very happy man. His former manager Simon Napier-Bell reflects and compares:

> *When they broke up, Andrew Ridgeley, who was self-confidence personified, just stayed as he was — totally at ease with himself, got married, went to live in Cornwall, took up wind-surfing, accepted the benefits that Wham!'s success had given him and opted for early retirement at 23. George, though, seemed unable to live without the uniform. And ever since, every time he tries to throw it off, every time he tells everyone he will no longer be a pop star, he's forced to put it on again, false name and all, because, presumably, he can't find anything solid enough underneath on which to build.*

As a summation of two men he once knew well, this is perhaps fair enough. But as Napier-Bell is well aware, people who feel as comfortable with themselves and their lives as Andrew simply don't have much of an impetus to create anything. By the former Wham! manager's own

---

* As perhaps befitting a man of his years, he's now a member of CAMRA, the Campaign for Real Ale.

admission, Andrew Ridgeley is a very likeable guy with a happy-go-lucky temperament, while George Michael, the more significant half of the equation, is stricken with insecurities and – in pop music terms at least – a true artist.

★★★

The completed demos for *Listen With Prejudice, Vol. 1* were delivered to Epic/CBS in July 1990. Its enthusiasm for what were clearly George's most mature and engaging songs to date was unbridled. Yet again, it was decided that his contractual terms should be renegotiated – to date, he was obligated to deliver to deliver another six albums (including the current unfinished work) over the space of just over a decade. *Listen Without Prejudice* made the company or label think differently; this was, in the jargon of the industry, a 'longevity performer', and terms needed to be revised in order to keep him on its books as a permanent fixture.

It sounded ideal, but in reality it was another contributing factor to the crisis point that the artist and his label would eventually reach. For while Columbia – which had now been swallowed into Sony Music and was firing its veteran music-biz staff at a rate of knots – was making plans for the best way to promote its artist's scheduled new release, the artist was contemplating withdrawing from promotion altogether. As George would explain in detail to Chris Evans in 1996:

I was unhappy because I just didn't spend enough time doing what I had originally wanted to do, which was making music, writing. It was all about promotion, you know, it was all about the videos, it was all about the touring. Touring is just not rewarding when you get to the stage of playing in huge arenas and you can't hear what you're singing, either because people are making too much noise or because you're playing in a big, cavernous hall.

Doing what I ended up doing was what entertainers do, right, and as I've said before, I never expected to be an entertainer. I thought I was going to be a singer-songwriter, and you get to a certain status in the pop field where you can't do that any more, it is impossible for you to play a reasonably small place, even secret shows or anything like that. You can't do the things that would actually improve your singing live. I would love to do something that would improve my voice greatly; the way that I sang in the eighties – and the places that I sang at and the types of shows and the whole thing – was just not about me being a musician at all. It was about me selling the record and about entertaining people, and it really wasn't what I was out there to do.

In the run-up to the album's release, it began to dawn on CBS/Sony that the usual itinerary of video/TV/touring wasn't going to be an option this time around. 'Without prejudice', as the main part of the album title, wasn't so much intended to suggest a legal letter (as in 'read without prejudice') as it was to impel the listener (and particularly the critics) to judge the songs on their own merits – rather than being by 'pop superstar'/'ex-Wham! man' George Michael. As part of this process, the peripheral selling point of the promo video was an aspect that the artist was actively kicking against.

At first, it seemed as if the corporation was ready to go with the wishes of its artist. As George retrospectively recalled:

I was very honest with Sony. One of the reasons we went to court [in 1996] is that I was so honest with them about what I wasn't prepared to do with Listen Without Prejudice, *that if they weren't prepared to deal with that then they would tell me – but they didn't. So we went to lunch and everybody told me what a fantastic album it was, and then came back to New York and told everybody that it was George Michael's* Nebraska. *Which was Bruce Springsteen's eighties album that he recorded on a four-track and it sold nothing because it's completely introspective. But I'd just presented them with* Listen Without Prejudice *which, I'm sorry, is not* Nebraska.

Nebraska is, in fact, one of Springsteen's best albums, which made up for its initial modest sales by picking up a cult following over the ensuing decades. But still, George had a point. As introspective as *Listen Without Prejudice* can sometimes be (check the celebrated first single from the album, 'Praying For Time'), there's nothing within its tracks that's distinctly less commercial than *Faith*. The difference this time would be in how the game of pushing the record was played.

In early August it was announced that the Kahane-Lippman partnership that acted as worldwide management for George Michael was dissolving, as agreed by each party. George cast his vote of confidence for the man who had brought him into the business relationship. For the time being, he would be solely managed by Rob Kahane.

This was followed by a dissimilar event of equal significance to the artist's career. 'Praying For Time' was debuted as the first track off the imminent new album. With great trepidation, CBS/Epic was forced to go along with the artist's wishes in issuing what is effectively a kind of anti-video. Featuring a dark blue-on-black screen, with only a few shifting shapes to suggest movement, it consisted basically of the song's lyrics appearing a line at a time as white-on-black lettering.

The lyrics, cryptic as they are, deserve the attention. They're the simple but powerful product of an unquiet mind, the composer's "scream from behind the door" set to a repetitive, almost mantric wave of acoustic guitars and drums. The audible anguish of a successful and sophisticated man, 'Praying For Time' attracted criticism for its lyrical obliqueness, for not being obviously 'about' anything. Those who have ears to hear will perceive a guilty man haunted by his inability to do anything to change the world outside his luxurious surroundings – an almost reclusive Citizen Kane figure, tormented by images on his television set.

The vocal is beautifully controlled yet suffused with despair. As a lyricist, George Michael fits the present-day stereotype of the person who is not strictly religious but 'spiritual' – there's no evidence, for instance, that the Greek Orthodox Church has ever been an influence on his upbringing. The narrator of the lyric, however, is clearly troubled by what the Buddhists would regard as karma, or the Christian fundamentalists as divine retribution.

In *Bare*, Shirlie Holliman, who speaks sadly of the distance that set in between George and her, tells the following story: "I had a dream about him last night. I dreamt that he died. He went missing and me and all these girls I didn't even know were crying our eyes out, trying to find him. I remember screaming, 'No he can't, he can't...'And everyone was saying, 'Are you *sure* you don't know how he died?' And then this Buddhist monk came up to me and said, 'You can't have everything, you know. George had too much. He had to die.'"

Ms Holliman seems to have become interested in Eastern mysticism in the way that many pop performers did, when they tried to reject the materialism of the eighties. And her old friend George seems to have borrowed her dream's theme of paying a karmic penalty. In 'Praying For Time', the consciously affluent and privileged man who knows that he has too much cries out that he's ready to take his chances, "because God's stopped keeping score". But this is no lifeline, just a denial of worldly hope "when there is no hope to speak of". The lyric and the vocal remain the most powerful in George Michael's entire repertoire.

'Praying For Time' is a monument in the career of its composer. It was a hit on both sides of the Atlantic, although it fared very differently. In Britain, where fans still seemed to be pining for the cuddly (and visible) George of Wham! days, it was in the Top 10 for several weeks. In the US, its mournful, almost apocalyptic tones struck a greater chord; 'Praying For Time' received saturation airplay and topped the *Billboard* chart.

Not only had promotion gone back to the hard sell of emphasising the music rather than selling it as a by-product of an MTV video (and the music industry used to have the perfect vehicles for promoting their artists – they were called 'records'), but press was limited too. In the US, George gave interviews to only a handful of the big papers – the *New York Times*, the *LA Times* and *USA Today*. Back in the UK it would be more limited still, though he did agree to a one-hour special for ITV's *South Bank Show*. The great leveller of arts shows, Melvyn Bragg's documentary series gained a reputation for populism as it veered away from high art towards pop culture. It also had a tendency not to be critical of its subjects – at times it could be outright sycophantic – in return for that all-important exclusive access.

When *The South Bank Show* aired on September 2, 1990, George Michael made the following statement about how he saw himself as a recording artist:

> *I believe that I am a writer more than I am anything else. Certainly for the first album I didn't believe that I'd ever make a decent singer, although I had belief as a writer then. The second album I started to believe in myself as a singer and I think it showed, because the second album sounded different vocally. But at the end of the day I don't think it matters what I do, I don't think I'm important as a pop star. I don't think that there are many people who are important as pop stars in the sense that they used to be. I don't think I will leave a great mark as an 'entity', I think I'm more realistic than that. I do believe that I'm a lot better singer now than I ever thought I would be, but at the end of the day I want to leave something as a writer... I want to leave songs, I believe that I can leave songs that will mean something to other generations.*

If he comes over as a little over-earnest and precious (perhaps what Boy George meant when he cattily described George Michael as having "no sense of humus"), perhaps it should be kept in mind how some of the tracks on the album reveal a self-consciously successful performer who is overly sensitive, perhaps too neurotic, to relax and take his situation for granted.

The TV show was closely followed by the release of *Listen Without Prejudice, Vol. 1* in the UK. The singer had even retreated from the cover – instead of a picture of him, there was a photo entitled 'Coney Island 28th July 1940 4pm' by newspaper photographer Weegee (real name Arthur Felig). Weegee often specialised in crime photos, but in this case he captured a seething, joyous mass of overcrowded humanity at the beach. In the tradition of rock albums from the sixties and seventies, the artist had chosen a striking image, then left the listener to ponder as to whether it had any relevance to the record.

Other standout tracks on the album include 'Mother's Pride', an antiwar ballad with Satiesque piano backing and simple but poignant lyrics. It laments the war dead from a mother's perspective ("the time has come to lose a son") and a promotional video – albeit one in which George doesn't appear – shows scenes from World War Two and Vietnam interspersed with shots of the mother at home, stoically accepting the "We regret to inform you" letter about her son, in the way she once did for her husband.

'Cowboys And Angels' is a wistfully melancholic love song. With its light, delicate vocal and waltz-tempo backing redolent of European cinema, it's about as far from George the white soul man as it was possible for him to be at that time. It's also the only George Michael single up till then to fail to make the UK Top 40, but for all that it's still sublime.

The last (videoless) single release from the album would be 'Waiting For That Day', a rather traditional piece of rock songwriting about a broken relationship which laments how, "My memory serves me far too well." In fact, the songwriter's memory seems to have dredged up a similar shuffling guitar-and-vocal backing to Lou Reed's 'Walk On The Wild Side', while the song ends on the title refrain of The Rolling Stones' 'You Can't Always Get What You Want'.

Listen Without Prejudice was a hit album. It went straight in at number one in the British charts while taking several weeks to reach number two in the US; in both cases it stayed on the chart for most of a full year. But it was damned in the eyes of CBS executives by its high-performing forerunner. As the record struggled to reach half the sales of *Faith* (while being, as George asserted, a much better album), its performance relegated it to the status of a relative failure. In November, the *LA Times* printed a headline which ran, 'Why Isn't This Man's Album Selling? Maybe It's Because George Michael Has Taken Himself Out Of The Picture'. And this, remember, was an album that was in the gradual process of selling well over a million copies.

The press controversy over George's perceived stand against the industry began at the time of the album's release. Rock critic Robert

Hilburn's September piece in *Calendar*, the weekend entertainment section of the *LA Times*, was prefaced by the following heading: 'The former Wham! star thought he'd walked away from teen adulation with his *Faith* album, but his sexy image became a nightmare. Now he's trying to make sure it doesn't happen again.'

The entertainment world quickly became divided between those who sympathised with George in his predicament and those who thought he needed a quick shot of reality or a swift kick in the butt, whichever would wake him up soonest.

(The following weekend's *Calendar* carried an outraged letter by another distinguished resident of Southern California, who'd said goodbye to public performance more than once. "Come on, George," the elderly Frank Sinatra scolded him. "Loosen up. Swing, man. Dust off those gossamer wings and fly yourself to the moon..." At least he didn't advise him not to lose his ring-a-ding-ding.)

As Andy Stephens, the ex-CBS man who would take over George's management later in the nineties, concisely explained: "The decision was taken in 1990 not to promote. It was felt that if he was to carry on, on the bandwagon as it were, that he would burn out. He had to get off it, and he explained to the record company that it was something that he had to do. And whilst most of the world accepted it, America couldn't."

Inevitably perhaps, there was a lot of cynicism about exactly why George was choosing to opt out of the fame game at a point when he'd already become so hugely, almost monstrously famous. Interviewed shortly after on one of Madness singer Suggs' earliest TV shows, Simon Napier-Bell was sceptical about his motivation: "It's quite a good trick, he's made quite a big thing out of not appearing in [videos] – sufficient for it to be a promotional technique in itself. Although I'm quite sure that if nobody appeared in their videos, it became the done thing not to appear in videos, he'd be the first one to get back to videos."

His ex-manager's comments flew in the face of how George had asserted, to Hilburn, "If my life goes the way I want it to, I would like to never step in front of a camera again." It seemed a sincere enough statement as far as promotional videos went, but how literally could it be taken? Did he never want to be filmed in live performance again? Never photographed for the press? Was there any way for a superstar to live so far apart from the entertainment media, save losing his fame and fortune altogether?

In any case, George had tried to explain that the root cause of his anxiety was not so much the product as his own state of being: "I'm not stupid enough to think that I can deal with another 10 or 15 years of major exposure. I think that is the ultimate tragedy of fame, people who are simply out of control, who are lost. I've seen so many of them, and I don't want to be another cliché."

For better or worse, George Michael was intent on eking out his own less-trodden path. In the wake of the *LA Times* piece, CBS Records president Tommy Mottola expressed sympathy with the artist: "I think you'll have a lot of disappointed fans because there is no video, but when they get to understand his point of view and hear the record, I don't really think there will be any problem... if doing those things are going to cause that kind of reaction in an artist, then what's the point of doing them?"

But the resentment between both parties would continue bubbling under until, eventually, it boiled over and someone got burnt. It would be a few years before Sony executive Rob Stringer (by now Chairman of Sony Entertainment) could matter-of-factly state, "There was a basic falling out over the philosophy of not promoting the record, and not providing a video for the first single. That's what it stemmed from." There would also be some serious battles fought along the way.

In late October 1990, in the spirit of compromise, the next single from the album came with its own promo video – although the singer was nowhere to be seen in it. 'Freedom 90' was so called to distinguish it from the Wham! hit of 1984. The funkiest number on *Listen Without Prejudice*, its video cost £300,000 to make – 10 times the budget of 'Careless Whisper' five years earlier, which seems to belie the idea of opting out of the promotion game. Most of the money went to the cast, however, a line-up of the world's five top supermodels at the time:

Naomi Campbell, Cindy Crawford, Linda Evangelista, Tatjana Patitz and Christy Turlington.

Playing it like an upmarket lingerie ad, each of the models mimed to George's defiant words about personal freedom and overcoming emotional possessiveness. The video was directed by David Fincher, who would go on to make such disturbingly film noir-ish movies as *Se7en* and *Fight Club*, but it played like a standard (albeit expensive) promo. Perhaps the only vaguely edgy moment was when the Triumph biker jacket that symbolised the *Faith* era was set on fire. But still, the "I don't belong to you and you don't belong to me" sentiment of the lyric was in a sense an introduction to a new George Michael, an older, less morally fastidious, more relaxed man who would gradually surface over the coming years.

"I was just totally naïve and felt that if I was open and honest and truthful that it would pay dividends," George would say of his relations with Epic/CBS at the time. "What a fool!

"As it turned out, one of my better ideas was getting five gorgeous supermodels [miming to the song] that people still want to look at today. If you're going to say to your record company, 'Look, I'm not going to be in this video,' I'd say that's a fairly good consolation prize really, you know, those five gorgeous babes."

Meanwhile, in that same autumn of 1990, the star who didn't want to promote anything bar the music alone had made an extraordinary move. *George Michael: Bare* was published by Penguin Books on both sides of the Atlantic. Basically the authorised autobiography of the 27-year-old star, it was co-credited to former *NME* journalist/future *Telegraph* music columnist Tony Parsons. Parsons had interviewed George throughout 1989 and early 1990, editing his words into the main narrative of the book, augmenting it with interviews with other main players in his life and the journalist's own written links. The performer had generously split his £430,000 advance 50-50 with his biographer. As premature as it may have seemed to immortalise his life in print at this stage, *Bare* remains essential reading for anyone who wants to understand the passion of the young George Michael.

Retrospectively, the book also reads like an adept PR job – as notable for what it leaves out of its account as for what it includes. "It's not badly written, Tony Parsons did a good job of writing it," an older, more worldly George would reflect on *The Graham Norton Show* in 2003, "but 'Bare' my arse!" The singer's self-deprecation raised hilarity among the audience. "Do you know what I mean? It says 'Bare' but I'm 24 or 25 [at the time the book was written] and absolutely sod all had happened to me by then."

Host Norton regained control by stating a simple fact: "This came out before you did."

The singer and the audience responded as if to a one-line gag. But Norton insisted, "It wasn't even a joke! But do you know what I mean? This wasn't your life as a fiction, but when you were with Wham! you were shagging girls."

"Absolutely," conceded George. "Well, you would, wouldn't you? You've got so much opportunity there."

The audience groaned. Social mores had shifted by this time; George, as a gay man making references to his butt, was good fun, but his boast about having been a sexual opportunist around girls was seen as distasteful.

There would be much shifting sand over the years that followed, not least in the life of George Michael himself. But back in 1990, things were a little different. Anyone reading *Bare* at the time could have been excused for believing its subject was a strictly hetero man. To paraphrase the song, what is now over here was over there.

In the early nineties, George Michael was leading the life of a lonely and successful young bachelor. Kathy Jeung, for a while his companion and briefly (in the 'I Want Your Sex' video) his artistic muse, was no longer part of his life. The only other living being to permanently share his home in Hampstead was a golden Labrador puppy gifted to him by his publicist, Gary Farrow. George named the Labrador bitch Hippy, and they would become a regular sight out walking on Hampstead Heath together.

In January 1991, as US troops prepared to invade the Persian Gulf region to counter Iraq's invasion of Kuwait, word got around that the most requested song on US forces radio was the much-played 'Praying For Time'. In fact, many of the troops seemed to consider it a personal anthem, in the way that the movies would have us believe that, say, the Stones' 'Paint It, Black' was a Vietnam war anthem. "I'm very uncomfortable with any connection," confirmed George, who had made his pacifist views clear in the song 'Mother's Pride'. But no composer can be said to fully own his own songs and, given the bleakly dramatic feel of 'Praying For Time' and its potent line about "the wounded skies above", it's little wonder that young men steeling themselves for mortal combat might feel the lyric was talking to them.

This gap between intention and perception was difficult for the songwriter to accept, however. As for his own instinctive resistance to warfare as a means of conducting international affairs, it would become much more vocal and more controversial by the time of the Second Gulf War.

In mid-January 1991, as America and her allies (including the UK) prepared to go to war, George Michael was in his homeland, beginning a brief 12-date world tour at the NEC Arena in Birmingham. Backed by a nine-piece band and the London Community Gospel Choir, the title and theme of the tour was Cover To Cover – a selection of covers of some of the singer's favourite songs by other artists. The tour was effusively received, with notable standouts including such danceable classics as Adamski's 'Killer', The Temptations' 'Papa Was A Rolling Stone' and David Bowie's funk lament, 'Fame'. But the only showcased tracks from *Listen Without Prejudice* were 'Freedom 90' and the Stevie Wonder cover. This latest bout of reluctance to promote the album dragged relations with the vocalist's record label to a new low.

In the spring of 1991, there was talk in the press that the singer would undertake a small, seven-city world tour early the following year, in aid of AIDS research. CBS/Epic was rumoured to be cagey about the prospect, believing that Michael was only serving to alienate his original, mainly hetero audience by being associated with "gay causes".

"By that time the relationship in America was already over," George would later remark on dealings with his record label, "so 'Freedom' peaked at 12, I think, in the States. Normally I'd be jumping up and down about it and really pissed off, but I was just back from Brazil and something amazing had happened to me, so all of this seemed relatively unimportant at the time."

The next dates on the Cover To Cover tour took place in Rio de Janeiro, at the massive Rock in Rio II festival. At the 100,000-capacity Maracana football stadium, as part of a starry line-up that included Prince, Guns N' Roses, Robert Plant, New Kids On The Block, Run DMC and white British soul singer Lisa Stansfield, George was booked to perform at two dates. At the second of these he would hold an ace in the deck, the latest (and to date the last) of his occasional reunions with Andrew Ridgeley, briefly returning to the Wham! era for the duration of a few greatest hits.

But the life-changing events in store for him would make even this concert promoter's dream seem insignificant.

CHAPTER 12

Heaven Sent And Heaven Stole

The first night of Rock in Rio II was something of a disappointment. In late January 1991, George Michael played his Cover to Cover set to a mere 30,000 – a sizeable crowd for any other concert tour but a poor showing for the massive Maracana Stadium.

But this was the night when the singer showcased his personal style for the first half of the nineties: brushed-back hair cut tidily close to the skull; pointed, almost devilishly trimmed beard; small-lapelled suit jacket, redolent of sixties Carnaby Street but soon to invade the modern high street. Then of course there were his two piratical hooped earrings and his ever-present shades – with smaller frames this time, like cooler versions of the spectacles he'd been made to wear as a boy.

The smaller crowd and muted enthusiasm would be forgotten by the closing night of the festival, in mid-February. This was when George promised to take a trawl back through his musical history – including Wham!, a scheduled reunion with Andrew Ridgeley set to earn both men a cool £500,000.

The duo closed the festival in front of a sell-out crowd of 170,000. "On the night of the Rock in Rio concert in Maracana Stadium," he would later reflect, "[there were] 160,000 people – it was going to be the biggest audience I'd ever played in front of. But in front of this 160,000 people, there was this guy over on the right hand side of the stage that had just fixed me with this look."

As the resurgent Wham! frontman stalked around the stage in a leather waistcoat to the strains of 'Everything She Wants', a twenty-something Brazilian was effectively stalking him in the nicest possible way. The singer's sexuality was becoming one of the worst-kept secrets in showbiz; rumours were crossing the ocean to South America and encouraging an admirer to try his luck.

"He was so cute, I was so distracted by him that I stayed away from that end of the stage for a while," the singer remembered. "And that was Anselmo – that really was the moment that my life changed. For a while it was just like, 'Wow, I've met somebody that I actually think I'm going to fall in love with, rather than just want their body for a while,' you know."

Wham!'s reunion was a final triumph, never to be repeated. That evening, the celebration party took over an entire floor of the Copacabana Hotel. Among the celebrants was Anselmo Feleppa, George's new, rather forward young acquaintance. In the days that followed, a big party of old friends would head up the coast from Rio to the beauty resort of Armação dos Bízios. Among them was Feleppa, the lithe, 29-year-old son of a successful clothing manufacturer.

It seems to have been an infatuation which turned to love on an accelerated timescale. And while it lasted, certainly in the early days, the love of these two young men seems to have been transformative. "For the first six months of our relationship at least, I felt better than I had possibly in my entire life," George would later admit. "It's very hard to be proud of your own sexuality when it hasn't brought you any joy. Once it is associated with joy and love, it's easy to be proud of who you are."

Ever since the early days of Wham!, George Michael had displayed a physicality that would have been alien to his nonathletic younger self. But his relationship with the Brazilian led to a greater engagement with the physical world. He would fly above the ocean by hang-gliding and explore its coral depths by scuba diving, whether with or without Anselmo. He even dived from the 1,300-foot peak of Sugarloaf Mountain into the waters of Rio's Guanabara Bay. "I didn't know how to enjoy myself before I met Anselmo," George would testify. His Brazilian lover made him lose his English reserve, also becoming more openly affectionate and tactile toward others.

They became a team. A partnership. A couple. When the Cover To Cover tour moved on from South America, George promised Anselmo that they would meet up again as soon as his itinerary allowed.

To the north of the continent, tracks from the artist's previous album – 'Mother's Pride', 'Heal The Pain', 'Cowboys And Angels' – continued to be released as singles to little avail, the first of these running contrary to the patriotic fervour of a nation that had recently fought a brief, victorious war. For a time, it seemed as if George Michael's old hits had dated him, that he somehow belonged to the previous decade. But the awards for *Listen Without Prejudice* kept on coming – Best Album of 1990 in *Rolling Stone*'s poll, Best British Album award at the Brits – before the Cover To Cover tour climaxed at Wembley Arena in the same month as the Brits, March 1991. On the final night, Elton joined George onstage for 'Don't Let The Sun Go Down On Me' and for a brief moment the triumph of Live Aid was revisited.

In LA, the latest negotiations between CBS, George Michael, Rob Kahane and Tony Russell resulted in further revisions of the artist's contract. Among the extra financial incentives shown to him was an investment of around £100,000 sterling in his own subsidiary record label, Hard Rock Records, to be part-financed by George to the tune of £250,000 and run by cousin Andros (whose involvement in the record industry thus far was mostly confined to a UK Top 20 cover of The Bee Gees' 'Jive Talkin''').

Business was secondary to the agenda at that time, however. As soon as the tour ended, George returned to Brazil. Cruising on a private yacht off the coast of Rio, he and Anselmo were seen in the company of Brazilian socialite-celebrity Lucia Sednaoui and her husband. Anselmo was noted around this time as wearing a new gold Rolex watch and to be driving a new Mercedes. As had been displayed to George's closest friends and family, his new lover's generosity knew few bounds.

As George Michael became decreasingly visible on the world's stages, much of his time was spent privately with Anselmo Feleppa. The Brazilian became an increasingly frequent visitor to the singer's homes in Santa Barbara and London. George reputedly bought a remote Brazilian farm as a love nest.

"People will find this hard to believe, but Anselmo and I didn't hide," said George, who attended Andros's wedding in Los Angeles to his long-term partner at this time. "We hid to the degree that I was living in LA; but that's hardly hiding from the media – you're a phone call away as far as *The Sun* or the *Mirror* is concerned."

In April 1991, George went back to the studio to complete his next album, *Listen Without Prejudice, Vol. 2*, which was (ironically enough) to be followed by a major promotional tour. It apparently elicited little more enthusiasm from CBS than the singer's AIDS campaigning; the blueprint album, *Vol. 1*, was regarded as a failure for only coming close to half of *Faith*'s sales. To put it in perspective, this meant that the record would sell *only* a maximum of around seven million copies.*

As absurd as it seems from our current vantage point, with CD sales at an all-time low, this lack of enthusiasm by the record company would couple with George's resentment of its attitude to ensure the album was never released. Intended to be the funkier, more dance-oriented counterpart of *Vol. 1*, the full track listing has, to date, never surfaced on the Internet. The first of the four tracks to eventually see daylight would be 'Crazyman Dance', a piece of urban funk with electro frills about New York's disenfranchised and destitute – surfacing as a B-side two years after a snatch of it was first heard in the Diet Coke commercial. The other three tracks – 'Too Funky', 'Do You Really Want To Know?' and 'Happy' – would be donated to *Red Hot & Dance*, 1992's charity compilation to raise money for AIDS research. Other featured

---

* At the end of 1990, George Michael had been ranked as 128th richest person in Britain, with a personal fortune of £65 million.

artists included such popular acts of the time as Madonna, Seal and Lisa Stansfield, plus pioneering funksters Sly & the Family Stone, but Epic/ Sony would apparently do little to promote the album or the cause.

For all his agonising over the issues of public and private sexuality, George Michael continued to nail his colours to the mast. In October 1991, he made a speech at the first of two concerts at the Great Western Forum in LA. California Governor Pete Wilson, having presented himself as a moderate Republican to the electorate, had previously solicited the support of gay and lesbian pressure groups in the state; now he was vetoing rights bill AB101, which would have legally protected gays against discrimination in the workplace. As a result, Wilson found himself the target of a series of protest rallies. "I know some of you were out marching today," acknowledged George from the stage of that day's rally in Santa Monica. "For all those protesting up there, I'd like to add my voice to theirs."

One month later, the cause closest to the singer's heart would make itself felt with a wounding vengeance. Like an echo from the previous decade, the Cover To Cover tour's duet with Elton John on 'Don't Let The Sun Go Down On Me' was released as a single in early December, making number one on both sides of the Atlantic and around the world. This revisit of Live Aid would be good for business and good for charity, raising more funds for AIDS research and for the Rainbow House charity for seriously ill children.

"Everything was okay with Sony for a while," George would later recall, "the single with Elton did really well. I was very happy, I guess it was the calm before the storm. I was about to become a grown-up, and I wasn't prepared for it."

According to his old club buddy Fiona Russell Powell, George had stayed in contact with American "fuck buddy" Brad Branson throughout this period. "They carried on and they kept a friendship for years and years," she observes. "George was still friends with him when he was with Feleppa. He was *moaning*, because George was very generous with his friends, and he was complaining, 'Oh, all I got from George for

Christmas was a Bang & Olufsen stereo, I didn't get a Mercedes like Anselmo did.'"

But for George, Christmas 1991 would have a more serious agenda than an old boyfriend's sense of disappointment. "I remember..." he paused, collecting his thoughts, "I remember the moment [Anselmo] told me about the test he'd been advised to have. I remember him leaving the house, and to this day I remember looking to the sky and saying, 'Don't you *dare* do this to me.'"

When recollecting the event in his biographical documentary, *A Different Life*, George's words were matched by a photo of the smiling, dark-haired young man with a large sore growing on his nose – Kaposi's sarcoma, one of the only visible signs of AIDS.

Meanwhile, on the other side of the Atlantic, a more advanced tragedy had entered its final act. Freddie Mercury, the truly mercurial vocalist of Queen, had never officially come out of the closet as gay – although, with his handlebar moustache and macho biker chic in the eighties, it's hard to imagine that anyone thought of him as straight. As with George, his sexuality had become a very open secret. Now though, after a protracted period of illness and persistent hounding by *Sun* reporters wanting to confirm the rumours, Mercury went into terminal decline. His press agent put out a statement on his behalf, confirming that he was suffering from AIDS, on the day before he died. On November 24, 1991, the rock legend succumbed to bronchial pneumonia, a by-product of his terminal disease.

"I remember my publicist phoning me to tell me that Freddie Mercury had died and that they wanted a quote from me," George recollected the passing of one of his seventies idols. "I remember I was trying to give her the quote and I was crying – I mean, bless him, I was really sad that Freddie had passed away. But of course I was crying about somebody else entirely."

On returning to London for Christmas, George made a more personal statement to the converging press: "I was very, very sad to hear of Freddie's death. I am still deeply upset by it – it's a tragedy." Along with a number of other top-line performers, he entered into discussion with the surviving members of Queen about an event that would commemorate their late frontman and raise awareness about the epidemic that had taken him.

But George was also haunted by the spectre of AIDS on a personal level. "Anselmo had the test in Brazil, over the Christmas period," he'd later acknowledge. "I went home to my family for Christmas and sat at the table not knowing whether my partner – who the people sat around the table did not know about – this person I was in love with, was terminally ill. And therefore not knowing whether I potentially was terminally ill, sitting there at Christmas. And it was possibly the loneliest time in my life, I think. But there you go, that's life, that's the chance you take, isn't it? And definitely, unfortunately, in 1991 that was the chance you took with a gay man, for sure."

Just as the last months of Mercury's life had inspired the press's worst bloodhound instincts, so the word about George and his gay lover in Brazil would be the cue for a new feeding frenzy. For the next few months at least, however, the papers would remain ignorant of the situation.

On April 20, 1992, The Freddie Mercury Tribute: Concert for AIDS Awareness took place at Wembley Stadium. By now, George had long been aware that his lover was HIV positive – and that he, mercifully, was not.

The line-up of the all-day event ran from top-ranking names including George himself, Elton John, U2, David Bowie and Annie Lennox to more conventional hard rock and heavy metal bands, reflecting the range of Queen's own music. Intriguingly, Axl Rose of Guns N' Roses – the man who famously sang how "immigrants and faggots... spread some fuckin' disease" – duetted with Elton on 'Bohemian Rhapsody'. Other bizarre highlights included Bowie, who'd had a deeply serious flirtation with the occult when he was managed by Michael Lippman, dropping to his knees onstage to recite The Lord's Prayer, and ageing Hollywood icon Elizabeth Taylor telling the crowd, "Protect yourselves. Every time you have sex, use a condom." (As one commentator pointed out, if this advice was followed 'every time', it'd put an end to the human race far faster than the HIV virus was able to.)

But amid all the grandstanding and pious gestures, George Michael's performance shone out like a beacon of pure joy. As one of a number of performers scheduled to take the tragically vacant Queen frontman slot for the night, he sang three of their vintage numbers dressed in his trademark hoop earrings and a pink jacket with a red AIDS awareness ribbon on the lapel.

"For many months I was kind of sworn to secrecy by Anselmo," the singer recalled of this period. "I went out there knowing I had to do two things: I had to honour Freddie Mercury and I had to pray for Anselmo. So it meant so much to me, all in that one performance; I'm so proud of the fact that I held onto that feeling, because I wanted to die inside. It was just overwhelming for me, and I think what that did was turn on one of the best performances of my career."

Indeed, the range of Queen songs chosen by George spoke of a truly confident performer. The lesser-known '39' was not a Mercury composition but written by astrophysics-graduate guitarist Brian May, a pseudo-folk song telling of space pioneers passing through a time warp; 'Those Were The Days Of Our Lives' was Freddie's swansong, the kind of ballad that led Bowie to credit him with turning every cliché to his advantage, duetted beautifully by George and Lisa Stansfield; the real show-stopper was Mercury's semi-operatic party piece, 'Somebody To Love', belted out with gusto by George and the London Community Gospel Choir.

After the show, drummer Roger Taylor was quoted conjecturing as to whether Queen might continue as a band with George Michael as vocalist. If the quote was genuine, then it was no more than wishful thinking. However, as later 'reformation' gigs with ex-Free/Bad Company vocalist Paul Rodgers (a fine blues-rock singer but totally lacking Freddie's vocal nuances and flamboyance) demonstrated, the only post-Mercury incarnation of Queen worthy of the name was briefly fronted by a man who was 12 when 'Bohemian Rhapsody' first topped the charts.

George committed to mixing his performances from the Mercury Tribute to a releasable standard, for a charity EP. In the UK, his own Platinum Trust foundation had been running in aid of children with disabilities and special educational needs for 18 months, since the release of *Listen Without Prejudice*. George himself had already contributed over £1 million of his personal wealth in that time and would continue to do so at a similar proportionate rate.[*]

When the *Red Hot & Dance* benefit album was released around this time, its main man conceded to make a promotional video for his track 'Too Funky'. Once again though, there was no sign of himself onscreen – co-directed with French fashion designer Thierry Mugler, the promo featured more world-famous models (including Linda Evangelista) wearing some of Mugler's more fetishised leather and plastic catsuits. Among these striking women was the drag queen Lypsinka, an entertainer renowned for miming to records on the New York gay scene. Epic/Sony seemed to have little interest in either marketing the album or promoting the cause – 'Too Funky' hit number four in the UK, but the album would go on to sell around 60,000 copies at first, which would be considered disastrous if it was a George Michael album per se.

For all the minor career setbacks and the stress in his private life, the performer was still determined to enjoy life in style. In the summer, he arranged for a group of 20 close friends and employees to fly to a private villa in Nice with him, to celebrate his 10 years in the music industry. (Andrew Ridgeley flew in with Keren Woodward, who would become his long-term partner.) At home, he bought a racing stable for his racehorse-owner father.

But within the music industry itself, relations were not getting any warmer. George's next mooted project was an album of new songs entitled *Trojan Souls*. Swiftly moving toward an impasse with Epic/CBS, the singer courted further hostility by making clear that he would not be

---

[*] A broadsheet newspaper survey would rank him as Britain's most philanthropic entertainer around this time.

singing the songs himself. Instead, he would delegate the vocals to such luminaries as his friend Elton, Aretha Franklin, Bryan Ferry and Seal.

The move seems to have had the desired effect. His label was indifferent to the project, not regarding it as a proper George Michael album, leaving the artist free to negotiate with Warner Bros Records in Burbank. (To date, *Trojan Souls* has never been completed or released. Despite recurring rumours of completion that lasted 10 years, it seems to be a casualty of the legal black hole that was starting to form around the Michael–Sony business relationship in the early nineties.)

In the autumn of 1992, George became one of the first celebrity guests on UK morning TV show *The Big Breakfast*, which would run for over a decade. On the early days of the show there was a regular feature called 'In Bed With Paula', where a male star would be verbally seduced (or later, in the case of INXS vocalist Michael Hutchence, continue the seduction himself after the show) by kittenish blonde Paula Yates.

Ms Yates, then the wife of Bob Geldof, had the youthful-looking but bearded George on the bed, ostensibly to be grilled about his 10 years in showbiz. He was still speaking in the controlled, accentless tones which he seems to have shed over the ensuing years, while in retrospect Paula appears to be teasing him about the most open secret in showbiz.

Paula: *Do you find girls a great inspiration, are lots of your songs written about girls?*
George: Of course.
Are they written about actual *girls?*
Oh, you mean any girl in particular? Yeah, any actual one relationship you've had has be the inspiration for a song – otherwise you're writing, '*To all the girls I've loved before,*' something like that.

After dancing around the subject, Paula decides to get naughty, playing footsy with George as she does so.

A lot of people find sex more exciting if it's a bit 'wicked' – things like being unfaithful, stuff like that.
Is that your idea of wicked? [grins]

Yeah, I think that's quite naughty. Or in the car park.
You mean anything that's slightly forbidden.
Yeah. Do you think that's true?
Yeah, I think so, yeah. I think you've always got to have one or two in reserve.
Do you ever feel guilty?
Feel guilty about sex? No.
Never ever?
I do feel it's dirty sometimes, but that's just part of the fun.[*]

In October 1992, George Michael, his manager Rob Kahane and his publisher Dick Leahy attended a meeting at the Sony building in Manhattan with Michael Schulhof, chairman of Sony Music Entertainment. The aim was to try to lever the singer-songwriter out of the business relationship that he now felt was constraining him. Schulhof apparently regarded the three men's visit as little more than a talking shop, even asking George if he could have autographs for his kids at home.

It was almost a provocation to the singer's more ruthless business side. A further meeting was arranged with Norio Ohga, world president of Sony, who flew into New York from Tokyo. On October 26, Ohga was flanked at the meeting by Schulhof and Paul Russell of Sony Music UK. After the preliminary handshakes, the Sony executives sat in silence to listen to their artist's misgivings.

He left them in no doubt. Despite the fact that his contract had a further 11 years to run, he'd long reached the conclusion that his relationship with his label's parent company was no longer sustainable on either a creative or a business level. In short, he wanted out. George

---

[*] When the scattily coquettish Paula Yates died from a heroin overdose in 2000, she would be mourned at her funeral service by the Live Aid generation of pop and rock performers – including George Michael.

Michael was making a straightforward request to be released from his contract with Sony Entertainment.

The management heard him out with quiet courtesy. As the meeting ended amicably enough, the singer had every reason to expect his strong will and impassioned argument had won the day.

But it was not to be. On his return to Santa Barbara, George was informed by Sony Entertainment that it had decided the terms of his contract would stand. It was prepared to fight any legal claim to the contrary in court, if need be.

"I remember sitting with my lawyer, Tony Russell, being asked basically, 'What are you going to do? Are we going to go for it?'" the singer would recall. "And of course they were itching for me to go for it. And I remember looking my lawyer in the eye and thinking, 'Well, you might as well. What the fuck else am I going to do for the next couple of years other than be terrified?'

"I will never know if Sony and I would have ended up in court had Anselmo not become ill."

The agonisingly protracted legal process would become both a catharsis and a distraction from George's intense anxiety. However, rumours also circulated (and persist to this day) that the moment George Michael decided to fight Sony may have come when he was on the phone to CBS top brass, hearing himself unguardedly dismissed as a "limey fag".

On October 30, 1992, Tony Russell issued a 30-page writ at the High Court in London, making the case that the singer's contract amounted to a "restraint of trade". It was claimed that EU rules were being contravened by Sony's/CBS's powers of veto over the artist's product being released in European member states – if Sony decided against a CD being released in a particular territory, it was argued, then the artist had no recourse to marketing and distribution via any third party.

Terms of trade aside, the Michael-Sony case threw light upon the long-accepted iniquities of the record industry. On sales of *Faith*, for example, the artist received UK royalties of 69p per copy calculated from the full retail price, while Sony made £3.38 – almost five times as much. The real problem with these figures is that for so long it had been accepted by industry and artists alike that it was simply the way things were done – the record label took the commercial risk and the costs of producing, promoting and distributing the product, and so therefore the lion's share of the profits was theirs.

Where this argument fell down, according to George and his legal representatives, was in the matter of who controlled copyright of the artist's original recordings (as opposed to copyright of the songs themselves, still assigned to Dick Leahy as publisher). The artist pointed out that all his record royalties contained a withholding clause which allowed the label to fund his next recordings via profits he had already produced. And yet the copyright of those recordings was held by the label, rather than by the artist who had funded them.

In this argument, George Michael found an unlikely supporter. Ex-manager Simon Napier-Bell, who at times would be a sceptical observer of his former client's actions over the years, later observed how the artist's legal battle had encapsulated his own views of how the record industry worked:

George Michael attempted to terminate his contract with Sony, which had now purchased CBS. It was rumoured what had triggered George was hearing the company's new president referring to him as a 'limey fag'. If a Sony employee were referred to in the same way, the company would probably end up in court and be fined. But an artist was not an employee, he was just an ingredient. Under advice from his lawyers, George didn't sue over this but instead claimed his contract was invalid. It didn't win him his case, but it told people a great many things they hadn't previously known about the record business.

Artists had to pay their own recording costs yet companies ended up owning the records. "The bank still owns the house after the mortgage is paid," is how Senator Orrin Hatch described it. Could we imagine film stars having to pay the costs of the movies they starred in and then giving the rights to the company that distributed it?

Artists also had to pay a packaging deduction of around 15 per cent.

This despite the fact that packaging rarely cost more than five per cent. The remaining 10 per cent was enough to pay the record company's entire cost of manufacturing the record. All in all, it meant an artist who sold 200,000 copies of a first album would still owe the record company although the record company had made a profit of a million.

But the worst thing about being signed to a major was that you lost the freedom to run your life. And though top artists could sometimes renegotiate an unfair contract, it soon became clear that in the music business you didn't get out of an unfair record contract to get into a fair one; you got out of an unfair contract to get into another unfair one, but with slightly better terms.

At the time the writ was presented on his behalf to the High Court, George issued a press statement: "With CBS, I felt I was believed in as a long-term artist, whereas Sony appears to see artists as little more than software. Musicians do not come in regimented shapes and sizes but are individuals who evolve together. Sony views this as a great inconvenience."

Sony countered with its own statement: "We are saddened and surprised by the action George has taken. There is a serious moral as well as legal commitment to any contract, and we will not only honour it, but vigorously defend it." This one was clearly going to run and run.

At the beginning of 1993, George took a Caribbean holiday with Anselmo Feleppa. The break was much needed and formed a peaceful prelude to the legal battles which had to be fought later in the year. But it was also a constant reminder of his lover's ailing health.

"The whole process of waiting and knowing and then grieving, that was about four years," he'd retrospectively reflect. "I tried to make that time for him happy. I think it was, actually.

"A lot of people would have run away from that situation. It wasn't an option for me to run away, you know. Even if I'd wanted to run away, I'm not the sort of person that could live with myself."

The court case was not scheduled to begin until the autumn of that year. Before then, as the winter passed into the spring of 1993, George returned to London to work on the mixing of an audio souvenir of the previous year's Freddie Mercury Tribute Concert. The five-track EP, with all royalties going to AIDS charities, would feature George's covers of 'Killer' and 'Papa Was A Rolling Stone' alongside the three tracks where he fronted Mercury's former band. Released under the title *Five Live* and credited to George Michael and Queen, it was a further sidestep from Sony, released to most world territories by Queen's label, EMI.

"There was one last moment when Freddie and Anselmo's paths seemingly crossed," he'd later reflect. "I was in LA and I remember I was on the floor signing the artwork for *Five Live*, the charity record based on my performances from the tribute concert, when the phone rang and Anselmo's best friend in Brazil was on the phone. *Phhhhh...* then it all goes blurry for a long time."

On that previous evening in March 1993, Anselmo Feleppa had suffered a sudden, fatal brain haemorrhage. It was as a result of the terminal virus he was suffering, but neither that knowledge nor the short time he'd had to prepare for his death could cushion the blow for George. He was left absolutely bereft.

With the passing of time, the performer would be able to look back on how his lover had briefly shared and transformed his life as nothing but the most positive of experiences. "He was just very funny, very full of energy, very loving," he'd say, "and I think Anselmo was the first time that I really loved someone selflessly – you know, where it really was about them."

At the time, however, it was a draining experience that threatened George's vital energies. With the aid of counselling for bereavement and depression, he would eventually overcome his negative emotions. But it would be many years before he could speak about the relationship in perspective; at that time, he believed the tabloid press would regard the death of Anselmo as less a personal tragedy than a 'smoking gun', which could serve to prove all the rumours about George Michael's sexuality.

For his part, and for several years to come, it would be a game he was loath to play along with. As he would tell Chris Evans in 1996:

I think people really seem to like to talk about it. I totally understand the debate, I have a real strong theory as to why people are so obsessed with one another's sexuality. And because I have that belief, I feel no obligation to join the debate, put it that way. I have no problem with everyone thinking I'm gay, or some people thinking I'm gay, some people thinking that I'm straight or whatever. I think it's totally, totally, irrelevant to my life, because all the people that I know and care about are perfectly clued in – I mean, everybody knows who I am. So for the sake of people that I never speak to, I really don't feel any desire to define myself, because I'll tell you what I really believe: we all sit and look at each other, and every human being constantly questions their own position – whether it be their race, their religion, their sexuality, their looks – we all question ourselves and use other people to define ourselves.

I think that one of the things that is so difficult in the modern world to actually accept is that sexuality is a really, really blurry thing. I know lots and lots of people who I thought were of one sexual persuasion, but they turned out to be the other – or sometimes to be the other. All I know is that I have never, never regarded my sexuality as a moral question of any description or anyone's sexuality as a moral question, other than when it is some kind of twisted sexuality that involves people that do not give their consent, you know. But I personally have never thought, 'That would be wrong, that would be right, that's what I should do.' I think most people do regard their sexuality as a moral question, and I think that they look to one another to reinforce their ideas of themselves. In other words, if somebody looks at me and says, 'I think he's gay,' and then next week I make a statement saying, 'I am gay,' right, that guy feels a little bit more secure in the fact that he knew that was my sexuality. Whether he was right or wrong, you know, whether I'm telling the truth or not. It's the typical old thing: the queen that stands in the gay club, or in the straight club, pointing out all the people that he thinks (or hopes) are gay.

Now, why is he really hoping that they are gay? It's like people who talk about me, in other words they're saying, 'I know what a gay person looks like, I know what a straight person looks like.' Therefore, in most people it's an effort to prove that they are straight themselves, because obviously being straight is the socially acceptable and most common human form of sexuality. But most people have some questions at some point in their life, even if they are very young, and those questions scare the shit out of them. One of the ways that they reinforce their own idea of their own sexuality, whatever it may be, is to tell themselves that they can spot it in other people and that they can spot people who are of different sexual persuasions, right, and that's why you get a huge debate about somebody like me. You've got all these guys, maybe their girlfriend likes me or whatever, and they're like, 'Oh, he's a fairy, it's obvious to me.' Now, if they were proved to be wrong that would be unsettling for them. If they were proved to be right that would be comforting for them. That's what I mean, it is literally as simple as that: 'I'm right, I know who he is because I know who I am; I know his sexuality because I know mine.' Now, I have got absolutely no desire to be that for people. Do you know what I mean? I've got no desire to stand up and define myself to a whole bunch of people who say, 'Yes, I was right,' or , 'No, I was wrong,' or, 'No, you were wrong.'

Anselmo Feleppa was buried in a Catholic cemetery on a mountain ridge overlooking his hometown, Petropolis, 50 miles outside of Rio. His black marble tombstone was inscribed, in Portuguese, "The tears of the interred will turn to joy in Heaven. Love has made your life eternal."

George was conspicuously absent from his lover's funeral. As the press had not yet picked up on the story, he stayed away for fear of turning the family's grief into a media circus. He would make his own personal pilgrimage to the graveside several days later, alongside Anselmo's mother.

In London, the tabloids had yet to pick up on the tragedy. But George's state of depression and the pressure he was already feeling produced prickly answers to any questions relating to his sexuality. When the connection to the deceased young Brazilian was finally made, it seemingly answered all the media's suspicions as to why the singer had invested so much time and energy into fundraising for AIDS charities.

The music network MTV was among the first to directly suggest his charity work was born from his own sexuality. "It's really sad to me that people think in order to work towards a cure," retorted George, "you have to be affected yourself." As far as he was concerned, it was a simple matter of humanitarianism; to the media, however, the human element of having been personally touched by the disease could not be ignored. 'So What If They Think I'm Gay?' was the *Daily Mirror* headline, spinning George's insistence that his own sexuality was irrelevant into a heavy inference, almost an admission, that he was in fact a gay man.

In an interview with DJ Simon Bates for Radio One, George started to unravel. Bates, who was by now as aware of the Anselmo connection as anyone who skimmed the tabloids, was considered a safe pair of hands; his show had for many years featured the maudlin 'Our Tune' section, where 'Hearts and Flowers'-type music introduced a listener's personal story and choice of record – often touched by some personal tragedy.

So when cuddly 'Simes' asked George about the loss of his close friend, without naming Anselmo, it was less of a brutal interrogation than a gentle probing. But the singer was momentarily lost for words. Mumbling his response, it took a good few moments before he was able to reconstitute.

Before the interview was out, George was able to return to his usual state of amiability. In fact he was professionalism itself. Before he left the studio, Bates had conceded to edit out the Q&A that had produced such a stumbling response.

CHAPTER 13

'Professional Slavery'

In early May 1993, the *Five Live* EP with Queen entered the British charts at number one, complete with liner notes on the AIDS epidemic written by George Michael. It would be one of the few times that he actually bothered the pop charts in the mid-nineties, given that its nearest companion was an underperforming 'mash-up' of two other covers from the EP ('Killer'/'Papa Was A Rolling Stone') that scarcely managed to enter the US charts – although it was promoted by a skilfully produced video combining elements of early nineties street fashion (which still look strangely contemporary today, illustrating perhaps how youth culture no longer evolves), TV advertising and an apparent nod to French fantasy film *Subway*.

There was still no sign of the artist himself in his promo video. But then, during this period, his career was less about performing than it was about litigation.

Early summer was a time of celebration though, despite all the recent stress and sadness. George celebrated his 30th birthday that June in a protracted fashion, with a weekend of partying that included all his family and close friends. All were ferried to the races at Newmarket on the Saturday, where Jack Panos's racehorse Nikita was running.*

Perhaps appropriately, given some of the male friends in attendance, the evening's party was held at Jack's stud farm in Hertfordshire. Among the 200 invited guests (including Andrew Ridgeley and the girls from Wham!), most made an effort to represent the garish fashions of the party's seventies theme. George himself briefly got into the spirit of the thing, jumping up on stage in an afro wig to sing Rose Royce's disco hit 'Carwash', before opting to change into a more sober designer suit. His elation may have been partly due to the fact that, according to his old friend Fat Tony, who was deejaying at the event, there were "buckets of MDMA" (ecstasy) to be had.

According to the version of events given by Fat Tony to his and George's old mutual friend, journalist Fiona Russell Powell, "all the boys were snogging each other, which greatly upset George's Greek-Cypriot father. George had to run around, looking incredibly embarrassed, begging everyone to tone it down. His father was the only one there not aware of his son's sexual orientation. He comes from a culture that finds it hard to accept homosexuality, and this explains much of George's failure, for so long, to come to terms with his sexuality."

This is probably true to a greater or lesser extent. But George would offer his own explanations of his personal reticence as the years, and the more dramatic events, unfolded. For all the sex and drugs and house-inflected dance music, however, in 1993-4 the real game for George Michael was being played elsewhere. For him, the most significant events of the year would take place in London's High Courts.

The first minor win in the legal war of attrition came in July 1993, when the Chancery Division of the High Courts allowed the singer's legal team to issue a request of disclosure to Sony's offices in New York

---

* The horse was named after the Elton John song about a Russian lover – assumed by 1980s pop-radio listeners to be about a girl, though Nikita is of course a man's name.

regarding the terms of its contracts with other major artists. (Among the names with CBS/Sony at the time were Michael Jackson, Bruce Springsteen, Bob Dylan and Barbra Streisand.)

Sony felt predictably undermined by any attempt to make its most confidential business dealings public. The legal team representing litigant Georgios Panayiotou – seeking the annulment of his recording contract with Sony Entertainment – sought to draw comparison and sound out any disparities of terms in the corporation's roster of major artists. It was an unapologetic opening salvo. Things could only get uglier now.

After spending much of the summer at his luxury hideaway in Santa Barbara, the recording artist known internationally as George Michael prepared to engage in the cut and thrust of legal argument and counterargument in central London's Chancery Lane district. As he would later concede, much of his obsessive focus on litigating against his label was born out of emotional pain; it was a combative distraction from grief: "I think to some degree the Sony court case was a perfectly good place to put my anger," he said. "This bloody six-month case that went on, I used to run on the treadmill every day for an hour before I went to court and run on the treadmill for an hour after I went to court, and played squash and did everything I could to get rid of all this anger and fear. But the best place for it was Court Number One really. Would I have been angry enough to take them on [if Anselmo had not died]? I think the answer to that is probably no, actually, if I'm really honest."

With proceedings due to start in October, the Panayiotou team found themselves approached by Sony's representatives prior to the opening of the case. As the performer himself recounted it: "They then called up and said, 'Can't we patch things up?' but I knew in reality that was a formality. They had to do that. But ultimately the whole thing was a complete waste of time – I went to them before it happened and said, 'Please let me go, I'm really unhappy, you don't want to work with me the way that I think [you should], let somebody who will work with me the way that I think by the contract. I've been with you for 10 years, everyone will think my contract's up, we'll keep it quiet and just make it civilised.' Instead, what we had was a two-year battle [from the beginning of hostilities to the court judgement] that got everybody loads of press, took two years out of my career and was an embarrassment, I'd imagine, to Sony. At the end of the day we came up with the same thing: they sold my contract to someone else. Why couldn't they have just done that and saved us all the time and trouble?"

Sony made an out-of-court offer to annul its client's contract for an undisclosed and presumably hefty price. For a short while, George procrastinated while seeking advice from his manager, Rob Kahane. Kahane advised that Sony's strategy showed it was in a tactically weak position and that the Panayiotou team should proceed to litigate. Temporarily reassured that he was on the winning side, George rejected the offer and proceedings got properly under way.

On October 18, 1993, Georgios Kyriacos Panayiotou v. Sony Music Entertainment UK Ltd finally opened at the High Court. Postponed for a week due to the injury of a member of the legal teams, the first day of the hearings saw a rare convergence of press, paparazzi and public outside the formal chambers. As the singer stepped from his chauffeured car wearing shades, a dark Versace suit with an AIDS awareness ribbon and steel-tipped cowboy boots, he studiously failed to respond to calls from photographers and love-struck female fans alike. Present in the public gallery most days were the ever-supportive Jack and Lesley Panayiotou, convinced of the rightness of their son's legal and moral case. Support from within the music industry itself was more muted – although the endearingly eccentric Sinéad O'Connor did turn up to pass the singer a note of support.

As QC for the plaintiff, barrister Mark Cran opened proceedings with a statement read in open court about how the Michael/Sony rift had developed as a result of the artist's reluctance to push his visual image on the *Listen Without Prejudice* album, and its singles' corresponding promo videos. The failure of CBS in the USA to respect the artist's wishes was, Cran asserted, at the root of the legal wrangles now playing out in open court. As George himself would acknowledge in the interview preceding his celebrated *Unplugged* performance, several years hence: "One of the difficult things about taking on Sony was that I knew a lot of people's attitude would be, 'The silly git doesn't want to do any interviews, doesn't make any videos, he's not going to do this, he's not going to do that, and then he complains that they don't push his music.'

"I was very confused, very unhappy, and the stance that I took to try to redress the balance in my own life was not offensive, [though] it may not have been ideal for the Sony executives in the UK and the rest of the world – far from ideal, I'm sure. They have an artist who sells 15 million albums, does the videos, goes out and does the tour and then says suddenly, 'No, I just want to sit in my room.'"

As the performer correctly anticipated, to a large proportion of the general public his actions would be interpreted as the strange whim of a man who already had everything. Former manager Simon Napier-Bell acknowledged this, later articulating, in an interview with Paul Du Noyer for *Word* magazine: "George Michael went to war with Sony saying, 'I am a pure artist, I don't want to promote the record or do videos.' Well, if you're an artist, go sing in the garden. Why do you want to sell records if you're just an artist? Being an artist is a cry for help. All artists are very insecure people. They are desperate to get noticed. They are looking for an audience. They are forced to be commercial, which makes their art, I think, all the better."

For all his cynicism, Napier-Bell would at least sympathise with his ex-client for having the guts (or the naivety) to challenge some of the record business' long-established practices. It would also be stressed by the Panayiotou legal team that their client's supposedly obstructive attitude had not stopped *Listen Without Prejudice* outselling *Faith* in the UK (though not in the US, where the first album's performance had been phenomenal).

But for now, the internationally renowned performer's motive was open to question – not least in the witness dock of the High Court. At the end of October, he was called to undergo three days of examination by the defendant's QC, Gordon Pollock, which cherry-picked what the barrister clearly saw as the more contentious moments of the plaintiff's career: Wham!'s conflict with Innervision and the attempt by George to hold his album's master tapes to ransom; the inherently (and sometimes explicitly) sexual nature of his promo videos; the sudden volte-face whereby the performer no longer wanted to inhabit the hugely successful, brooding persona that had helped sell *Faith*. All was fair game and all, it was implied, was symptomatic of the artist's perversely capricious nature.

"I remember seeing him on the news and it all looked so scary," ex-Wham! girl Shirlie Kemp later recalled of the court case, "and I thought, 'Why is he putting himself through all that?'"

Within a couple of years, George would gain enough perspective to become a little more objective about his motives: "Suddenly, I realised I didn't have complete control. I'm a control freak – I'd gone through my career having success after success, everything was sweetness, everything was perfect, so I didn't really think about the fact that I hadn't got any control. And then suddenly, when things go wrong, you think, 'Shit, I can't do anything about this! I've had all these years of success, I've made all this money, all these people want my music, etc, and ultimately I cannot have my own way.'"

George Michael had encountered relatively little resistance to his strong will and his personal game-plan every step of the way; the man who was now one of the planet's most recognisable entertainers had come to expect life itself to accede to his every wish. This, remember, was the man who had looked skyward and issued a warning to his personal God, warning Him not to harm his ailing lover.

In the courtroom, Mr Pollock QC enquired of George exactly how much his career with CBS had earned him. At first he refused to answer the question. After consultation with the judge, Mr Justice Jonathan Parker, he agreed to write down the figure for the QC rather than answer in open court. "This is supposed to be a decimal point?" joked Pollock when passed the note.

The defence's contention was that the plaintiff's action was brought not on the basis of any legitimate grievance, but because the singer and his manager – Kahane's testimony and attitude called very much into question – had taken an active dislike to the new Sony management at CBS. On one level, it was a difficult accusation to refute. George

Michael was a phenomenally wealthy entertainer, and was forced to agree that everything he had was at the behest of the industry he was now fighting against.

But as Mark Cran QC put it, "This case is not about money." It was, according to the plaintiff's barrister, about the equitable principles denied when an artist was forced to take the far lesser proportion of the many millions of pounds earned by his recordings; when his previous royalty payments were clawed back to pay for future recordings, and yet the products of those recordings remained under the sole copyright of the record company.

Sony's executives, unsurprisingly, saw things very differently. Theirs were the standard terms under which the recording industry operated, and they had served to make their artist, Mr Michael, a particularly wealthy man. If the case was not about money, well then, why was the plaintiff's QC arguing that the label's territorial rights amounted to a restriction of trade? Did his client not understand the basis of an exclusive contract, whereby he was restricted to working with one company in return for appropriate (and in his case substantial) remuneration? Why had the plaintiff immediately accepted Sony's early nineties offer of a huge advance of $11 million, if he did not intend to adhere to the terms of his contract and deliver the requisite product? Was it, the label mischievously implied, because he was about to undertake a world tour and would therefore be outside the UK long enough to avoid paying domestic income tax on such a huge sum?

Only when the motivation for the plaintiff's actions veered away from the fiscal toward the personal was the defence prepared to concede ground. While the British press was starting to buzz again with rumours about George Michael's sexuality and the general public were largely unsure of (or indifferent to) his orientation, in open court it was conceded that his record company had behaved with open homophobia toward him. Sony admitted the existence of a tape recording of a conversation between Rob Kahane and the new president of CBS Records, in which the latter referred to the performer as "that faggot client of yours". (Other rumours of the time suggest George was routinely dismissed by one of the label's executives as a "limey faggot".)

Sony's defence barristers swung the argument back in their favour. According to them, this was the essence of why the performer was litigating against his own record label; it didn't have its foundation in any of the business arguments that were being cited but in personal dislike and verbal abuse. It didn't seem to have occurred to them that, in most modern industries, an employee abused in this way might have recourse to legal action. In the record industry, contracts were perpetual and exclusive and made no allowance for an artist reaching the stage where he or she felt they could no longer work with the executives involved.

As George said in an impromptu press conference conducted outside the law courts: "I have absolutely no right to resign. In fact there is no such thing as resignation for an artist in the music industry. Effectively, you sign a piece of paper at the beginning of your career and you are expected to live with that decision, good or bad, for the rest of your professional life."

At its own press briefings, Sony offered the further rationale that George Michael was suffering from an intense writer's block and using legal action to retreat from his contractual obligations. This line was picked up on by a scandal-hungry Fleet Street. "There are those who believe that Michael's litigation is not a way of asking for a nice life, but a way out, that he has dried up and peaked at 30," ran a *Sunday Times* piece on October 24, 1993. More obvious in its gagging for a good story was *The Sun*, which selectively translated and reprinted sections from an article in the Brazilian magazine *Interview* about the singer's relationship with the late Anselmo Feleppa, which stopped just short of making the obvious point that the relationship was (in part at least) sexual.

The Mail On Sunday, the most right-wing of the UK's weekend tabloids, was in high dudgeon. Here was a pampered pop star daring to rattle the bars of his gilded cage, while seeking to suppress the fact that he was (in the viewpoint of mid-nineties British tabloids, anyway) a sexual deviant. *The Mail* felt qualified to ask whether the motivation for his legal battle sprang from the loss of his close friend Feleppa (which was, in fairness, similar to the conclusion reached by George himself years later). Curiously, after an article which went to some lengths to persuade its readers of the very opposite, the piece ended with a legal disclaimer stating, "Although striking up a friendship with Anselmo, Michael, of course, is not gay and has always denied he was such."

(If such caution seems oddly hypocritical, it should be remembered that the press were still wary of the super-rich singer and his litigious nature. If he was bold enough to take on the record company which, in many people's view, had made him a wealthy man, why would he think twice about seeking a court injunction to protect details of his private life?)

After many weeks of hearings, the court case would recess for Christmas. In the interim, George Michael made a comeback from his self-imposed career limbo by appearing at an AIDS charity event on December 1, 1993, in front of a capacity crowd at Wembley Arena. It would be the first public performance he'd given in the land of his birth for more than 18 months – since the similar event in memory of Freddie Mercury.

The Concert of Hope took place on what was designated as World AIDS Day, in the presence of its royal patron, Diana, Princess of Wales. It was hosted by David Bowie, further transformed from the most charismatic rock star of the seventies to a stick-thin uncle figure who turned up as cheerleader for the younger guys and gals. The three headliners were safe crowd-pleasers – George and Mick Hucknall of Simply Red, performing their different brands of blue-eyed soul; then there was the more recent phenomenon of k.d. Lang, the modern-girl folk and country singer. While George was still resolutely in the closet, his parading around the stage at the end, with his arm around the unabashedly 'out' Ms Lang, was seen by some as a message of support to what was becoming known as the LGBT (lesbian, gay, bisexual and transgender) community.

Of most lasting note would George's first one-on-one meeting with Princess Di, the woman whose charity work did much to diminish the stigma imposed on AIDS victims. Hitting it off from the beginning

(George cheekily dedicated 'Freedom 90' to the princess, then instigating a lengthy divorce from Prince Charles), these two eighties pop kids would enjoy a chatty, close friendship over the next couple of years. More startlingly perhaps, George would later let slip how he believed that – as Diana was living by the credo of 'what's good for the goose is good for the gander' in terms of royal adultery – they could easily have become lovers. As he later put it over a decade hence: "I think we clicked in a way that was a little bit intangible, and it probably had more to do with our upbringing than anything else. She was very like a lot of women who've been attracted to me because they see something non-threatening.

"I feel guilty because she did really like me as a person, and I tended to shy away from calling her because I thought she must have so many people calling her for all the wrong reasons. I knew she was suspicious of people by then, so I would almost treat her the way I know some people treat me. I would presume it was an intrusion to call, when actually you know they're lonely and would love to hear a friendly voice."

Just how deep the late princess' affections for George Michael ran can never be known. As a sexually active woman in the wake of Prince Charles' much documented playing-away-from-home, it's possible she may have realised early on that she was barking up the wrong tree.

For all that, George's cousin Andros has told of a night when, the both of them arriving back at George's place stoned on weed, he was stunned to hear the voice of Diana on his cousin's answer-phone, talking unguardedly about her divorce proceedings and the general state of her life.

"There you go," George reputedly told Andros, handing him the tape, "there's your pension." (Andros, to his credit, seems to have taken it in the jokey manner in which it was intended and has never made the contents public.)

If Diana's apparent attraction toward George had ever been consummated, however, it would have been the ultimate liaison between two celebrity idols, putting any Hollywood/footballer and WAG romances truly in the shade.

The case of Panayiotou v. Sony ran on for close to six months, a total of 178 days. The final summing-up statements were made on April 13, 1994, after which it would be a further two months before the High Court judge delivered his verdict. (Such litigation is legally regarded as beyond the ken of a jury.)

George and his close retinue of supporters returned to the High Court to hear Mr Justice Parker articulate his deliberations on June 21. "I thought it was 60/40 in my favour, easily, on what the case was," George recalled. "Then I got in there and felt the atmosphere and saw the judge and his reaction to the two QCs, and I knew."

As best friend David Austin remembers, "I think it was about six or seven o'clock in the morning when the guy sat down and said, 'Well, you've lost.' And it was like, that was it."

In his summing up, the judge read from a 280-page case document that had been put together over the last six months. According to him, the terms of the performer's contract with Sony were "reasonable and fair" and had placed him at no disadvantage. The corporation had shown a continual willingness to let the artist and his representatives renegotiate his contract; negotiated advances of, in the first instance, $1 million and, secondly, $11 million paid in several tranches had been willingly met. Singling the artist's manager out for particular criticism, the judge described Rob Kahane as a "thoroughly unreliable and untrustworthy witness" who, in his estimation, in acting out of self-interest had served to poison the relationship between his client and the entertainment corporation.[*]

George walked away from the High Court stony-faced. He would later claim: "It was really about the attitude, it wasn't about anything

---

[*] While the fallout was not immediate, it sounded the death knell for the Michael-Kahane relationship. By October of that year, the alliance was terminated and the singer would go through a brief period of managing himself. Kahane went on to found Trauma Records in LA, which would also end in acrimony – though not before he'd also discovered the British post-grunge band Bush and become instrumental in their success.

else. It was all about, 'Well okay, if he doesn't want to make videos, then we've got loads and loads of other artists. The fact that he's sold however many million records is completely without relevance,' you know. I couldn't work with people that didn't care. I think that my judge was really misled into thinking that somehow free agency within the music industry would kill the music industry. It was a six-month trial and a lot of people talked a lot of crap. I think that the issues got lost. Four days after that case ended, a friend of mine signed an eight-album deal with Sony."

As the performer himself suggests, the verdict seemed to be coloured by the belief that if musical artists were allowed to walk away from their contracts at will, then the industry itself would collapse. While there may have been some common-sense logic in that, it would never be put to the test in the sense of both sides being allowed to make a clean break, with the label relinquishing its claims and the artist being forced to return the proportion of his advance that he had yet to justify.

Outside the High Court, however, in a hotel at nearby Temple Place, George swore to a coterie of reporters that this was not the end of it. His legal team were already filing an appeal on his behalf and he was confident that the iniquity of a creative industry that denied the freedom of its workers could not withstand scrutiny. In a phrase that would echo around the industry, he announced, "I am convinced that the English legal system will not support Mr Justice Parker's decision or uphold what is effectively professional slavery."

Having already spent between three and four million pounds in legal fees, George was adamant that the case would continue. Justice Parker's judgement would be challenged in the Court of Appeal; if that court failed to see the merit of the appeal, he would then take his case to the European Court of Justice in Strasbourg. His resolve was firm, as was his contention that, as long as he remained under contract to Sony, he would never sing another recorded note.[*]

---

[*] Rumour has it that callers to his private number at the time were treated to the singer's parody of his own 'Careless Whisper': "I'm never gonna sing again…"

But it was the 'professional slavery' comment that most onlookers picked up on. It elicited bemusement from the general public, ridicule from much of the press and a smattering of sympathy from the creative side of the music industry. As the singer himself later had to acknowledge: "I called it 'professional slavery' because I knew it was a good sound bite, for God's sake, I knew it was going to get out there. Of course, you can be an incredibly wealthy slave – but at the end of the day, if you can't work anywhere else and you can't leave your boss or tell him to get lost, you're a slave!"

For all the expense and bitter resentment behind the war of words, neither the artist nor the record label he was contracted to can have had any inkling of how history and consumer technology would soon overtake them. Within a decade of their court battle, the new age of the internet would ensure the labels struggled to retain copyright control over their wares while artists would be hard-pressed to make any revenue at all from their recordings.

For now though, both sides continued living in a kind of fools' paradise – where the all-consuming industry believed it could go on turning the same kind of gargantuan profits as before, while some artists continued to search for greater autonomy without leaving the industry's great financial cushion behind.

Within several days of the verdict, George appeared on a major TV interview with Sir David Frost, effectively serving to warn Sony that the appeal was going ahead and the battle was not over. To most of the public (except the most die-hard female fans), he seemed to be pointlessly tilting at windmills; one decade hence, he would look back on his own quixotic battle: "I do remember being *absolutely* gutted – not that I'd lost, but that the record companies were absolutely outside reasonable law, there was absolutely nothing that required them to pull their socks up in any way. Okay, there was an inevitability to the end of youth culture as we loved it. But I think if artists from the early nineties on really had been masters of their own destiny, there is a possibility that *Pop Idol* wouldn't have ruined everything."

While George undoubtedly led the charge for himself as an artist, however, it's a moot point as to whether he truly had the interests of *all* recording artists at heart. He had, after all, initially offered Sony the choice of allowing his contract to be secretly sold, keeping the arrangement out of the public record so that no one else could use it as a precedent to get out of their own contract.

When offered moral support by Prince (or The Artist Formerly Known as Prince, as he was then, identified by some kind of runic symbol), George became positively tetchy, ignoring a series of supportive phone calls; when they appeared on the same bill at George's next major public performance, the Anglo-Greek singer would seethe with resentment when Prince performed with the word 'Slave' scrawled across his cheek. ("Wipe that fucking word off your cheek," were the words he used to describe his own attitude to the stunt. "You're not exactly doing me any favours.")

As has become customary, ex-manager Simon Napier-Bell has his own take on what motivated George's legal battle. It was, he claimed, the singer's own way of playing (if not praying) for time: "Many people think the golden rule is that publicity can only be as valuable as the music it's selling. But that's not quite true. The real media kings can cover a bad musical patch. Again, George Michael is the ultimate, if unwitting, example. When he sued his record company, it prevented him making a new album for a full two years, allowing him to emerge at the end of the dispute creatively refreshed while keeping his face on the front pages day after day.

"Using the media to lengthen and underwrite a career in this way is a trick many singers have played deftly, the essential thing being 'not too much, not too little'. Occasionally, though, a hit song can be a good idea."

The first new George Michael song to be unveiled for many a moon was debuted in November 1994 at the MTV European Music Awards in Berlin, at which George shared the bill with Prince and was introduced by the original old blue-eyed soul man, Tom Jones. In the early part of the show, he effectively re-created David Fincher's video for 'Freedom 90' by singing the song surrounded by a string of strutting supermodels led by Naomi Campbell. Later, he sat alone in the spotlight to sing a new ballad that was delicate to the point of fragility: 'Jesus To A Child'.

As its composer later described of the song's post-litigation origin: "Creatively, I was stifled in so many ways; I don't think I actually admitted to myself that I couldn't write till the whole thing was over. I flew to New York, had a very quick meeting there where basically we agreed that the contract would be sold; I was in seventh heaven, came home and started work immediately. And at that point I realised – at that point I wrote 'Jesus To A Child' and I realised that I could really start again, and most of the stuff I recorded in the couple of years before had just not been up to par."

The quietly atmospheric, seven-minute track was first performed to the well-lit backdrop of Berlin's Brandenburg Gate. Gently floating to the rhythms of Brazilian bossa nova, its minor-key emotions gently stroked by Spanish guitar chords and an airy flute, the song managed to be an elegy for loss and a heartfelt dedication of love, all in the same breath.

When the singer precisely intones of how, on finding love, "when you know that it exists", even a lover you have lost will stand next to you on the coldest nights, there is little doubt of whom he sings. At the time, the song's love object was a subject of tabloid speculation; with the passing of years, the semi-whispered dedication to the lover that "heaven sent and heaven stole", the gay man who George acclaimed for transforming his life as profoundly as the Christian messiah, is obvious.

"I was so excited that I'd finally been able to put my feelings for him into words," the song's composer later confirmed. "The kind of catharsis of that record for me was massive, and within a week of writing it I was singing it in front of the Brandenburg Gate with an orchestra behind me, and paying my first kind of public tribute to him there."

"I can only imagine what the Sony executives were thinking sitting in the audience in Berlin," said Andy Stephens, the former CBS man who would soon replace Kahane as the singer's manager. "I don't believe there's a soul in the audience that could have sat there and gone, 'It's over.' It was obvious that he was back on form."

Between the song's first airing at the MTV Europe Awards and its release as a CD single the following year, the speculation about the person at the heart of the lyric became intense. It was all the more frustrating for Fleet Street, who by this time assuredly *knew* just who had looked on the singer and smiled at him with kindness in his eyes. In deferential fear of the singer's lawyers, however, they would skirt around the subject without saying it outright.

George articulated his own response to the speculation when appearing on Chris Evans' radio show a year after the song's release: "I obviously knew when I made lyrical references on the record to somebody that I knew that died, a man that I knew that died, and I've absolutely no problem in saying that I loved him very much. I have no problem in writing about that experience; I've got no problem with people reading my lyrics about that experience; I've got no problem with the honesty that's there. I've got a real problem with this constant need for definition."

As the New Year of 1995 rolled in, the performer's legal team were intermittently pushing the Court of Appeal to bring their client's appeal date forward, which as yet wasn't scheduled to be heard till the late summer. In reality, they must have been aware – as George himself certainly was – that negotiations were afoot for a third party in the US to buy out their client's contract from Sony at massive financial cost.

In April 1995, the singer, who had not issued any new original material in over three years, was honoured with the accolade of Best Male Vocalist at the Capital FM Radio Awards (for the second year running). In fact, George had a long-term relationship with Capital, the sound of suburban London, going back to his childhood. Capital had launched in October 1973, with heavy airplay and coverage of Elton John's new double album, *Goodbye Yellow Brick Road*.

It was traditional by now for him to match the station's listeners' contributions when they requested any of his own songs – usually

'Careless Whisper' – on the annual Help a London Child charity weekend.*

This year he would auction 'Jesus To A Child', which had not yet been committed to record. Promising to match all contributions by listeners who pledged to pay to hear the song's radio debut, George generously added £30,000 to the £20k contributed both by the general public and a mobile phone company, to bring the song's Easter weekend takings to a round £70,000.

It would also ensure a thriving trade in bootleg tapes and CDs of the track, in Capital's broadcast zone of London and the Southeast and far beyond. It was a fitting metaphor for the Easter weekend: the resurrection of an artist's career; the gentle lyricism that equated gay love with the blessings of Christ. The latter would obviously be blasphemy in the eyes of any religious fundamentalist who might become aware of the song's content. For his part, the composer was not trying to be provocative but merely honest; while not in thrall to any religious dogma (indeed, his personal sexuality excluded him from it), he was nonetheless very far from being a materialistic atheist: "I've always used religious references although I'm not a religious person, I'm much more of a spiritual person. But I've always been drawn to words like 'heaven' and 'angel', you know. I suppose they're the easiest way to reach people in terms of their own idea of spirituality, they're little stock trademarks for spirituality.

"I learned a lot of very, very incredibly important lessons in the last five years, things that have left me feeling so much better about myself, feeling so much more able to cope about whatever's coming in the future.

This very positive sentiment tapped into the whole essence of modern religion: if it can still inspire with hope, with the sense that existence is imbued with more profound levels of meaning that somehow make

---

* Rumour also had it that if you were passed by an expensive car on Oxford Street with George Michael's music blaring out of the sound system, you'd probably just been passed by the singer himself.

sense of all human suffering, then religion still has a purpose. Without buying into any specific belief system or religious denomination, George Michael was still influenced by the gentler, more merciful aspects of the Christian tradition.

Over the months and years to come, however, he would need to draw on those feelings of hope and positivity in order to survive what had yet to announce itself.

CHAPTER 14

Working For The Dream

The cavalry that rode to the rescue of George Michael's recording career came straight out of Hollywood. DreamWorks SKG was a powerful conglomerate put together by three luminaries of the motion picture and music industries – Steven Spielberg, the king of the movie-brat generation who had more recently become a serious filmmaker with the harrowing *Schindler's List*; Jeffrey Katzenberg, the former head of the Disney studio who pulled Uncle Walt's dream factory back into profitability; and David Geffen – veteran of the West Coast music scene and head of Geffen Records.

If DreamWorks today more readily suggests the hugely successful animated *Shrek* films, it's because the Disneyesque element of the venture was the most successful. In fact, Geffen Records and its subsidiary label, Interscope, would jump ship fairly early on, moving back into the mainstream of the US music industry and amalgamating with MCA Records.

In early 1995, however, David Geffen was a trusted ally in the upper echelons of the music business, looking for a new outlet for his talents. George had actually first met him in the early-mid eighties, on Wham!'s first US tour. This was in the early days of the Geffen label, when the former Asylum Records producer (and rumoured one-time lover of Carly Simon – see Chapter Two) was in the process of establishing himself as one of the US industry's main players.

Geffen had also been publicly coming to terms with his own sexuality back in the eighties. Having enjoyed relationships with both women and men, he felt it was time to put his head above the parapet as a gay man. This was at precisely the same time that his younger Anglo-Greek friend was suppressing any indication of his own sexuality, in apparent fear of it harming his career prospects. But still, the two had remained friendly over the previous decade.

By the mid-nineties, David Geffen had been lauded by America's premier gay lifestyle magazine, *The Advocate*, as one of the nation's foremost individual promoters of gay rights causes. For all George's reticence about putting his private life on display, he obviously admired Geffen's forthrightness. On a more personal level, his friend had long been cultivating him with a view to getting out of the much-disputed Sony contract.

As George told Chris Evans a year later: "David Geffen was initially trying to talk to me in terms of stopping us all going to court, because I didn't want to go to court. David was obviously hoping that I was going to sign to his label, which I eventually did, but he also believed, as I agree, that a successful artist should not be spending their time in courts, a successful artist should be making records.

"He paid millions and millions of pounds, and I think that his relationship with Sony was good enough to spur things on. I honestly think that, without David Geffen, it would have been very possible that I would have been in the Court of Appeal.

"I'm contracted to both labels [DreamWorks in the US/Virgin in the UK] for a period of two albums. You've got to remember that they'd paid somewhere in the region of $50 million, just to get me out. If I had really been in a position where I was free, I would have done a one-album deal with Virgin and a one-album deal with DreamWorks in America, because I think that is the way that business should be done. At the end of a business project, if one partner has failed or the relationship is not good, I think people should be able to walk away."

As Tony Russell and the rest of his legal team continued to file appellate motions, behind the scenes Geffen had been endeavouring to ensure any further protracted legal action was redundant. By June 1995, the story broke in the US press ('Spielberg may rescue George Michael' was the not-strictly-accurate *New York Times* headline) before crossing the Atlantic. Negotiations continued, but the number two favourite in the running, Time Warner Music, seemed to put itself out of the game when its MD kept referring to 'George Michaels', as if he was interested in buying out the contract of an up-and-coming bar mitzvah singer.

Eventually, in July, a deal was struck which would allow Sony to fast-track a George Michael greatest hits compilation while he would go into the studio to record new material for DreamWorks. As a further concession to Sony, three of the new tracks could also be included on its greatest hits collection. This was at a cost to DreamWorks of a lump-sum payment to Sony of $40 million, while the singer himself would receive an advance against royalties of $10 million. Further to this, to ensure the company's new signing was kept satisfied, George's legal representative negotiated an increased royalty rate of 20 percent of cover price for each unit sold (then an industry record), while DreamWorks would also cover the legal costs, which now ran to several million pounds.

In some ways, the enterprising David Geffen was an unlikely champion of George Michael's creative freedom. In the early eighties, he'd signed rock veteran Neil Young to Geffen Records; emerging from the folk-rock and psychedelic scenes in the sixties, Young was long noted as a musical maverick whose style veered from country ballads to all-out electric attack. He also championed the young Elton John during the Brit singer's early LA residence, reflecting the more pop-orientated side of his own repertoire. It might have been expected that his recordings for Geffen would follow an unconventional path, but when Young respectively recorded an electronic album, a rockabilly album and a country album, David Geffen filed a lawsuit against him for making "music unrepresentative of himself".[*]

But no such acrimony was anticipated for the Michael–Geffen deal. After all, it wasn't as if George was about to record his singing voice through an electronic vocoder, as Young had done. (He'd wait another 15 years for that – until the record industry as he'd known it was all but deceased.) For now, it could be assumed that Geffen was familiar enough with the singer–songwriter's music to be sure of what he was getting, and that both men knew each other well enough to have faith.

In the first instance, it would be a while before the recording sessions bore anything ready for release. In the early summer of 1995, George kept his hand in by singing backing vocals on British singer Lisa Moorish's slightly odd cover of his 'I'm Your Man', which she promoted by dressing androgynously in a suit with short hair. (Ms Moorish herself was all-woman, as she'd later prove by giving birth to the children of Britpop brat Liam Gallagher and the shambolic Pete Doherty.)

The record did not bother the charts overmuch, but George did invite Ms Moorish's producer, Jon Douglas, onboard for his own scheduled recording sessions at Sarm Studios West in London's Notting Hill. As with the singer's other collaborators, Douglas would make his own creative contribution to a long-anticipated album.

As with the older Neil Young, the north London superstar went back to using herbal cannabis for musical inspiration. Unlike most old-school smokers, however, George was by now smoking weed continually as part of a daily regime to keep him detached from everyday concerns or anxieties. As he'd later admit, since the death of Anselmo he'd worked his way up to a mind-melting 25 spliffs a day. This wasn't recreational drug (ab)use so much as compulsive self-medication; in the semi-psychedelic state of being perpetually stoned, his memories and dreams of love were as real and as ever-present as his immediate physical surroundings.

---

[*] Young told of how, just before he got the call from his lawyer to tell him he was getting out of his Geffen contract, he'd smoked a big spliff; when he got the news he became so uproariously happy that he feared he'd have a heart attack.

"I think from then on I was recovering and I started recording *Older*," he'd recall of the origin of his third solo album through an attack of good-natured giggles. "It was a long process, probably because I was so stoned! Considering the album, as far as I'm concerned the album's great, so it's a great advert for grass."

While cannabis was clearly conducive to his well-being at the time, there was still a compulsive element to his smoking of both marijuana and tobacco. In their 1996 interview, Chris Evans tried to tease out of him what lay behind the compulsion:

Why do you want to give up smoking? Why do you smoke first of all? Why do you smoke?
I smoke because ...
You don't like it really, do you?
No, I don't like it.
Do you smoke incessantly?
I smoke incessantly when I'm with people who smoke incessantly, Chris. I smoke because I started when I had real kinds of reasons. I had a real low point about five years ago [at the time of Anselmo's diagnosis] and I smoked, I started to smoke grass to relieve stress and whatever, and because I didn't want to be on any kind of sedatives or ...
Can you roll a joint?
No.
Who does it for you?
Anyone who will. I mean, this is incredible when you think about it, because smoking is the most stupid thing I've ever done, it's the worst thing for my health, it's completely out of control, but somehow I think I've got control over it because I don't roll my own joints; which means I can't go home with a bag of grass and sit and get stoned out of my head. I have to have someone smoking with me.
Let me tell you, if you had to, you would roll your own joint.
Oh I'm sure, but I'm not saying I haven't attempted the odd really nasty-looking sausagy thing, but the truth of it is that I started

smoking grass for whatever reasons at that point in time, and what happened was that …

So how long is that from now?

That was about four years ago.

Now you've said to me that you desperately want to stop and you've tried three different ways of stopping, I think you said?

No, not three different ways, I've been to three different hypnotists, right.

Why? Only pop stars do that stuff. Don't do that.

No, lots of people do that. Lots of people do that.

Not three different ones.

No, not three different ones, they normally give up after the second because they can't really afford the third one.

Why don't you say you like it?

Why did I say I like it?

No, why don't you say you like it?

I don't like anything that has control of me, basically.

Give up now.

Would you stop this? I get this the whole time, I get this at home, I get this everywhere. Stop this.

Stop now, just put that out and stop now. Just stop.

I've stopped, Chris, look, we're on radio. I've stopped. I'm just putting it out now.

I think you should do what you want, mate.

Absolutely, I know. Actually, there's another thing, it's always been a real issue. Self-control has always been a real issue with me and I really let go of a lot of that, four or five years ago, and I'm a much happier person for it. I'm much less cautious and much, much more about living for the moment than I was. I'm not as frightened of the future and everything. And it's just an unhappy coincidence that this change, this big change in my life, started at roughly the same time that I started smoking. Smoking was obviously one of the results, and I have this fear that controlling my smoking is somehow going to set this reverse pattern, and I'm suddenly

going to start controlling everything again. I kind of associate the
immediate gratification of picking up a cigarette and inhaling it
somehow with freedom. I know it's really odd.

It's very odd.

It's really odd, but as a child I was always told, "You will not
ever smoke."

By the summer of 1995, the perpetually stoned sessions for what would
become *Older* were under way. Marking his return to the industry
proper, George had secured the services of calm, businesslike Brit Andy
Stephens to replace abrasive American Rob Kahane as manager. Their
business relationship had been a decade in the making, as Stephens was
one of the first management figures that Wham! had sought out prior to
the Nomis deal. Over the ensuing years, his new manager's unflappable
demeanour would prove a boon to the artist at times when his life
appeared on the verge of unravelling.

In the summer, George took a break from recording to purchase
his third home – this time in the South of France. Set on a cliff top
overlooking St Tropez, the circa £2 million property was named 'Chez
Nobby', after the singer's alternative nickname. ('Yog' we all know
about; 'Nobby' is probably best left to the imagination.)

On his return to Sarm West, George supplemented his own multi-
instrumentalism (playing keyboards, bass and drums) with keyboardists
Jon Douglas and Dave Clews, saxophonists Andy Hamilton, Chris Davis
and Phil Smith, and guitarist Alan Ross. As if to emphasise the more
languid, late-night jazz-inflected air of his new music, the line-up also
included trumpeter John Thirkell, trombonist Fayyaz Virji and Stuart
Brooks on the flugelhorn – the northern European brass instrument
ominously used in the past to signify death.

While he worked on the album throughout the year, the public
resurrection of George Michael wouldn't really get under way till
the cusp of 1996. By then, George had had his former brushed-back,
semi-quiffed hairstyle shortened to a 'Caesar cut', close to the skull and
redolent of some of the Britpop bands then at their peak in the mid-

nineties. His designer stubble was thinned out too, cut to a pointed, almost Mephistophelian goatee beard. Suddenly, the eighties seemed like a much bigger jump away.

Although 'Jesus To A Child' wasn't scheduled for release till early January 1996, the singer was adroit enough to ensure it was one of the most played songs over the Christmas holiday period. With a duration of nearly seven minutes, it almost doubled the average length of airplay afforded to most singles; however, as the record label (Virgin in the UK, DreamWorks in the US) and its pluggers offered advance promo copies of the disc only on the basis that the track would be played in its entirety, no national or major regional radio station wanted to miss out. The first original new material from George Michael in five years was too much of an event for that.

When the record went on sale in the UK in the New Year, it was further boosted by a first near-giveaway batch retailing for 99p, a good £2.50 below the average DVD price. It had the desired effect; 'Jesus To A Child' entered the UK singles chart at number one. When the album was eventually released, this smooth yet melancholic elegy to a love that persisted beyond death would open the CD as the first track. The album itself would carry the dedication, "To Anselmo Feleppa – who changed the way I look at life."

While 'Jesus To A Child' stayed at the top position of the British charts for one week only, it also made number one in 15 other countries around the world. It was promoted by an atmospheric video filmed by music industry specialist Howard Greenhalgh. Delicately surreal, it featured the lithe bodies of male and female ballet dancers, for whom collapsing piles of dust and a swooping pendulum ball signify the passing of time and the loss of love, as well as their own mortality. Typically, the BBC insisted on inelegantly pixillating the nipples of the dancers for broadcast, while MTV restricted it to late-night play. But most notable perhaps was the presence of the singer himself in the video, his slimmer, short-fringed face intoning over the proceedings. George Michael was back in the business of promoting his own music.

Further away from the bombast of rock music than ever, the new rhythms of *Older* were also infinitely subtler than the thump-thump-thump beat of nineties rave music. The album would also mark the most significant musical collaboration between George and his old mate David Austin.

"'Jesus To A Child' went to number one," recalled guitarist/songwriter Austin. "We went out for a big celebration lunch, Andy [Stephens] did, the whole team. And [George] put a Walkman across the table and said, 'Have a listen to this,' played me 'You Have Been Loved' and I just couldn't believe what the man had done with that."

In its original conception, David Austin's lyric for 'You Have Been Loved' was a third-person narrative describing both the grief and fortitude of a mother losing her son. In the description of her taking the back road and the lane, "past the school that has not changed", it evokes the landmarks of suburban England. In its title refrain and its description of children dying in their mothers' arms, it may also suggest the 1993 murder of young black student Stephen Lawrence in a southeast London suburb; his mother would unsuccessfully seek justice for her boy, who died with his head cradled in the arms of a Good Samaritan who whispered "You are loved" in his ear.

Whether or not this recent London tragedy had inspired the song, as the singer George would further adapt the lyric and make it more personal to him. In the line, "Don't think that God is dead," he defies despair. The sense of him sharing the loss of the grieving mother suggests the predicament of Anselmo Feleppa's mother, who welcomed George into her family as if one of her own. In this, 'You Have Been Loved' becomes an understatedly moving companion piece to 'Jesus To A Child'.

If the music of his third solo album was less chained to a dance rhythm than of old, that didn't mean its creator had left the disco entirely. Following 'Jesus To A Child' into the charts by several months and pre-dating the album itself by a similar period, 'Fastlove' was the slickest dance track on the album. "The album didn't come out till a good year later [than the first tracks were laid down]," confirmed Andy Stephens, "but with 'Fastlove' coming from that it just exploded the *Older* album for us."

Almost liquid in its feel, not for the first time it contains no conventional chorus – though it does have a refrain from the early nineties dance hit 'Forget Me Nots', not sampled but sung by Siobhan Fahey (ex-Bananarama/Shakespears Sister). Its lyrical inspiration would later be revealed as a quickie affair with banker Brett Charles, who George met in Kazakhstan during a spate of globetrotting. Though it would be immortalised in musical form (and presented in hetero parallel in the video – where a slightly androgynous black guy and a brunette white girl give each other an animalistic come-on), the fling would be just one more erotic interlude before the entrance of a truly significant other into the singer's life.

The video, by TV commercial directors Vaughan Arnell and Anthea Benton, was budgeted at a full quarter of a million pounds just over a decade on from the cut-price promo of 'Careless Whisper'. It parodied the commercial world in which its creators worked, its fast-cutting edit featuring a group of slick-suited record company executives with the logo 'FONY' on their lapels. (No one ever said satire had to be subtle – as George himself later proved with his comment on the second Gulf War.) The vocalist himself is seen in corporate yuppie mode, spinning around in a revolving office chair before soaking by an indoor cloud – though the drenching doesn't stop him determinedly throwing some moves.

'Fastlove', as a single, exceeded the success of its more serious predecessor, hitting number one in the same number of countries and staying at the top in Britain for three weeks. At the time of its release in April 1996, George also attended that year's Capital Radio Music Awards in his now trademark shades and goatee. "The first half of the nineties was pretty crap for me, and 1996 has made it all worthwhile. Thank you very much," he said of the ever-faithful music station's award for Outstanding Contribution to Music.

"The kind of optimism that I showed on *Older*," George later appraised the album that less perceptive critics complained of as too downbeat by half, "I kind of took my first experience of bereavement and tried to take all the best, most positive lessons from it. It was totally the album that I had to make at that time, it was where I was. Definitely by the second half of making that record, I was a happy man again."

The upturn in his emotional state was due almost entirely to an event in his private life. During the latter part of the album's recording, the singer met a flight steward named Kenny Goss in LA. A tall, blond, physically fit Texan, the former high-school cheerleader coach Goss's appearance belied the fact that he was four years older than George. What the performer wasn't sure of was whether he had the slightest chance with his new acquaintance; for his part, the budding new friend was uncertain of whether he was in the presence of somebody truly famous.

"Where we met was this famous spa," Kenny later recalled. "It's not gay or anything. I wasn't sure it was him [i.e. George Michael, superstar]. I didn't grow up in a musical family."

"No, I don't believe that for a second," laughed George as their exchange of reminiscences was edited on film for his bio-doc. "I believed it at the time, but I know him now. Our relationship was kind of chats, me plucking up the courage to ask him to go out for dinner with me."

"He actually asked me out. He said we should go out for a meal – I'm like, 'Yeah, yeah!'" Kenny panted light-heartedly, sending himself up. "I think he thought, 'Maybe I'm picking up this straight guy,' which he wasn't."

"I wasn't sure he was gay, and I wasn't sure he was gay on the first dinner date," confirmed George, laughing. "The second night, I became *very* sure he was gay. From that point on, from the third day he was around me, I felt that my life was about to change drastically again."

So it was. The sexual liaison of George Michael and Kenny Goss would soon outgrow the bedroom to become a more stable, permanent relationship. "Everyone knew," asserted Kenny. "We would go out to restaurants, hold hands and all sorts of stuff. I think it was just he never went on a television show and said, 'I'm a gay man.'"

Older, the third solo album by George Michael, was released in mid-May 1996. It was the herald of a renaissance for the artist, on a musical, business and personal level. Besides the dedication it bore to its creator's deceased Brazilian lover, it also carried the following tribute: "To Antonio Carlos Jobim – who changed the way I listen to music." Jobim was the Brazilian songwriter who composed the sixties classic 'The Girl From Ipanema', which was translated into English and covered by everyone from Frank Sinatra to Eartha Kitt, who sang it as 'The Boy from Ipanema'.* Its gently sensual bossa nova tones were back in vogue as part of the nineties vogue for retro-easy listening, but it was this very same aesthetic which would make the album difficult listening for pop-music critics who habitually related 'gentle/quiet' to 'downbeat/depressing'.

The final dedication of the aptly-titled *Older* was to the fans: "Thank you for waiting." Only a very few would be disappointed enough to suggest its six-year gestation period had not been worth it.

Besides the standout tracks discussed above, 'To Be Forgiven' continues the ethereal South American atmospherics, its lyric of personal despair ("I'm going down, won't you help me?") delivered in a delicate vocal free of histrionics, backed by trilling acoustic guitar and airy flute. 'Free' is an instrumental with barely a whisper of George's voice ("Feels good to be free," is the only line); the most cinematic track he'd produced since 'Careless Whisper, it was almost *Twin Peaks* in its intensity. 'It Doesn't Really Matter', on the other hand, was so laid-back it was almost laid out, its regret-tinged lyric shuffling along on a rhythmic bed of electronic bleeps and synthesised drums. The title track, 'Older' itself, played in part like a fortiess film noir soundtrack,

---

* George further displayed his liking for all things bossa nova that same year with his contribution to another AIDS-benefit album, *Red Hot And Rio*. This was a gently laid-back Portuguese duet, entitled 'Desifinado' ('Off-Key'), with original 'Girl From Ipanema' singer Astrud Gilberto.

overlaid by George's lyric about letting go of an old love affair and hints of greater hope in the future ("Something good has happened to me").

'Spinning The Wheel' was the funkiest number this time around – though even here, the semi-whispered lyric about the lover who hasn't returned home by four o'clock in the morning possesses more texture than beat. When released later as a single, its video would merge the jazz dancers of twenties New York with modern breakdancers, including a striking mixed-race girl resembling the iconic Josephine Baker. 'Star People' is more conventional smooth funk, with a lyric set in the place where celebrity high-life meets the late-night life ("your secret's safe with me"). 'Move On' is the most overtly jazz-inflected track, a wistful, finger-clicking number about falling "out of favour with Lady Luck" which would be promoted by a black-and-white performance video shot at what appears to be a late-night jazz club.

Older was met with a mix of anticipation and bemusement. Disappointingly, most British reviewers chose to harp on its supposedly downbeat and depressive nature, which was a rather superficial view. (*Older* was not Leonard Cohen, after all – though even that lugubrious singing poet had smoothed out his rough edges in recent years and had more in common with George Michael than one might expect.)

While the still-just-about-hip *NME* (prior to its conversion to a kind of *Smash Hits* for students) saw fit to give to their one-time cover boy from Wham! an effusive nine out of ten stars, *Older* was mostly met by shrugs or thumbs-downs. The charts told a different story though. Well within one month of its release, the album had sold over two and a half million copies worldwide. All the signs were in place for this being the start of phase two of George Michael's career – which, if fate hadn't intervened, is surely what would have happened.

In the meanwhile, Virgin and DreamWorks SKG were met by the same dilemma that the much derided Sony had once faced – their artist's reluctance to get out on the road and tour in support of his product. As a compromise, the singer and his management started to put in place some personal appearances that would serve the promotional purpose by being broadcast around the world.

The first of these would be an MTV *Unplugged* concert. While *Unplugged* generally meant an artist turning down the volume and performing an acoustic (or semi-acoustic) set, much of the highly orchestrated new music of George Michael was perfect for the show's format. It was filmed in London's East End, at Three Mills Studios in Bow, where the River Lee flows into the Thames.

To accompany the worldwide broadcast of his performance, George gave an interview that mostly concentrated on the downside of his celebrity: "The things that are written about me normally revolve around three things: either my sexuality, my beard or my dog [Hippy, now seven years old]. I have a dog that if I was doing interviews every five minutes no one would notice, I have a beard that if I was doing interviews every five minutes no one would notice, but because I don't talk to people the things that they can write about are fairly limited. So they end up being: what shape is his beard this year – oh, the other thing is how much money have I got? I manage to accrue about another $20 million a year – I don't know where it comes from but I do, apparently, just by being famous. And the other one is my sexuality – and ultimately, there is not a person in my life I care about, or that cares about me, who doesn't know who I am or what my life is. But outside the people in my life, who am I clearing it up for and why am I clearing it up for them? I have absolutely no problem with people speculating about my sexuality – is he gay? is he straight? or whatever – no problem with that, everybody does it, we all do it with each other. I have a *real* problem with people who think it's somehow strange that they're not given the answer. People are surprised when they don't hear some response to that kind of speculation – like you're supposed to deny or you're supposed to confirm whatever the rumour is. I don't know when it became part of the job that you had to give your *entire* life. Everybody knows that when you become a public figure you give up a lot of your life, but in the nineties it's like *don't do it* unless you want everything raked over, and if you've got anything to hide, don't do it."

Despite these old bugbears, the performer announced that he was happy to be putting on the show and that it was part of his way of announcing to the world, "Hello! I'm still here!" In the years that followed, ensuing events would ensure an entirely different perspective on his performance.

"I remember the *Unplugged* really, really vividly," George more recently recalled. "I just lost myself in singing that night, and I'm so glad my mum was there. And so I'm glad that for the first time ever, and certainly the only time on film, I actually said hello to my mum in the audience."

In the film of the *Unplugged* concert, he gives her a little wave and a smile, calling out, "Hello Mum!" and self-consciously scratching his goatee. "And it was the last time she ever saw me play. So I have great affection for that evening, because I knew she was so proud of me, you know."

He was aware by this point that Lesley Panayiotou, the mother who had shown belief in and loyalty toward her son all his life, was threatened by illness. By his own account, however, George was probably not fully aware of how serious her condition was becoming.

"I think we'd met like a week," recalled Kenny Goss of the previous few months. "He was speaking to his mother, telling her that he'd met me, and she told him that she'd found a lump or something, but she kind of downplayed it."

In the bio-doc *A Different Life*, Jack Panos recalls of his wife, "She had a little spot, like a dark spot on her shoulder. And you know, you don't look at these things." As a tan-complexioned Greek Cypriot, Jack's own skin tones were more able to safely soak up the sun's rays than that of his light-complexioned wife.

For now, however, regardless of the potential threat of skin cancer to his mother's health, George had to continue with his comeback itinerary. In November, the month following the *Unplugged* performance, an interview with him was run in *The Big Issue*, the socially aware UK magazine sold by and campaigning on behalf of the homeless. In the radio interview accompanying his next major performance, he would make his sympathies clear: "I do actually believe that there shouldn't be people with their hands out on the street in this country these days, and half of me thinks the next government has to do something about it and half of me thinks no government is ever going to be able to do anything about this ever again."

After more than 17 years of Thatcherite Conservative government, his pessimism seemed well founded. In the next year, however, George himself would become part of a new dawn in British politics – even if many would subsequently regard it as a false dawn.

"Sometimes I'll put my hand in my pocket [to make a donation to *Big Issue* sellers], and nine out of 10 times I don't have any money on me, you know. Because I don't carry cash, I'm like that," he confessed. With his political credentials on display, George was about to become part of an affluent but socially conscious generation who would be labelled 'champagne socialists'.

For now, however, it was time to take care of business. For his second live performance broadcast that autumn, he would appear in November at the BBC's Broadcasting Theatre at Broadcast House in Portland Place, at the heart of central London. His personal choice of interviewer to accompany the radio show was a slightly younger man – Chris Evans, the chirpy carrot-top who'd become a hit on Channel 4's *Big Breakfast* and his own follow-up show, *TFI Friday*, before becoming a radio DJ.

Though the BBC considered Evans somehow an 'edgy' choice for an established singer and his response to *Older* had been outright sceptical, George couldn't have had a more sympathetic interviewer. Their 1996 BBC Radio One interview is a classic of its kind, and informs various parts of this book. Among many lesser little confessions, such as waking up every day to the *Richard And Judy* show at 10am on Channel 4 (as with many stoners, George had a deep and meaningful relationship with his TV set), he articulated what he hoped to achieve after performing for BBC Radio One, a station that now had a much younger audience demographic than his own 33 years: "I want to go all the way, I want to work until the day I die, I want to have something creative to do, somewhere to take things creatively; I want to drop dead in the studio...

"I'll just get on with making records; I've started a record label, I'm just starting one now [Aegean Records, run by Andros Georgiou], so

I'll have a lot of work going on with that and I'll carry on doing what I do. I'll just keep on recording and hopefully I'll get to record lots; you know, last time I said this I ended up in court for three years, but I really would like to record more…

"It's almost like I really do have this genuine feeling of starting all over again. And one of the things I intend to do in the, let's call it the second phase of my career or the second half of my career, is to make sure that when I sing, I sing in situations that I enjoy."

The agenda was clear. For all his dislike of the album-and-tour promotional treadmill, George Michael was now resurgent and he intended to remain consistently productive, dividing his time between the recording studio and a select number of specifically chosen personal performances.

But as one of his personal songwriting heroes, the late John Lennon, might have told him, life is what happens to you when you're making other plans.

CHAPTER 15

Waltz Away Dreaming

George Michael briefly became a poster boy for social causes (aside from the fight against AIDS) in the mid-nineties. At first, his attempt at direct engagement was a misfire. Around the time of his autumn 1996 *Big Issue* interview, he was a volunteer for an inner London soup kitchen, doling out food, tea and sympathy, the first of which was pre-prepared in his Hampstead home.

Within a short space of time, however, he was dissuaded from his good deed by the retinue of reporters and paparazzi who were starting to haunt the place to get a story on 'Saint George' – largely the same people who were always seeking an 'exclusive' on his sexuality.

Over the ensuing year to come, the singer would seek out a more practical method of working for the society that had granted him success and privilege. But in the earliest days of the New Year, there were significantly more personal matters to attend to.

★★★

In January 1997, the family and friends of Lesley Panayiotou attended a party for her, thrown and funded by her son. According to a tabloid report of the time, the party was a celebration of her positive response to treatment to diabetes. This seems to have been a PR smokescreen, as the reality was far graver.

One month later, George was due to attend the 1997 Brit Awards, for which he would receive the award for Best British Male. But this time around the tabloid headlines would be more accurate: 'GEORGE MICHAEL AGONY – He misses Brits to be at mum's bedside,' read *The Sun*.

At the Brits, Elton John, dressed in one of his best multicoloured pantomime outfits, accepted the award on behalf of his friend: "Now unfortunately George cannot be here tonight," he told the audience, "but I have a message from him and I've got to read it out. It says: 'To everybody here, and everybody watching at home, I apologise for not attending tonight's awards show.'"

As the man himself would later reflect, "My mother had the melanoma – 'melanoma' means a skin cancer – of apparently the most virulent form. And I think in reality she knew she had a far smaller chance of survival than she was letting on to us."

In fact, on her most recent admission to hospital, Lesley had been informed by her specialists that her situation was terminal.

For a sensitive man whose talent stems from his ability to channel the most tender of emotions, the cruelly short period of respite between getting over his lover's death and his mother becoming critically ill made it all the more agonising.

"In a way, if you're a glass-half-empty, you could say, 'Oh my God, you didn't get any time off!'" George would later reflect, having by now arrived at a more stoical state of mind. "'The minute you were in love again something disastrous happened.' But the way I look at it is I feel as though Anselmo sent me Kenny at the exact time that I would need him."

In his *Big Issue* interview, George had hinted at his happiness with his new lover, without revealing his name (or indeed his gender). But the fact that he'd reiterated his call for safe sex and the use of condoms in the same few column inches made the point: George Michael was a gay man who was, by now, quite comfortable with his sexuality – as long as he didn't have to stand up and announce it in public.

For all the emotional support he could offer, Kenny would find it would take many months – if not years – before he could start to ease his lover's pain. The extent of the loss he was about to undergo was too profound, far too deeply felt, to be suffered lightly.

"Unfortunately," as George later recalled, pausing to collect himself, "[the cancer] went into remission for three or four months, and then came back with a vengeance and within a week of that she was gone."

Lesley Panayiotou died, surrounded by her husband and children, in bed at Charing Cross Hospital, central London, on Wednesday February 26, 1997. She was buried in Highgate, north London, the area in which she was raised and which she still regarded as her roots. To the present day, according to the guide who conducts tours of Highgate's historic gothic cemetery, her grave is tended and fresh flowers are placed every week – "unless the person who does it is away or abroad".

The impact of her death upon her immediate family was as profound as can be expected. The effect upon her only son was, at first, too emotionally painful for him to even discuss it.

"Yog's always been a man who just bottles it up as well, you know," as David Austin later remarked. "And it was just devastating. This was one period when I just couldn't say anything to him. I didn't know what to say."

"I remember being somewhere on some other planet for weeks," concurred George. "I don't really remember the days afterwards. I don't really remember who tried to comfort me, you know. I know I was in shock, I know I wasn't prepared – I was *not* prepared."

As befitting a musical performer, perhaps, one of the only ways he could attempt to expiate his grief was through his art. In a truly poignant piece of synchronicity, during his mother's final week George had first heard the demo of a song entitled 'Waltz Away Dreaming', by his Aegean Records signing Toby Bourke.

221

"He told me he played it in his car just hours after his mother died and knew that he wanted to release it as a single," recalled Brit folk-rock singer Bourke. "I did a small rewrite and agreed to let George sing on it."

The lyric of the final version is credited to Bourke/Michael. Irrespective of how far the Aegean boss contributed to the final words, 'Waltz Away Dreaming' is itself a dreamy modern folk ballad, tinged with a kind of romantic Irishness but still smoothly English and polished. (In this it predates acts like Mumford & Sons, the almost forgotten Bourke pre-empting the modern Brit-folk scene by a full decade.)

'Waltz Away Dreaming' is a tribute to a lost love, but far too upbeat and romantic to be a lament. It mythologises the departed woman who now flies "like an eagle above" and who may or may not have departed this life. In fact, in the original lyric the suggestion is merely that she chose to leave, but in the verse that George sings, the line "every grown man cries with his mother's eyes" has a definite and deliberate poignancy.

His collaboration with George Michael would provide Bourke with his only hit record, but he found the sessions far from a standard exercise in cutting a track. "He was stoned all the time," the folk-rock singer recalled a decade hence. "It was pretty much a haze of dope the whole way through the recording sessions.

"He would smoke skunk joints in the studio when we were meant to be working. He was easily getting through 20 joints a day. The joints were in a Marlboro box and had been rolled by one of George's lackeys. He would smoke one, take a break, then spark another one up.

"Another time he was so stoned he forgot he had left his dog Hippy in the car outside the studio. Fortunately, someone told us and we went and rescued the poor thing."

For all Bourke's moral disapproval, the stoned aesthetic seemed to suit the song perfectly. When a video was produced, vivid CGI graphics showed the songwriter and his mentor in a fantasy woodland that might have come out of *The Lord Of The Rings*, surrounded by half-animal nymph girls.

At the end of March 1997, George attended the Capital Radio Awards at the Royal Lancaster Hotel in London, where he picked up the gongs for Best Male Vocalist and Best Album. Dedicating the awards to his late mother, with Easter close at hand he pledged the first playing of his and Toby Bourke's collaboration to the Help a London Child weekend. As with his launch of the unreleased 'Jesus To A Child' two years previously, George offered up to three times the amount promised by Capital listeners in order to hear the song's debut. In the event, he exceeded his own previous generosity, stumping up £166,000 as a healthy supplement to the £35,000 pledged by listeners. 'Waltz Away Dreaming' would become Toby Bourke's only Top 10 single when it was released two months hence, in June 1997.

It was in the interim that George found a practical outlet for his own need to 'give something back' to the modern society that made him famous and successful. In late April, he made an unannounced guest appearance at that year's VH1 Honors concert, held at LA's Universal Amphitheatre. As with the Motown Returns to the Apollo concert 12 years previously, he would duet with one of his greatest musical influences – Stevie Wonder, Motown's musical polymath. In fact, as he sang a verse on 'Living For The City', Wonder's innovative electro-backed anthem of urban grit, George was looking ever more like the young Stevie Wonder himself: short-cropped hair, dark shades, trimmed facial hair. If he had caused a controversy by being the first white man to win a Best R&B Performer award in the late eighties, this time he looked like he was actually morphing into a black man.

But it was the sentiments behind the gig that really chimed with the Anglo-Greek singer. It was to raise money for VH1's Save the Music programme, which in the face of budgetary cuts would help provide musical instruments and training to pupils in the USA's public education system. It lit a fire under George that would stay ignited till he was back home in London. Having already offered his verbal support for the modern Labour Party (or New Labour, as it came to be known), he saw musical education as a means by which he could actually connect with left-of-centre politics.

"Until I was [in my] early thirties I'd never paid a penny that hadn't gone to the Tory government," he'd later tell interviewer Kirsty Wark, then the presenter of BBC2's *Newsnight*. "So I was used to the idea that I didn't like where my money was going."

Under the New Labour leader, Tony Blair, the singer who came to the fore in the Thatcherite eighties could see the potential for change. New Labour had shed much of the socialist ideology of the past, including the right of trade union leaders to place casting votes, in exchange for a political pluralism that combined social conscience and liberalism with the pursuit of wealth. As George told Ms Wark:

"I was one of those who sat up at night with a tear in my eye, thinking, 'My God, things could change.'"

"I'd gone to [Tony Blair's] house in Islington before he was elected – a very, very nice, decent man. I had said that I wasn't going to go to that 'Cool Britannia' thing – I'm a little smarter than that, a little longer in the tooth. I just knew that that was going to be a bit of a joke. I just said that if he wants my support I'll see him personally."

('Cool Britannia' was coined by a 1996 issue of Newsweek *magazine, lionising the resurgent Britain of the time. The ailing Conservative Party tried to hijack the label, but it didn't stop Blair winning the 1997 General Election at the beginning of May – one week after George visited his home. In truth, no politician can take credit for popular culture's ups and downs, but this didn't stop Blair hosting a celebratory drinks party at 10 Downing Street in the weeks after the election, with guests including fashion designers, Creation Records director Alan McGee and Noel Gallagher, guitarist of the then immensely popular Oasis. Perhaps wisely, George Michael didn't believe the hype in this instance and stayed away.)*

"I actually think that public spending is a good thing. Whether they're creating a few false jobs along the way or not, I do actually think that public spending and the money that's going towards it and the attempts that have been made in various areas are quite successful."

At his meetings with Blair, among the uses for public funds under discussion were access to musical equipment for British schoolchildren and the dawn of the Internet age. In those early, idealistic days of New Labour, George put himself on offer as public representative of a scheme that would take every British schoolkid online. (Over the party's 13 subsequent years of government, this at least was one aim that was almost met.)

But an increasing amount of factors would get in the way of George's initial crusading zeal – though the demands of what was, after all, his day job seemed to be becoming ever less significant.

The same month that Tony Blair became Prime Minister, George was presented by Queen guitarist Brian May with the prizes for Best Songwriter and Most Performed Work ('Fastlove') at the Ivor Novello Awards. His ongoing grief was underlined by his acceptance speech, in which he added, "I would like to thank my mother whose soul is in every note I have ever written."

"Everybody knows how long it took him to – not quite *get over* her," George's father, Jack, would acknowledge years later. "It's very tough for all of us," he added, as if to stress that, for his son, the period of mourning had proven especially difficult and protracted.

"My mum never, ever patronised me and always believed in what I was doing," his son elaborated on his own sense of loss, "and always believed in my right to do what I was doing. And I miss that so much, I miss that incredibly."

"His mother especially was a huge blow, after Anselmo, like a double whammy," reflected his friend and mentor Elton John. "So George spent a lot of time grieving for people that he really, really loved."

"Because he was so close to his mother," reflected new live-in partner Kenny Goss, "[it was] a really tough call. That kind of stopped his songwriting, all those things. That became not important at the time."

For a long time, the musical career of George Michael would be a sporadic thing at best, increasingly peripheral even to the life of the man himself. Deferrals were accepted by Sony/CBS, his former record label, who realised there was no point in rushing him to complete the three new tracks he owed to pad out its greatest hits collection.

For now, there were only memories, distractions, indulgences – and dope. As his former friend Fiona Russell Powell opined in her interview for this book, "The funny thing is he's definitely a depressive, and if you're depressed then smoking weed isn't a particularly good idea."

In the nineties, the abundance of hydroponically grown herbal cannabis had begun to outstrip the staple Moroccan hash, which in its widely varying potency had been the mainstay of Britain's dope smokers. The new strains – 'skunk', as they were generically known for their pungent smell – could be guaranteed to work well every time and contained less of the 'downer' chemical which could root heavy smokers to the spot.

The greater percentage of THC, the psychoactive ingredient, meant that skunk was a near-psychedelic experience. As a mild hallucinogenic it enhanced whatever way the smoker was feeling. Simple happiness could quickly reach a state of euphoric bliss; profound unhappiness, on the other hand, could open up a dark tunnel that led to the depths of the soul. Added to the herbal intoxication, it can be assumed that George was now also taking strong painkillers for the back problems that had been plaguing him intermittently since the days of Wham! Subsequent to his mother's death, he'd been told by a specialist that he'd soon need an operation to remove two vertebrae or else he'd face virtual paralysis.

At the end of the summer, the final single taken from the *Older* album, 'You Have Been Loved', was scheduled to be released as a double-A side with 'The Strangest Thing'. The latter track was a dope-influenced piece of world music with a haunting bouzouki motif, the nearest its composer ever got to traditional Greek music. Ethereally evoking a disorientated mind, the lyric happily acknowledged, "I don't even recognise people that I care for."

Just over a week before the single was due to be released, a national tragedy played out which impacted upon the ever more insular world of George Michael.

On the morning of Sunday 31st of August, 1997, George would go through his regular morning ritual of waking from a stoned slumber to light another potent spliff. It must have created a particularly sensitive condition in which to receive the news that Diana, Princess of Wales, had been killed in the early hours of that same morning.

The entire nation – and beyond that, the whole telecommunicating world – were waking to the news that Diana, her love Dodi al-Fayed and their driver had all died as the result of a crash in a central Paris traffic tunnel. (Diana's bodyguard, initially comatose, was the only survivor.) As seems to be the case with any tragedy involving an internationally admired figure, the death of Diana would breed conspiracy theories. All that can be known, however, is that driver Henri Paul died with a potent enough mix of alcohol and antidepressants in his system to impair his driving, while his employer, Dodi, was apparently goading him to go faster to escape the paparazzi.

In Britain, the period of national shock and mourning that followed was almost unprecedented in modern times. Prime Minister Blair adeptly judged the mood, stepping forward to acclaim Diana as "the People's Princess", as if she were somehow part of the New Labour project. The divorced princess was treated as a secular saint; the admirable fact that she managed to find time for charity work (particularly the battles against AIDS and land mines) in her playgirl lifestyle being her grounds for canonisation.

Despite her estrangement from the Royal Family, Diana was rightly accorded the dignity of a state funeral. In the week leading up to the 6th of September, 1997, masses of mourners from across the nation and beyond made a pilgrimage to her official residence at Kensington Palace. Every part as much a product of celebrity culture as any pop star, Diana's memory was defended by ladies from Middle England who baulked at the sight of a camera, believing that the press had killed her, while they themselves would not even have known what she looked like if not for her constant exposure in the news and entertainment media.

On the day of national mourning George Michael joined Elton John at Westminster Abbey, among the very limited ranks of invitees from the showbusiness world. Elton was also accompanied by his long-term boyfriend, David Furnish, having long since come out as a gay man.

As distraught as he and her showbiz mourners felt, Elton had to maintain his composure to perform his funereal tribute, 'Candle In The Wind', a rather odd rewrite of his 1973 hit about Marilyn Monroe, which now referenced 'England's rose' and had all the melody ground out of it. (For all that, 'Candle In The Wind 97' would become the UK's biggest-selling single of all time. It was also the record which kept 'You Have Been Loved'/'The Strangest Thing' out of the number one slot.)

On the day, George was not capable of showing the same restraint. Shaken by the sudden death of his contemporary – the woman with whom, he claimed, under very different circumstances he might have formed the most startling celebrity couple of all time, though they never spoke directly more than a dozen times – he frequently broke down in tears at the Abbey, in full view of the TV cameras. By his own admission, "I was one of the few people in that part of Westminster Abbey who was really blubbing."

In a telephone interview the next day, the unorthodoxly spiritual singer made his latest reference to the ethereal when he described Diana as "a gift from God". Echoing the national sentiment about protecting the young Princes William and Harry from press intrusion, he told his interviewer (on *The Pepsi Chart Show*, of all forums), "I pray that after time they will feel her presence in everything they do – and know their mother's love will never leave them."

It was strikingly redolent of recent public comments about his own late mother. As with the death of Freddie Mercury, six years previously, George's mournfulness in public was compounded by how the event impacted upon him as an echo of his own private pain. He was mourning the iconic figure in the spotlight, but in his dark corner of the Abbey there were other ghosts.

After dedicating his latest hit, 'You Have Been Loved', to the Princess, he would withdraw into luxurious reclusiveness for months to come –

moving in dreamily stoned sequence between his three homes around the world.

"I suppose [the tabloids] left me alone for a while because I was nowhere," George would later recognise. "I was stuck at home in my black hole, I was nowhere to be seen."

When he next exploded in the public consciousness, however, it would be with a startling vengeance.

CHAPTER 16

Outside/Outed

In late 1997, it was a disillusioned George Michael who first embraced the new culture of the Internet. In a posting on his first official website, www.aegean.net, he wrote: "So far my time with DreamWorks has been frustrating and disappointing. I would like to apologise to many of my fans, especially those in America, for the lack of availability of my work."

At the root of his discontent were the very moderate sales of *Older* in the US – 700,000 copies in the first six months, less than half of what it had sold in the much smaller UK market and proportionately much smaller than the album's performance worldwide, where it had gone platinum several times over. At that early dawn of the online culture, it was not yet evident to either George or his record label that the availability of music would be the very factor that radically decreased CD sales, rather than improving them.

With his greatest hits collection postponed by Sony, George was co-opted into playing the retro-promotional game for the release of a Wham! compilation. His part of the promo push was to give a one-off interview to his *Bare* biographer, Tony Parsons, now a columnist and feature writer for the *Daily Mirror*. It bespoke his ongoing state of melancholia. "I don't love this country any less than I did before my mum's death," George told Parsons, "but my ties with Britain are definitely less now that my mum's died. It's hard to work out if that's because she's gone or because there are too many memories here."

As intimated by the article, he intended spending a lot more time in his second hometown of California, where record sales dictated that he was no longer quite the international star he used to be. If the career of George Michael needed a shot in the arm, however, it would soon receive international coverage that (in its early days at least) was less of a publicist's dream than a PR catastrophe.

The early days and weeks of 1998 were mostly spent in southern California, where George alternated between laying down the odd track, socialising with boyfriend, Kenny, and their mutual friends, or just chilling out. As when he was at home in north London, he'd also developed a few little private routines that he tended to adhere to.

One of these was to randomly jump in his car (a sleek new black Mercedes) and drive over to the Will Rogers Memorial Park, a pristinely kept piece of public land adjacent to Hollywood's legendary Sunset Boulevard. By his own later admission, he was in the habit of cruising the park in the afternoons or early evenings in a series of loose-ended, lonely adventures.

Tuesday April 7, 1998 was one such afternoon. George drove over from his rented luxury home on Calle Vista Drive, Beverly Hills (his own home in Santa Barbara being a little further out from the hub of LA society) to take in the sights at the park. This sunny day, however, he headed straight for the public restroom – the almost reflexive action of a gay man who'd grown used to hiding his sexuality. Ironically perhaps, the namesake of the park, Will Rogers – early 1900s America's beloved vaudeville cowboy, silent-movie star and popular wit – had once coined his own epitaph as, "I joked about every prominent man of my time, but I never met a man I didn't like."

This was one day when the latter part of the sentiment might have been attributed to George Michael, though for a while at least he'd find the joke was on him.

Dressed casually in a blue T-shirt and tracksuit bottoms, George entered the public toilets at 14.50 hours, according to the Beverly Hills Police Department report. From here, we follow the timeline of the police's official version of what transpired:

A Caucasian male in his early-to-mid-thirties walks toward the public urinal, later identified as UK citizen Georgios K. Panayiotou. He makes eye contact with a well-built young man of approximately 30 years old (later confirmed as BHPD Officer Marcelo Rodriguez), but no words are exchanged.

By motioning and silent inference, the man later identified as Mr Panayiotou indicates that the police officer should enter the toilet cubicle next to him. Officer Rodriguez complies.

Mr Panayiotou next begins to visibly masturbate his own sexual member. He walks towards the open cubicle, penis in hand, to demonstrate his actions to Officer Rodriguez. (To substantiate his account, the officer will state that he witnessed a nicotine patch designed to combat smoking attached to one of Mr Panayiotou's buttocks.)

After apparently watching Mr Panayiotou masturbate for several moments, Officer Rodriguez brushes by the man to wordlessly exit the restroom. Outside, he informs a uniformed colleague patrolling the park, who consequently enters the restroom to arrest Mr Panayiotou for performing a lewd act in a public place.

"It's nice to make people laugh once in a while, isn't it?" George would later make light of the scenario. At the time, however, becoming a public laughing stock seemed an altogether more serious proposition to him.

"This is entrapment!" he reputedly shouted at the scene of his arrest. It was an allegation he would continue to assert over a number of years.

Unable to produce valid ID, the suspect was searched (and found to be in legitimate possession of prescription antidepressant Prozac), arrested and 'taken downtown', as US cop-show parlance has it, to the

Beverly Hills County Jail – where he was fingerprinted, photographed, charged and bailed at $500 to appear at the Beverly Hills Municipal Courthouse on the morning of May 5.

"You know the really weird thing?" George would later ask his bio-doc interviewer in the more relaxed (and slightly more camp) tone of voice that he gradually adopted throughout the nineties. "That day I remember so clearly being in the car and it was really windy; there were these two guys that I think were also part of that entrapment setup, they were going in and out of that bathroom. And something in me said, 'You shouldn't go in there, there's something really dodgy going on'. But I went in there, *you know what I mean?*"

Back home in London, many of his old friends made a collective cringe on his behalf – even if they weren't overly surprised by George's actions. "I just thought, 'You silly fool, how could you have got caught?'" laughed ex-Wham! girl Pepsi. "You see helicopters flying over the house and you just think, 'Oh my God, how embarrassing!'" seconded her ex-singing partner Shirlie Kemp.

(Ms Kemp was by this time running the information service for Aegean Records. Having nursed her husband, ex-Spandau Ballet bassist and *EastEnders* actor Martin Kemp, through treatment for a brain tumour, she'd had to declare bankruptcy before George rescued the Kemp family by employing Shirlie.)

The helicopters that Ms Kemp saw on TV were not the property of law enforcers (who were hardly dealing with a major crime, in any case), but the TV and radio networks who were suddenly ablaze with the news. The official police department statement, as read to the media, ran, "Beverly Hills officers arrested the singer known as George Michaels," and any suspicion that law enforcement were unsure of exactly who they'd had at the station were later compounded by a judge who referred to the defendant as 'Michael George'.

The news and entertainment media suffered no such confusion. Hungry for any scandalous detail of the star's recklessness, they were officially reassured that the policing of Will Rogers Memorial Park was not some kind of covert anti-gay operation but a precaution to ensure acts of indecency did not intrude upon families and children who used the park. The actual nature of the charge was described as "committing a lewd act with no other persons present" – which, by a process of grammatical mangling, ended up being described back in London as "committing a homosexual act alone". ("He's a gifted boy!" quipped comedian Paul Merton on TV show *Have I Got News For You?*)

The management went into action. Andy Stephens flew to LA with lawyer Tony Russell, seemingly in fear that, after several years of minor controversies and drawn-out legal disputes, George Michael's career could finally be going into meltdown. The news that – after years of evasion – their client was being 'outed' as a gay man needed to be carefully managed.

Two days after the arrest, on the Thursday of that week, the singer felt secure enough to go to dinner at Spago, an exclusive showbiz restaurant on Sunset Boulevard. Despite his initial trepidation, he was greeted by old-school Hollywood hedonist Tony Curtis, who told him to "keep smiling", and applauded by a crowd that included singer Lionel Richie at that awkward moment when he needed to visit the toilets.

It's tempting, if rather cynical, to think that the Sunset celebs were having a joke at the outed singer's expense. But this was Hollywood, where the sleaze which went on even in the days of Will Rogers was celebrated in Kenneth Anger's classic series of *Hollywood Babylon* books. As George would gradually come to realise, great careers had survived much more than a pissy little scandal such as his.

As the next step in their news and crisis management strategy, Stephens and Russell arranged for George to be interviewed that Saturday, April 11, on CNN, the most relatively liberal of the rolling news networks. Interviewed by anchorman Jim Moray, George's responses seemed heartfelt and forthright. Seen through the prism of the passing years, however, it's clear how he was seeking to control the public perception of him even when he was at such an apparent disadvantage. His address to the public is summarised as follows:

"I've been living in a circus, you know, in the middle of helicopters flying around my house. Literally hundreds of people outside the house waiting day and night for something, I don't know what exactly. But I just want to tell my fans, who I feel, apart from embarrassing myself, I've embarrassed to some degree. I just want to let them know that I'm okay, that I know a lot of them realise I've had a very tough time over the last five or six years. And I want to let them know this is not going to finish me off. This is really nothing compared to the bereavements I've had to deal with. Even compared to the legal situations I've had to deal with, this is kind of – I was going to say a walk in the park, but I don't think that would work here.

"I'm not at liberty to talk about it, not because I'm afraid to talk about it but simply because it's a legal situation that's still up in the air and I don't know whether or not I'm going to be charged with anything. I've been advised that I am not really allowed to talk about the detail of it.

"I put myself in a position where I risked all kinds of things. I risked prosecution. I risked all of the things that happened to me and I'm not proud of that at all. But the actual moral question at the centre of it – which ultimately would not be a huge deal if it was a heterosexual moral question – I'm not ashamed of it at all.

"With pop stars or film stars, we become the object of people's self-definition, as well as the object of sexual definition. I think people like to think they can spot a gay person as opposed to a straight person because it makes them feel, in some way, a little more defined in themselves. And if someone is on the borderline, which I've always considered myself in terms of the way I appear to people, ambiguous, I think while it works very successfully in pop culture – especially if you are trying to communicate something emotional, or sexual, that you're communicating with both men and women – my sexuality was not cut and dried. I spent the first half of my career being accused of being gay when I hadn't had anything like a gay relationship. In fact, I was 27 before that happened to me. So I spent years growing up, being told what my sexuality was really, which is kind of confusing. And then by the time I'd kind of worked out what it was and I'd stopped having relationships with women, I was just so indignant about the way I had been treated until then, I just thought, 'Well, I'll just hold onto this.

They don't need to know. I don't think I should have to tell them.' But, you know, this is as good a time as any.

"I want to say that I have no problem with people knowing that I'm in a relationship with a man right now. I have not been in a relationship with a woman for almost 10 years. I do want people to know the songs that I wrote when I was with women were really about women, and the songs I have written since have been fairly obviously about men. So, I think in terms of my work, I've never been reticent in terms of defining my sexuality. I write about my life and I want people to know, especially people who loved the earlier stuff, especially if they were young girls at the time, there was no bullshit there.

"And I think, having done something as stupid as that – I'm a very proud man – I want people to know that I feel stupid and I feel reckless and weak for having allowed my sexuality to be exposed this way, but I don't feel any shame whatsoever.

"I don't think I ever really wanted to address it and certainly not quite this way. I think it was the danger of the situation that must have compelled me to do it because it was absolutely compulsive. I have no problem in saying that I am a human being and I think for most of us our biggest frailties are sexual.

"I made some pretty important decisions at the end of the whole *Faith* period. I don't think that they were entirely divorced from my feeling my sexuality was changing, or that I was defining myself in a different way, but it was far more to do with the fact I was feeling very unhappy. I was very miserable at the centre of that kind of fame at 23 to 24. I just couldn't cope with that. I don't think that is altogether that surprising considering that I left school at 17 and was a star by the time I was 18 – a star in certain parts of the world anyway.

"I think it's just something you have to accept and I think if I wasn't prepared to accept that I wouldn't have put myself out there again. I really did at one point believe that I never wanted that sort of success. My success over the last seven years really has gone from strength to strength in the rest of the world. So I achieved what I wanted, which was to hold onto my ability to do something that was going to please people and write something that meant something to me and to them. I also gave myself the chance to quietly slow my life down and grow up a bit, even though this week has not been the most grown-up of my life.

"I think I'm angry at media generally about a lot of things, but not just for myself. I mean for all of us, whether we're famous or not famous, or just happen to get caught in the glare of publicity over one issue or another, I think the media is a real demon. But from my own point of what's happened, I can't be angry with anyone but myself. I mean, the only people I've really hurt are myself, the people who love me and my partner, who has been absolutely amazing and understands me, thank God. I owe those people apologies, as again, I probably owe an apology to fans that have been supportive and have not wanted to believe that any of this was true. I know it really takes a little bit of the sheen off of the mystique, to put it mildly, but other than that I really don't have apologies to make.

"I knew I was going to do this from the moment I was arrested. Absolutely, I knew that this was the only way to go. I've seen too many people run away from situations like this and I'm thinking, 'Just go on TV; you're a human being, just go on TV and get it sorted out as quickly as possible.'

"I define my sexuality in terms of the people that I love and my life right now is very happy, living in a gay relationship. I'm very happy with that; I don't look to the future and think I might change my sexuality, because I'm hoping that my relationship is the one that is going to last me for the rest of my life. I mean, I could have tried to put any number of angles on this tonight, but ultimately, at the end of the day, I'm not ashamed; I'm just pissed with myself for having been so stupid. And I'm perfectly prepared to believe that as long as I am truthful to myself and truthful to the people who are out there with my music, then I have nothing to fear."

In many ways, it sounded like a courageous if overearnest statement. George Michael was finally staking a claim to his own sexual identity and refusing to apologise for it. It's only in the linear sense of what preceded and followed it that a controlling agenda becomes clear.

To take him at his word, George's life had been divided into two distinct personal segments – hetero and gay. He never had a gay relationship until he was 27 years old. (In time, this statement would be refined so that a distinction was claimed between 'relationships' and 'sex' – and then a further distinction between 'relationships' and 'live-in relationships', of which Anselmo Feleppa certainly seems to have been the first.) His early songs were all about women and nothing was ever hidden – even when Paula Yates was trying to tease out of him exactly which "actual girls" he was writing about, at a time when his male partner Anselmo had been diagnosed as HIV positive.

In one sense, he was underplaying his talent – in the universal language of the love song, there is little that's 'obvious' about whether the love object is male or female, and in terms of the emotions invoked sometimes it's not even relevant.

But for all the attempts to manage the public perception, the singer had at last arrived at a place when he could finally and unapologetically be himself. After the CNN interview, George and Kenny decamped to the Beverly Hills branch of The Ivy to celebrate the singer's coming out with mutual friends. It was the beginning of a new personal era.

"To come out of the closet and be busted in the toilet is probably not the best way of coming out really," Elton John would laughingly acclaim, "but he coped with it really well."

"Would there ever have been a day when I said, 'Yes, Mr Such-and-Such from *The Daily Mail*, or *The Mail on Sunday* maybe, 'I am gay'?" George conjectured aloud. "Would I have been able to do that? That probably would have been harder than all the flak I took."

Despite the triviality of the court case, the legal proceedings continued to reverberate throughout most of 1998. At home in Britain, the inevitable scandalous headlines seemed comparatively muted – as did any opposing voices of support.

One perhaps unlikely detractor was journalist Tony Parsons, George's former co-author on the *Bare* autobiography. Having interviewed the singer for the *Daily Mirror* only a few months previously, he now expressed outrage at the Beverly Hills incident, decrying the undeniable indecency of 'cottaging' in a public park and condemning George as, "way out of line. Nobody wants to see this kind of thing when they pop to the loo after feeding the ducks." Except perhaps for a certain kind of park visitor, among whom George surely numbered.

Parsons would later state in print that he'd been offended by how manipulatively George had treated him during their last interview – though he'd been willing to let the singer retract his extraordinary comment about how he and Princess Di might have become lovers. Whether he was further offended by the huge gap that existed between the George Michael arrested in LA and the George Michael presented in *Bare* remains a moot point, but from here on any misadventures in the singer's life would earn only scorn from his former friend.

The trial proceedings themselves were dealt with neatly and quickly. George's management appointed showbiz lawyer Ira Reiner to plead no-contest to the charge of committing a lewd act in public; the defendant didn't even have to appear in court on May 15, when he was sentenced to a fine of $810 plus 80 hours' community service, preparing meals for the Project Angel AIDS charity with whom he already had a working association. (He was also barred from the Will Rogers Memorial Park for a probationary period.)

But the matter didn't end there. Having realised that he was coming out the other side of a scandal far more intact than he might feasibly have hoped, he actively tried to turn the situation to his advantage. As his old friend David Austin put it, "I knew he'd *fly* through that. I knew him so well. And he handled that like George Michael."

In early November 1998, freed of the constraints of the court case, he gave an interview to MTV which went out under the heading of what *really* happened: "I got followed into the restroom and then this cop – I didn't know it was a cop, obviously – he started playing this game, which I think is called, "I'll show you mine, you show me yours, and then when you show me yours, I'm going to nick you.""

"Actually, what happened was once he got an eyeful, he walked past me, straight past me and out, and I thought, that's kind of odd. I thought, maybe he's just not impressed. And then I went to walk back to my car, and as I got back to the car, I was arrested on the street... If someone's waving their genitalia at you, you don't automatically assume that they're an officer of the law... I've never been able to turn down a free meal."

In the space of a few months, George Michael had passed from being reluctant to openly address his sexuality to joking about his voraciousness as a gay male. ("I'm not saying that I have an open relationship with my boyfriend but he... knows that I'm generally oversexed," he matter-of-factly claimed. "We love each other and he understands that it was a stupid mistake and he's forgiven me, I hope.") He was also quite unambiguous about how the investigating officer in the case had allegedly enticed him by revealing himself first, and suggested he may have been set up for a fall by a conspiracy between the Beverly Hills PD and the hated British tabloids.

"I really thought, to my fans, I outed myself with the last album because ... there's been a lot of publicity about my sexuality over the years in Europe and my ex-partner's death was reported very widely, so when I dedicated the album to him and wrote the album for him, I felt like I was coming out to my fans, and I didn't really care about people who weren't interested in my music ...

"So, really, this doesn't feel like an outing, this is just public outing. But any gay person who comes out realises that the tough bit is your friends and family and that was a great thing – it was a great, liberating thing and I did it a long time ago."

The theme of alleged entrapment was continued in his interview that same month for *Late Night With David Letterman*: "This week the DA's office has issued a statement, I don't know why, they've done it several times over the past six months, saying that if I believe I've been entrapped – the one thing that I know about the police report that they had to put down is that I stood in the middle of the street surrounded by people saying, 'This is entrapment!' So that's in there, because I said it publicly to people watching and listening. But they said if it was entrapment, as they saw [in] an [MTV] interview I did last week, then why did it go to court? If anyone can tell me that a sane celebrity involved in a lewd conduct arrest can go in front of international cameras, you saying, 'Yes you did!', him going, 'No I didn't!', you going , 'Yes you did!', there's no way that I'd put myself through that and no way that I'd feed the circus to that degree. I was tried by the media."

The case and its aftermath sent George into overdrive. Rather than breaking him, it seemed to bolster his belief in his own moral correctitude to an overwhelming degree. And he was going to fight back, in the best way that he knew how. "I also knew that, having made such a fool of myself, I'd better come up with a hit song," he'd later admit.

During the fallout from the case, his old nemesis Boy George had been noted for his goodwill in saying he hoped that George Michael wasn't punished for what was, essentially, a victimless crime. Several years down the line, when interviewed for George's bio-doc, he decided to revert to bitchy type.

"I did laugh," sniped 'the other George'. "I mean, it's not very dignified being caught in the toilet by a policeman with your trousers down, is it, and it certainly wouldn't have happened to me. I wouldn't be all kind of self-righteous about it, you know, go and make a *video* about it."

'Outside', the single that was launched by George's MTV interview, and its notorious promo video were his first overtly gay artistic statements. In the video, young male lovers groping become LAPD officers arresting a respectable-looking businessman-type in the toilets. Amid the lavatorial imagery and muscleman bodysuits, the police in the toilets turn into an all-dancing chorus line. LAPD officers kiss as George struts around in uniform with a truncheon.

The song itself had the same fluid electro-soul feel as 'Fastlove'. Despite its relaxed admission of, "And yes I've been bad," however, there was little doubt of who the main targets were. In early 1999, Officer Marcelo Rodriguez would file suit against George Michael, seeking $6.5 million in damages for the emotional distress arising from the satirical video. The court would deny his suit.

'I'LL MAKE GEORGE PAY FOR WILLY PORKIES,' ran the memorable headline in *The Sun*. 'Toilet cop sues for slander over star's allegations.' In 2002, Rodriguez was invited to file an appeal against the original decision. This too failed – as a public employee, it was ruled that the policeman had no legal right to sue for emotional distress. The same principle also applied to the singer's accusations against him of entrapment.

'Outside', perhaps unsurprisingly, did not do great business in the US – while it went to number two in the UK singles chart. It did, however, serve to show that its creator could show balls of brass and turn humiliation into victory, when he was forced into a corner.

"Looking back on that period, the media did some interesting things," he later opined. "First there was this absolute dependence on the past in terms of what was going to happen inside to me as an individual. The headlines [*The Sun*: 'WE'RE SO IN LAV – Loo shame George and his boyfriend'; *The Times*: 'Tortured artist whose dream of celebrity turned into a complete nightmare'] were all about shamed this and shamed that, 'the tortured artist'. The homophobia was just flying! They were *loving* it! To be able to say that this man who had hidden from them for the best part of six years – or seven years it was by then – had been this *tragic*, stereotypical, old-fashioned cottager, they just *loved* it!"

But then, in the final days of the nineties, there was the sense that the popular press might just have misjudged the popular mood. As indeed George himself might have done, having guarded the truth about his sexuality so jealously for so long.

"There was obviously a general feeling of, 'Poor sod, and who cares anyway?'" he'd observe retrospectively. "Then of course I spoilt all their fun because I made the record and I made the video, then kind of cleaned up the mess that was left with the Parkinson interview."

George's late autumn 1998 appearance on Michael Parkinson's chat show was the final *coup de grace* in his personal relaunch. He made quips like, "I never even think about masturbation before calling my lawyer!" to applause, laughter and adoring female screams. Old veteran 'Parky', as reassuringly Northern English as an old cricket pullover, was the perfectly sympathetic foil against whom George could state his case. When Parkinson commented, "It was so blatant, the entire thing, maybe you wanted to declare what you were?" George replied, "Now that I look back there were certain elements that are just undeniable. Apart from the fact that it was Beverly Hills – it was probably the most glamorous toilet in the world. 'If you're gonna do it, do it right,' and everything." When the laughter died down, Parkinson asked, "So what you're saying is there was an element of collusion?"

"Yeah," said George, "I think subconsciously that was my way of coming out. Talk about showbiz or what, that was like *The Full Monty*... If it hadn't happened I don't think I'd have been heartbroken, but I think my subconscious definitely allowed it to happen."

From sleazy alleged entrapment in a Beverly Hills toilet to a necessary psychological catharsis, it was a PR masterpiece. 'The night George showed his real asset – honesty,' read the headline in the now strangely sympathetic *Sun*.

Former Wham! manager Simon Napier-Bell has his own theory as to why the time was right for George to finally come out: "With Elton taking legal action [back in 1987] and the papers full of it every day, the public found themselves bored to death with the words 'rent boy' and 'gay'. By the time Elton had got *The Sun* to settle with him, those two words had become so overused that the public hardly noticed them any more. Ten years later, when George Michael was arrested for almost indulging himself with an LA cop, the tabloids sensed this change in public attitude."

"He was gorgeous," George told Parkinson, trying to make us understand why he'd been tempted. And to some extent he succeeded. The tabloids avoided gratuitous gay bashing and even showed him some sympathy.

In fact, one week after the Parkinson interview, George was given a standing ovation by diners in a central London restaurant just as he had in Beverly Hills. Fiona Russell Powell, who had been a contemporary of George and his clubmates in the early eighties, believes that everyone – including the singer himself – had been at least a couple of steps behind the changing public mood.

"I don't think it was as big a deal," she claims. "I don't know if you can call *Sun* readers en masse 'sophisticated', I just think we've all become a little bit more sophisticated about it. Do we get those headlines any more – '*Sun* Says – Shock Horror – Really Gay'? They report it, but it doesn't become headlines.

"I bet you George probably thinks, 'Oh, if only this had happened sooner!' Because that video was him going right out and embracing it. 'Why didn't I do that before?'"

For all her obvious empathy, when the Will Rogers Memorial scandal broke in '98, Ms Russell Powell earned herself ostracism from George's circle of friends by writing a piece in *Punch* magazine which recalled him as a young gay man on the club scene of the early eighties. Neither George himself nor the occasional fuck-buddy she identified (Brad Branson) would ever have any contact with her again.

As to George's insistence that he'd already come out to his family, it's believed that this was in the form of a letter to his parents and sisters after Anselmo had died. Ms Russell Powell and mutual friend Fat Tony are insistent that his father still didn't know by the time of George's 30th birthday, however; to muddy the waters further, George himself has been sometimes contradictory about just how much his mother knew before her death. In his interview with Kirsty Wark, he related his mother to the memorial park incident: "It wouldn't have happened if my mother had been alive. Because it was obviously my way of... it was self-destructive and angry, I think, but it was also my way of saying, 'I can't be dealing with this any more,' in terms of privacy and being quiet about my private life. And I think that, were she alive, my subconscious would never have found such a ridiculous way to do what I did. I think I would have just had to bite the bullet and tell an interviewer. But absolutely, I'm sure it wouldn't have happened with my mother in the world."

Over the course of a decade, the performer had come to regard his most startlingly scandalous moment as an unconscious cry for freedom – something that just had to happen. As to whether he ever fully came out to his late mother, in a 2008 interview with the *Good Morning America* programme on which he was asked whether his mother knew he was gay, he responded, "Oh yeah, I think so. I remember her saying to me when I was about 17, 'It must be so much easier for the parents of gay people now.' And I didn't even hear it at the time, I just thought, 'Oh God, she said the word 'gay'!' And when I look back I think, 'Oh bless her heart, she just wanted me to tell her.'"

For all its comical absurdity, the 'Outside' incident (and particularly the correspondingly camp video) was a watershed in George Michael's career. The ensuing years would witness a transformation into possibly the most 'out' gay man in showbusiness. It would be quite something to behold.

But for all the personal politics involved, the ultimate fear that his sexuality would damage his career was shown to be outmoded and outdated. Not only the tabloid media, but George himself was also shown to be way behind the modern public's mostly tolerant-to-the-point-of-indifferent attitude.

"There's no question – I told the truth and showed more of my personality than I'd ever had the courage to show before, and sold two million records!"

Sony, the corporation whose executives had previously dissed the artist as a 'limey faggot', must have been particularly pleased with sales of *Ladies & Gentlemen – The Best Of George Michael*. As, indeed, it must have been with the second supplementary single recorded for the collection – a cover of Stevie Wonder's *Songs In The Key Of Life* classic 'As', duetted with R&B queen Mary J. Blige, which went Top Five on both sides of the Atlantic.

"And I suppose from that moment till the release of *Patience*," he later reflected, "the press thought that they had not had their pound of flesh."

CHAPTER 17

Songs From A Lifetime

The end of the second millennium saw a great spate of inactivity from George Michael, which reached a kind of non-climax in 1999. It was then that his record label, Aegean, ground slowly to a halt.

In a later interview for the *Daily Mirror*, Aegean artist Toby Bourke (writer and co-singer of 'Waltz Away Dreaming') spoke of how it all ended not with a bang, but with hardly a whisper. "I hadn't heard a dickie bird from anyone on George's label for two months," Bourke retrospectively complained, "then the manager rang out of the blue and sounded really excited. I was hoping he was going to say that George was ready to get back in the studio. But instead he told me things would soon start going again – because they had feng shui'd the office."

As with many in those pre-millennial days, the spiritually minded George had a fixation on the Chinese tradition (cum superstition) of feng shui. Derived from Chinese Buddhism, the positioning of buildings and their internal contents was said to allow for the flow of positive energy between Heaven and Earth. For all his adherence to Christian icons, it was a fad that George bought into alongside New Age devotees – some of whom were, like him, profoundly stoned at the time.

It was his dope-smoking habit, according to the embittered Bourke, that put paid to Aegean Records. In fact, George was known to have sought release from his psychological addiction to the herb by hypnotherapy with stage hypnotist Paul McKenna. It proved about as successful as McKenna hypnotising UK heavyweight Frank Bruno to make him believe he could knock out Mike Tyson.

"The waste of young talent that went through Aegean was a disgrace," said Bourke. "It was almost as though George could not be bothered any more. We could do nothing without getting the okay from George, but he was too hammered to give us that okay.

"The label wasn't doing too great but George didn't seem bothered. He was too off his face to care."

It was in 1999 that Bourke received the phone message confirming that Aegean was folding. "To be honest, it was a relief," he claimed. "But it was a sad way to end. It was a good experience to be part of a bit hit single ['Waltz Away Dreaming']. But at the same time it was heartbreaking to see someone as talented as George in such a state."

Despite his obvious embitterment (at the time of the article, he was described by the *Mirror* as running "a successful telecoms business"), Bourke shared concerns with George himself about the singer's lack of productivity. While the former Aegean boss didn't blame it all on the weed, but on the emotional depression that spurred his overindulgence, he was only too aware of his own state of creative inertia.

"From my fans' point of view," he'd later admit, "I thought, 'God help them, they're going to have to wait again, because I can't come up with anything.' I personally wanted to stay afloat by having something to do, which meant learning, progress, working with Phil Ramone, singing songs that would stretch my voice."

The prolific and productive Phil Ramone is a veteran producer and sound technologist whose career stretches from Elton John and Burt Bacharach back to reputedly recording Marilyn Monroe singing 'Happy Birthday Mr President' to John Kennedy. An expatriate South African, his influence on the American music industry can be measured by how his record label was the first to record music for release on compact disc and his advancement of digital recording techniques.

In his collaboration with George Michael, however, he would hark back to some of the more traditional elements of his career. For what the Anglo-Greek singer had in mind was an album covering classic songs, with nary an original composition between them.

"I heard that people said, 'Well, he did the covers record to cover up his period of [not] writing,' or whatever," Ramone later acknowledged. "I think when you work with anybody who has any kind of tragic news – the loss of his mother, all of it – the parts that you use to come through it in the studio are what writers do."

But as the producer was well aware, that kind of creative catharsis was denied to an artist suffering from what seemed like terminal writer's block. Instead, George was putting his creative energies into his talent as an interpretive singer.

Released in late 1999, *Songs From The Last Century* was timed to coincide with the millennial mania that fuelled everything from New Age spiritual beliefs to the misplaced fear that the 'millennium bug' would shut down the world's computer systems as 1999 passed into 2000. By the time the album was picking up sales at Christmas, so the logic ran, it would be mere days away from the classic songs on the disc becoming remnants not only of another century, but of an earlier millennium.

Songs From The Last Century was released by Virgin Records on both sides of the Atlantic, the disappointingly abortive relationship with DreamWorks SKG (which had paid many millions of dollars for their short dalliance) now over. It was a cool, laid-back, jazz-tinged piece of easy listening, with a repertoire of all-time greats that spanned the decades.

'Roxanne', Sting/The Police's urgent, anguished 1978 love song to a prostitute, is rendered here as a languid piece with a down-tempo but swinging rhythm. 'The First Time Ever I Saw Your Face' is one of those songs George Michael was born to sing; taking its cue not from folk singer Peggy Seeger's original but from Roberta Flack's slower, achingly beautiful 1972 hit version. Next to this more obvious choice is an understated reading of Johny Mercer's classic 'I Remember You' – the 1962 hit version by Frank Ifield was beloved of his parents' generation, so it's disappointing that George doesn't attempt Australian crooner Ifield's yodelling. Still, it's a heartfelt number that testifies to the ability of popular music to evoke memory. (It's little surprise that George would dedicate it to his mother and Anselmo in live performance.)

George's mellow tones work their magic on quietly dramatic numbers like Johnny Mathis's impassioned 1957 film theme 'Wild Is The Wind' (also immortalised by Bowie) and U2's eerily cryptic 'Miss Sarajevo'. But the standout track of the album is 'Brother, Can You Spare a Dime?' An early thirties show tune which both epitomised and became the anthem for the Great Depression, its lyric about the suffering of working people after the Wall Street Crash was best known through versions by Al Jolson and Bing Crosby. As the most passionate of champagne socialists, George's vocal eschews its usual gentle control to end by belting out the title line like an accusation. (Today, it plays like the anthem of a world economic downturn which would arrive nearly a decade later.)

Songs From The Last Century is a remarkable album. While the covers anthology is a well-worn genre, George Michael's contribution belongs up there with the very best of them – such as Bryan Ferry's 1973 *These Foolish Things*, another collection by a contemporary pop singer in which several eras collide.

Sadly, the reviewers of the time felt differently, with dismissive headlines like '100-Year Bore' by post-Britpop critics who found it all too subtle for their liking. Airplay was limited, as was TV exposure after the effective video for 'Roxanne' (featuring real-life female sex workers and brief moments of nudity) was predictably considered unsuitable for daytime or primetime broadcast.

"I was offered the opportunity in the year before to take those standards and do a big New Year's Eve show," confirmed George, "which would have sold the album through the roof, no question. But for someone in my position, I just would have looked like an old crooner – no, I'm sorry, I would have felt like Rod Stewart: 'Well, I'll do a bit of this now.'"

Due in part perhaps to this characteristically perverse reticence, the album remains a career oddity, undervalued and underselling. Reflecting what had by now become a tradition, George declined to 'tour the album'. Instead, in the early noughties he joined the bill for a major US music-industry consciousness-raiser at which he was the main attraction – though he still managed to berate the audience for not buying his last two albums.

Equality Rocks took place on April 29, 2000 – the day after the Millennium March on Washington DC, to promote equal rights for the LGBT community and protest against anti-gay violence. Topping a bill at Washington's Robert F. Kennedy Stadium which also included k.d. Lang and Melissa Etheridge, George's off-the-cuff greeting to the audience was, "A sports stadium full of queers? Fucking brilliant!" To echo an old joke, he was now so far out of the closet that he'd forgotten what a coat-hanger looked like.

Performing a set based around his most danceable hits, George took a brief interlude for an informational documentary film about dubious religious or psychiatric movements that claim to 'cure' gay teenagers. Returning to the stage to resume the tunes, George duetted on 'Freedom 90' with a most unlikely partner – Garth Brooks, the Stetson-wearing, hetero New Country star who was happy to lend his support and have George wrap a brotherly arm around him. Also sharing his stage and his arm was Geri Halliwell, the ex-Spice Girl, also straight but espousing gay causes like the trendy little fag hag she'd become.

Other musical collaborations of the time included a duet with Whitney Houston – whose own wild lifestyle and drug habits were soon to become public knowledge – on her single 'If I Told You', a 1998 album track re-recorded to flesh out her greatest hits collection. It first made the charts on both sides of the Atlantic in mid-May, three weeks before George appeared at a charity fundraiser organised by opera singer Luciano Pavarotti in his hometown of Modena, Italy. With a bill featuring the temporarily reformed Eurythmics, the musical line-up raised funds for children in the Far Eastern poverty black holes of Tibet and Cambodia.

But the name 'George Michael' was now almost synonymous with gay causes and the gay lifestyle, neither of which could be used by the press as a stick to beat him with any more. "They had to go along with it at the time: basically, 'Good old George,' and, 'Now you're out and isn't it wonderful – blah blah blah blah blah, we're so accepting,'" he'd reflect, perhaps with the slightest touch of paranoia. "But privately, these people who make it their *life's work* to upset people they feel are too privileged were like, 'Fuck, what is going to stick to this kid?' And then of course I went, 'Well, why don't you try *THIS?*'"

It was during this period that George Michael's musical output seemed to slow to a virtual stop – though his writing and recording throughout the period appear to have been fairly constant, little of it saw release till much later. As he himself so witheringly put it, he is not a Prince figure who sees his every outtake as worthy of release to CD.

Apart from that, relatively little was seen of the performer in the period spanning from mid-2000 till early 2002. From what can now be gleaned of his personal life, much of this time may have been spent wallowing in a luxurious miasma of chemical and sexual indulgence. That's certainly the impression one gets from the March 2002 single release 'Freeek!' – "I'll be your sexual freak of the week," promises naughty George in a hard-edged return to electro-funk. Littered with samples from earlier dance hits by various other artists, the song draws an analogy between the instant hit of drug-taking and internet culture, with its references to shooting up and online connections.

Suggestively giving the come-on to all and sundry, 'Freeek!' proved a welcome return to the Top 10 in the UK and on the Continent – although, for unspecified reasons, it wasn't released to the US market. Its lurid video, directed with full visual overkill by Texan promo maker Joseph Kahn, would be among the most expensive ever made at a budget of $2 million. Set in a science fiction metropolis reminiscent of

Blade Runner, its moments of semi-nudity and suggestions of fetishism ensured a limited broadcast. While George and the other (mainly female) cast members were dressed in a variety of skintight rubber superhero costumes and the CGI effects reflected what was going on in Hollywood cinema at the time, the rubbery nipples on George's lobster-red cyberpunk/X-Men suit were more suggestive of S&M than Marvel Comics.

Ironically perhaps, it would be George's return to making records rather than any personal vices that drew him back into unwanted controversy. His sin in this instance would be to use a pop star's shorthand vernacular to try to comment on current affairs.

What he failed to take into account was that the rules of the game had changed: on September 11, 2001, the atrocities signified by the term '9/11' had occurred; a murderous underground faction of Islamists (politically motivated Muslim radicals) had declared war on the West due to its allegiances with Israel and the Saudi oil sheiks. The infamous tally of that day was almost three thousand dead in hijacked plane attacks on the World Trade Center and the Pentagon.

The shockwaves were seismic. The revulsion was almost universal (though not in the Islamic world, where reactions varied greatly). As was expected of the world's last remaining superpower, America gathered up her military might quickly. First she instigated the invasion of Afghanistan, where ruling Islamists granted a haven to the cabal the West now called Al-Qaeda; then the 'War On Terror' began to open up a second front, when President George W. Bush let it be known that he was considering an invasion of Iraq, due to ruling despot Saddam Hussein's failure to offer up his reputed weapons of mass destruction.

As with the Afghan invasion, the mooted Iraqi adventure had the support of George Michael's one-time great political hope, Prime Minister Blair; unlike in Afghanistan, the murderous Saddam had no apparent links with the 9/11 plotters and had in fact been the target of a *fatwa* (Islamic death warrant) by Osama bin Laden.

Despite the USA's major country hit of 2001 asking, "Where were you when the world stopped turning that dark September day?", these were not times when the wisdoms (or platitudes) of pop stars were overly valued. As George would recall: "What was naïve about it was the timing. I genuinely believed that people were more concerned about it than they were already, you see. That's the thing about being a politician, you have to understand timing. If you are one of the earliest messengers of doom, people can react the wrong way.

"I wrote a song in the year 2000 about the fact that I thought it was very uncomfortable that our leader was so friendly with a born-again Christian at the moment when fundamentalism was the most dangerous thing on the planet. I had no idea what was going to happen; I had no idea that Tony Blair would make me look so astute over the next five years, but I really did something that was initially done to make no impression at all outside my fans, because it was just about a possibility, that was the thing.

"And actually, on the last day of recording 'Shoot The Dog', the planes hit the towers. It was so ridiculous, I just suddenly thought, 'Oh my God, this obviously can't come out now, it will be too offensive.' But then, a year later, when there was still some question about whether Tony would go ahead [in committing British troops to the invasion of Iraq], I had to go for it. I had to do something, because I was just eaten up with guilt that I had an opportunity to speak out and I wasn't taking it."

The title of 'Shoot The Dog' has a rather obscure origin, but is reputed to derive from *Wag The Dog* – the Clinton-era Hollywood black comedy about White House PR people who invent a fictional war in order to cover up a presidential sex scandal. In that instance, the title evoked 'the tail wagging the dog', i.e. the arse-end taking over the whole body politic. In the case of the George Michael song, it seemed that devious politicking and manipulation was fucking over everyone.

Or at least that's what it *seems* to be, as the song itself says very little. It's ironic, but the event that came closest to ending George Michael's career was a manufactured controversy that came from outside of the singer himself. In producing a video for 'Shoot The

Dog' – which, as a piece of music, is one of his more lightweight dance numbers – he elicited the services of the producers of *2DTV*, a knockabout satirical TV show. In the tradition of the rubber puppet show *Spitting Image*, the UK ITV network's *2DTV* used computer-enhanced animation to parody politicians, public figures and celebrities as cartoon grotesques.

The supposedly controversial elements of 'Shoot The Dog' arose entirely from the video on the song's late August 2002 release. By this time, the rumblings of war emanating from the US presidency had been heard since earlier in the year. (An insider's account of the 9/11 aftermath in the White House later described how the inner circle of the Bush administration decided Saddam was somehow involved in the attacks as far back as mid-September 2001.)

As for the song's rather less outrageous lyrical content, George later found himself coming to its defence in his 2004 interview with Kirsty Wark:

So you've been to the [Blair] house for dinner and then you have this cartoon where Cherie says, "Tony, are you horny?"

"It says, "Tony, Tony, Tony, I know that you're horny, but there's something 'bout that Bush ain't right." Which is a bit naughty really. But I did actually understand the concept that people would be scared to talk about it in some ways, which was why I used humour. I really didn't create anything too controversial, I think it was absolutely necessary to make it look controversial to shut a lot of people up."

You must have known of course that it would go down like a lead balloon in America?

"I knew it, but I was naïve. I just thought there were more people with their eyes open than there were, and of course now the majority of people have their eyes open [due to the admission that no weapons of mass destruction were found]. I don't think I'll be doing that again in a hurry for the simple reason that you have to be the right man for the job. You have to be somebody that your average male journalist doesn't want to jump up and down on [laughs] from a great height, you know."

'Shoot The Dog' was only the second single CD release of an original George Michael song since 'You Have Been Loved', five years earlier. It would prove to be the most controversial moment of his career, going wildly beyond its creator's rather milder expectations and taking him way outside of his comfort zone.

The animated video showed a guided missile hitting the Blair bedroom just at the point when Cherie is refusing Tony sex. In his regular *2DTV* depiction as an infantile idiot savant, George Bush rides the missile in a phallic *Dr Strangelove*-style and his pre-coitus interruptus of the Blairs was taken by many an offended American patriot to infer their president was having gay sex with the British prime minister. In fact the action is not so clear-cut, but the caricatures are so sexualised that anything could be going on.[*]

Next to all this, the song itself is a rather inconsequential dance tune with its most memorable moments sampled from 'Love Action (I Believe In Love)' by The Human League – an electro tune that topped the charts at the time that Wham! were just about hitting the dance floors of suburban London. But in the minds of many, 'Shoot The Dog' equated with the wacky video, not the song.

On the home front, criticism came from the man who, with the decline of the record industry, was starting to epitomise pop music to the general public. "I don't think that someone like George should necessarily be making political records," pronounced Simon Cowell, the impresario who began the *Pop Idol* and *X-Factor* TV franchises. "He obviously was going to offend Americans when Americans have made him a lot of money. I mean, that was a *brave* thing to do and I thought a stupid thing to do. He's going to have to eat a lot of humble pie – and so he should."

Under the influence of Cowell and his corporate partners, mainstream pop music would be reduced to karaoke, with the biggest 'stars'

---

[*] For all the charges of self-righteousness against him at the time, George was a good sport when it came to satirising his own sexuality. His own cartoon caricature is seen strutting campily out of the White House restrooms.

being those nearest to note-perfect on the cover versions assigned to them. It was a phenomenon that was supposedly anathema to George Michael and yet one from which he could not entirely divorce himself. Mainstream pop was his arena, after all, and the coming years would witness an uneasy relationship with the whole *Pop Idol* phenomenon.

Less close to home were the snipes from the musician who briefly epitomised cool in the Britpop era. "This is the guy that hid who he actually was from the public for 20 years, now all of a sudden he's got something to say about the way of the world," sneered Oasis guitarist and songwriter Noel Gallagher. "I find it fucking laughable! That's before you get to the song, which is diabolical."

In this instance, George felt compelled to defend himself when the Mancunian monobrow's comment was brought up in an interview. "I think that's a laughable statement," he simultaneously grinned and grimaced. "What, the fact that I didn't want to share my sexuality with the world, in this current media atmosphere, means that I have no right to talk about politics? This is not an intelligent man. This is not someone you should throw quotes at me from really."[*]

Ex-Wham! singer Pepsi was one of the few to step up to the bat to defend him, though few were listening "George is in a position to use his credibility to voice his opinions," she protested, "and his opinions are those of many people – not *everybody's*." This may have been something of an understatement.

There was a tense six-and-a-half-month countdown to war between the release of 'Shoot The Dog' and the invasion of Iraq by a 'coalition of the willing' (principally the USA backed by the UK) on March 20, 2003. In the run-up, George was offered a sympathetic platform via an interview in the *Daily Mirror*: 'George goes to war on The War,' ran

---

[*] "I respect George Michael, I really fucking do," Gallagher would protest four years later, before launching an attack on the singer's more reckless behaviour of the time. In the interim Gallagher, by then approaching 40, admitted that he'd managed to read a book for the first time in his life.

the headline. 'WORLD EXCLUSIVE: "It's the most dangerous time of our lives… being silent is not an option."'

The *Mirror*'s bigger-selling tabloid competitor, *The Sun*, had already gone in for the kill. Part of the News International stable belonging to conservative Australian media mogul Rupert Murdoch – proprietor of Fox News in the US – it knew how to potentially wound.

'COWARD – George refuses to release his anti-US "protest" song in States', ran *The Sun*, accurately reporting that there were no plans for 'Shoot The Dog' to be an American single release. 'POP PERV'S 9/11 SLUR – George Michael mocks Bush,' accused US sister paper the *New York Post*.

"U.S. CALLERS JEER AT GEORGE ON LIVE TV,' reported *The Sun* back in the UK, telling of how a phone interview with the CNN news channel, intended as a form of damage limitation, had drawn boos from the US audience and outraged phone calls. "By portraying [Bush] going to bed with your Prime Minister," accused Leah from Florida, equating the song with the video, "you slam our country. You can talk about your own family, but I'll be danged if I let anyone step in from the outside and talk about them." Leah seemed oblivious to how the US was about to step in from the outside and invade a country which – according to George and like-minded commentators – posed her no threat.

The Sun piece continued, "Gay George – arrested in 1998 for fondling himself in an LA toilet…" and the US tabloids followed suit: "GEORGE A GONER – George Michael's 'Shoot The Dog' has passed cleanly from the pan, navigated the pan and is now floating somewhere in the sewer"; "WHAM! That's the sound of pop star George Michael driving the final nail into the coffin of his sagging career by releasing a song that mocks President Bush… He should stick to what he knows best – perving in public restrooms"; "RIP GEORGE MICHAEL'S CAREER: 1982 – 2002," ran another heading, with George's eyes, nose and goateed mouth from the cover of the *Older* album Photoshopped to look almost as Arabic as those of bin Laden.

"After 'Shoot The Dog' and the kicking he had off the back of that in media terms, he was very down," manager Andy Stephens would understatedly observe. George himself saw it in rather more vociferous terms.

"Basically, Murdoch was getting his way," he said of the media mogul he by now saw as his nemesis and persecutor. "That was *massively* depressing to me. I got a bunch of homophobia that had been reserved for me since – as far as I'm concerned – I escaped the clutches of the press in LA, and it floored me. It was ironic, but the thing that floored me – for the first time ever really, in terms of the press – had nothing to do with my private life."

George's feelings of very personal enmity with Murdoch may have been fuelled by both a very real awareness of the media tycoon's influence and by a heavy dope smoker's paranoia. But there was no doubt that, for a while, it was open season on the singer.

In the couple of weeks before the single's release, the London *Evening Standard* ran a piece by a middle-aged journalist named Geoffrey Wansell, dramatically entitled 'The Fall Of George'. Based on little more than glimpses of George walking on Hampstead Heath, the subheading felt able to announce, "George Michael set out to shock with his latest single. By doing so, the rock superstar may just have committed professional suicide." What was remarkable was the fact that Wansell had published his 'official biography' of serial sex killer Fred West just two years previously; now, after wading through the deeds of the most callously sadistic criminal in modern British history, he could profess himself shocked by the wacky antics of a 'rock superstar' (sic).

"I think, at that moment in time, I and others close to him felt it could really be all over," Andy Stephens conceded. "He bounced back, but it was close. Very close."

The impetus for keeping his head above the tide of negative press seemed to come from his own sense of defiance. In late February 2003, the US and UK governments insisted that Saddam immediately comply with the United Nations resolution that he should give up his weapons of mass destruction (WMD) or else face imminent invasion; UN weapons inspectors countered that they had found no evidence of WMD on their visits to Iraq, but were politically ignored. Everyone knew that the Iraq War was about to commence in the following month.

It was at this point that George Michael decided to put himself back in the firing line by appearing on the BBC News 24 show *HardTalk*, to face a grilling by anchorman Tim Sebastian. With all the vehemence of a man who'd been under attack for a sustained period, he gave a pretty good account of himself:

Why Iraq? Because it's fashionable?
"Oh God, no. I've got absolutely no desire to be here today, I'm really reluctant to be here – in all honesty, because I was first out the trenches in terms of entertainers who were going to get behind something which, at the time, was so divisive. If you're approaching a subject that's as divisive as Iraq was six or eight months ago, then you're taking a big risk as an entertainer. Because you're going to alienate a lot of people, and I did, very quickly, and I was completely pilloried really for having the audacity to be a pop star who's in the mainstream – as opposed to a rock star or some kind of protest singer…"
Tell me what you're so scared about in Iraq.
"I'm not scared about Iraq. I'm scared about Mr Blair and his attitude to the future. I think we're at a watershed moment. September 11 was the first part of this watershed moment and this is the tail-end of it. September 11 was so obviously directed at America to provoke a response and the response was supposed to be revenge. We've spent something close to, what is it now, 18 months trying to prevent that kneejerk reaction, and if all that was is delay then what's the point?"
But there wasn't a kneejerk reaction, was there? There has been a properly considered reaction, consultation all around the world, hasn't there?
"Has there? I don't see any consultation. I see a lot of bullying. Do you hear them saying anything other than, "It's the terrorists or

us"? ... 91% yesterday said that without the UN they don't want to go in. Do you not think that that's close to unanimous?"

You said, "I'm still a believer in Tony Blair, I found him to be a charming and decent man." At what point did you lose faith?

"Well if I'm really honest, I've lost faith in the last five days."

This was three days ago.

"But on Sunday I was trying not to come across as too wound up, in all honesty, and what happened was I was quite polite and nobody reported anything, which is not what I'm here for. So today I'm speaking my mind a little bit more than what I did at nine o'clock on Sunday morning.

"I'll be honest – I've been very distressed by Mr Blair's behaviour for several years in terms of how I think he's removed the idealism from politics, by taking a supposedly left-of-centre party and calling it Labour, or New Labour, and saying, 'We have to be pragmatic,' in these overly consumerist times."

He also said we have to have an ethical foreign policy, didn't he?

"Absolutely, and this is not ethical, is it? This is a Christian country, with a supposedly Christian leader, who somehow thinks the answer to the future is pre-emptive action. Now to me pre-emptive action is every bit as dangerous as the initial concept of creating the atomic bomb. And by the way, that was created for the same deterrent purposes by the same nation, and I do not believe that this is any more safe than that."

So you've lost faith in him, have you?

"Well, until last week I thought that it was bluff, I really did. I thought, he's trying to keep the pressure up until the last moment. But he's making so many damaging statements..."

Are you writing him off or...?

"If I was writing him off I wouldn't be here. If I thought that man wasn't listening to anybody, I wouldn't be here."

You wouldn't vote for him?

"No, I'd never vote for him again, never. He's gone beyond the bluff, he's bullying the UN on behalf of Bush."

Bullying? Or persuading, you might say.

"[Exhales] I'd say bullying. You cannot ignore statements like, 'The UN needs to prove its relevance.' You cannot ignore the fact that America can say, "You either agree with us or you're irrelevant.""*

What kind of Prime Minister do you want, if you don't want a man who leads on his convictions?

"I want somebody who leads on his convictions until the point that 90% of the public disagree with him."

That's the hard time, but that's what he's paid for, isn't it? To take hard decisions, not to be a populist...

"No, you're not paid to put people's lives in danger and ignore their opinion on that very subject. No one's paid to do that."

He says: "Failure to act will lead not to peace but to a bloodier conflict in the future." That's what he says.

"I'll take the future compared to right now. Because – absolutely, we know the dangers of Saddam Hussein, we know that we can't afford to leave him alone. Why have we left him alone for 12 years, why did we leave him there and now, at the point when Sharon is bombing the West Bank, we're going to take on Saddam?"

So they gave diplomacy a chance for 12 years? Even you have to admit 12 years is long enough, isn't it?

"Absolutely, I have no sympathy for Saddam Hussein. He should be gone, we need him gone in order to stabilise the region, but you cannot do this at the moment when the entire fundamentalist terrorist network around the world is *waiting* for this to legitimise what they want to do."

---

* As with many liberals, George was quick to cite the authority of the UN, for all its very flawed record in terms of peacekeeping in war zones. As was also often the case, he was less keen on upholding the UN's absolutist 1971 resolution on drugs; the organisation continued to threaten expulsion to any nation that might dare to legalise cannabis.

How do you think you've contributed to the debate on Iraq? 'Shoot The Dog' makes Bush and Blair out to be fools and has been described as rather a vicious attack by some people.

"It's called satire – and by the way, satire from exactly the same people who show exactly the same stuff, with exactly the same animation and exactly the same character references every Saturday on ITV at 10.30."

But you wanted a serious debate – how does that kind of thing contribute?

"That's what I'm here for now. Eight or nine months ago, we're talking about a generation that has so little desire for politics in its music that if I knew I was going to be ahead of the game and try to get people to discuss this, I had to do it with some humour. And sure enough, even the humour at that stage in time was something that people did not want to hear about. Now that they're deluged with it, it's okay. I can come out here and I'm relatively safe. At that point in time, I wanted to make the statements as broadly and as funnily as I could in the video, to make sure that before people were too freaked out to talk, they'd laugh their way into it…

"I don't know how closely you were watching popular culture at that time, but I think I dragged that argument into the mainstream, out of the political chattering classes, whatever you would call them, two or three weeks before it was going to get there. And I would say at this point in time, when we're supposedly in such a bloody rush, that those two or three weeks were worth what I put up with, worth losing the record, no one playing the record, no one playing the video, it was worth it because when I was attacked for doing it, it came into the mainstream. And that's why I'm here today…"

What worries you about the New York Post?

"What shouldn't worry me about the *New York Post*? It's a fascist newspaper."

[Quotes] "A washed-up pervert."

"Well, why should I worry about that? Really, I don't worry about the *Daily Star*, I don't worry about the *Sport*, I don't worry about *The Sun* or the *Mirror*, why would I worry about that? I do find it absolutely unbelievable that they're able to call a homosexual man a 'pervert' for having been caught cruising, I do find it quite laughable that that is not sue-able…"

What do you want Saddam to do? What do you think should be done with Saddam? He's made it clear now he isn't going to disarm, he won't get rid of the missiles. Just talk with him?

"No, not with Saddam — Saddam has to be dealt with in the way that Saddam has to be dealt with. But not *now* — not until there's some effort shown in Palestine, because otherwise…"

Why are you linking the two together?

"They're not linked, but every terrorist in the world, who is an Islamic fundamentalist terrorist, links those two things. Would you agree with that?"

A lot do — but that doesn't make it right.

"Of course it doesn't, but this isn't about right and wrong. This is what makes it such a dangerous situation…"

Make you feel better if the UN had a second resolution authorising force?

"Slightly, but I feel that most people who voted against Mr Blair on this issue are not voting really on whether it's right for us to kill innocent people in Iraq… I think they're also saying we did not vote for this war in our backyard, we did not do anything to deserve it… I do not feel that Americans have the same point of view — I think that they have been attacked, they feel frightened, they understandably want a strong leader, they're not anywhere near as informed by their media as we are, and I honestly think that the majority of British people have no idea what we're doing here, on our own, with the Americans…"

What are the lessons for you from this protest? Is this a one-off as far as you're concerned?

"Absolutely. The only other thing I would put my neck on the line for…"

George Michael's going to stop caring and go back to the business?

"Well no, I think the only thing I can see myself going this far out on a limb for again is Clause 28. I would probably go that far for Clause 28."

On homosexuals teaching?

"Well, it's not just teaching, it's all kinds of things. As it stands, I can still be arrested just walking down the street holding my boyfriend's hand. I mean, it would never happen, but it's one of the ridiculous things that's in there. And I think it's time for gay couples – I have no particular views on marriage because I have no desire to ape heterosexual relationships, but I think it's time that people who live together their entire lives had the rights of spouses. The idea that if anything happened to myself or Kenny, the idea that our families would have all the rights and we would have none is just ridiculous."

At the end of the show the formerly sceptical Sebastian thanked George warmly. "Cheers," said the singer, leaning forward to shake his hand.

A more direct protest against the war was made at the end of the month, when the singer performed Don McLean's starkly melancholy depiction of trench warfare, 'The Grave' (from his bestselling 1970 *American Pie* album), on MTV Europe, the BBC's *Top Of The Pops* and Channel 4's *Graham Norton Show*. The McLean original opened hauntingly a cappella, but George sang plaintively backed by acoustic guitar. The lyrical lament for "a man barely 20" who answered the call "when the wars of our nations did beckon" evoked World War One, despite its Vietnam protest origins; but the image of the doomed youth who clings to the earth and effectively digs his own grave remained a timeless pacifist sentiment.

As the coalition of the willing went to war in March 2003, much of what the pop singer had claimed would happen in his strongly argued (if diffusely reasoned) interview came to pass. Innocent children were pinned under burning masonry as the allies attacked; Islamic fundamentalism became more prevalent, rather than less, in a nation where religious extremists had previously been reined in by an all-powerful dictator;

while the war was officially declared over by President Bush within six weeks, terrorist atrocities by 'insurgents' became such a regular event that they were sometimes barely reported in the western press. As George had also predicted, on July 7, 2005, four British Islamists would use Iraq as one of their rationales for a suicide attack on the London Underground travel network, leaving 52 dead and many more maimed.

As George articulated in his interview with Kirsty Wark: "I don't doubt for a moment that the vast number of Iraqis want this thing to work. Whether or not it will is another question entirely. And I think that they're locked into a dreadful, dreadful situation and it will be constantly a matter of trying to keep civil war at bay. And I think as long as that's going on, I'm just horrified [face in hands] by the number of speeches that ignore the amount of Iraqi loss and talk about terrorists as though there's a massive difference between blowing somebody up from a car 20 yards from them and dropping a bomb on them from a great height."

It's motive, isn't it?
"Well, the real difference is that one is an elected party and one is not. But ultimately it just breeds terrorism and death. Every time they kill an Iraqi civilian or soldier, they create a family at least one member of who will probably be prepared to die to avenge that death."
What did you think when the London bombings happened then?
"Well again, I think the media very cleverly tried to downplay what was actually being said, that very disturbing message from that guy with a northern accent, the one that was sent back [on] the tape about the bombings. What he was really trying to say – but unfortunately the rhetoric of it was a little dignified – was that we had been spared the bombing until the point when we voted Tony back in again."
But there's no justification for that.
"Oh no, there's no justification…"
But you understand what is happening?

"I think killing is killing, an absolute sin, and outside of very definite situations I think what we did in Iraq was absolutely terrible. I don't have any sympathy with anyone who straps explosives to themselves and kills total strangers, no, it's a horrific, dreadful crime. But to me the obvious dynamic is that the longer this war, or rather this 'insurgency', goes on in Iraq, the more bombs, the more suicide bombers, every day that passes you create new terrorists."

History may, of course, take a longer-term view. Despite the squeamishness of George and other like-minded people with regard to toppling Saddam, the fugitive despot was tracked down by the Americans and swiftly dealt with by the Iraqis, who hanged him for crimes against his own people. In the present day the violence in Iraq, while not entirely subsided, seems to be under control, with various Muslim sects seeking to work together to make their post-war nation succeed.

In the immediate aftermath of the war, however, there was no doubt in Elton John's mind, for instance, as to who had been right all along. "They're being told now, the American people, 'There were no weapons of mass destruction, the information we had was wrong.' But George said that 18 months ago."

Of course, little of this directly pertained to a very slight song entitled 'Shoot The Dog'. The record had shown George Michael's limitations as a writer of political lyrics, just as his interviews on the subject had shown his views to be heartfelt and reflective, if a little scattershot.

'Praying For Time' has been cited as an earlier (and much more successful) example of his political songwriting, but in truth that song adopts an entirely personal standpoint. It is an elliptical view "from behind the door" of an extremely privileged man, who despairs of the power to do anything positive about the world he lives in.

Interestingly, George himself would arrive at the view that his own reaction against the Iraq War had more to do with his internal psyche than any objective assessment of world affairs.

"There is something that I now understand, having been I think on a bit more of an even keel mentally," he told the interviewer in his

2005 bio-doc. "I think that I was suffering to a degree from that kind of syndrome that happens to people when they go through something as traumatic as bereavement. My fear, in terms of what the next blow in life may be, attached itself I think to my fears about the world in general."

To George, it was the personal that remained truly political.

★★★

'Shoot The Dog' was the second previewed track of the next fully original George Michael album, which would not see its much delayed release until a full year after the allied invasion force went into Iraq. "I came up to London [having recently bought another home in the West Country] and moved back into the house where I had written the first three solo albums," he explained of its origins. "It was the house [in Hampstead], incidentally, where my mother cleaned every week and the house I most associate with her, in my adult life anyway. And I got back in there and started to write.

"I can't think of any better way of putting it: I felt like God gave me my ball back. Whoever my God is said, 'Whatever the lessons you are supposed to translate back into your music are, whatever the painful lessons are, they're over for the moment at least.'"

With all the sniping and shooting over (at least metaphorically speaking), the singer was able to return to some of the quieter causes that had gained his sympathy. In October 2003 he lined up with other celebrities for the Rainbow Trust charity, in its campaign to raise £20 million for terminally ill children; as George said at the time, "Loss is such an incredibly difficult thing. I bow down to people who actually have to deal with the loss of a child."

In the closing days of the year, he partnered up with former Boyzone boy-band singer Ronan Keating for a Christmas celebrity edition of ITV's *Who Wants To Be A Millionaire?* The personal sadness George and Ronan shared in common was that both had lost their mothers to cancer; in George's case, his share of any winnings would be donated to the nurses of the Macmillan Cancer Trust, "to say thank you for looking after my mum". In the event, sister Yioda saved the day in a 'Phone a Friend' moment by correctly identifying the title of Tim Rice's autobiography. (George and Ronan walked away with £32,000 to split for their respective charities; if not for Yioda, the show might have lived down to its popular soubriquet of 'Who Wants To Win 16 Grand?')

In early March 2004, *Patience*, as the new album was ultimately (and very aptly) christened, took a number of further sidesteps into the areas of loungecore and electronica that George's last original album (a full *eight* years previously) had hinted at.

There was no 'thank you for waiting' dedication on the album's sleeve, as it was already inherent in the title, while the cover showed George at home with the stoner's best friend (his couch). Alongside the multi-instrumentalist composer/producer doubling up on keyboards, guitars, bass and drum programming ran credits for Johnny Douglas and James Jackman on keyboards and programming, plus engineer Niall Flynn. Alongside this 'A-team', additional credits also ran for keyboardists Ruadhri Cushnan, Chris Cameron, Pete Gleadall and old matey David Austin, guitarists Phil Palmer and Michael Brown, Wurlitzer organist Luke Smith, bassist Graham Silbiger and orchestrator David Arnold.[*]

The years of contemplative (and herbally assisted) moodiness had born some very interesting musical fruit, validating George's recent claim that Pink Floyd were up there among his major musical influences, alongside Elton John and Stevie Wonder.

'John And Elvis Are Dead' is a songwriting collaboration with David Austin, a stoned slouch with electronic choral backing vocals. It's a lyrical anecdote about a friend who awakes from a coma to find that the girls all look the same and youth culture, as he knew it, has vanished. "If

---

[*] Hippy the dog was credited with 'panting' on 'Shoot The Dog', while keyboardist Cameron was said to be playing a piano formerly the property of John Lennon – specifically the keyboard at which he wrote 'Imagine', which George had paid a cool £1 million to purchase.

Jesus Christ is alive and well," he rather confusingly asks of the modern world, "then how come John and (Marvin and) Elvis are dead?"

'Through' is more atmospheric, a piece of folk-ish musing which expressed fear about the fickle loyalties of an audience (rather unfairly, considering how long some of them had waited for this). Beginning with an electronic soundscape before slipping into a more acoustic folk mode, its emotionally insecure lyric promised, "They may take away the things I work for, but you pull me through, babe." Beneath all the emotional turmoil, it suggested, his long-term relationship with Kenny Goss was keeping him sane.

It was recorded at a time when George had already commissioned a film crew to make *George Michael: A Different Life*, his part-confessional/ part self-laudatory bio-documentary. One of the main onscreen enthusiasts for the singer's new material was his now middle-aged and balding ex-musical partner. "If Wham! were still around today," joked Andrew Ridgeley in a mock-Yorkshire accent, "that's what I'd like 'em to be doing. But I think it's much more than that," he demurred, "because I think it's a song that's really quite euphoric, but it's also tinged with bits of...'

"Bumming," interjected a laughing George, reluctant to submit to serious analysis by his former playmate.

'Round Here' is the now celebrated bittersweet reflection on the composer's origins – from 1957, when his mother "had a real bad start to the game" to the days of Bushey Meads School, when "we two [had] other plans". Gentle and dreamy, it makes biographical sense of the songwriter's life without imposing any grand statement or drama upon it.

Of an altogether bluer biographical tone, 'My Mother Had A Brother' was the album's quiet bombshell. When coaxed back out on the road over the next several years, George would explain the subject to a very vocal and adoring (and mostly female) audience: "My uncle Colin, who I didn't know anything about until I was 16 years old, killed himself and my mother never felt it appropriate to tell me. When I asked her why he killed himself, she told me that it was almost certainly because he was gay, although he never actually had come out to anyone. [*At this point, there were hysterical screams from early middle-aged women in the audience. George must retrospectively rue the times when he or his management feared his sexuality might have lost him his fan base.*]

"And it made me understand parts of my childhood a little better when I heard this, but more than anything the fact that this poor man killed himself a few years before things really changed – the 'swinging sixties', whatever – and changed for the better for people like me and him. But unfortunately he wasn't around to see it." [*This comment was met with mass applause and screams of "We love you, George!"*]

'My Mother Had A Brother' is one of the more atmospherically dramatic numbers in the Michael songbook. Singing of his uncle who was "oversensitive and kind", he articulates his belief that this secret family tragedy occurred on the day he was born in June 1963. "Oh mother, will you tell him of my joy?" he implores to the deceased Lesley, in the firm belief that her surviving spirit has communed with that of her suffering brother. It poetically articulates her fear that her son may have inherited his suicidal uncle's 'gay gene', and speaks volumes about why he chose to stay in the closet for so many years – even if, in her heart, his mother knew all along. As he would admit several years on, at the time of his next major tour: "It changed my opinion of her entirely because it wasn't just that – she'd also seen her own father die the same way. They'd both put their heads in the gas oven. And, lucky old Mum, she found both of them. She spent years being so remorseful that it's impossible to hold that time against her. And in the last 20 years of her life, I don't think we had a crossed word actually."

As to the question of whether he'd ever fully told either of his parents about his sexuality, he now told *Gay Times* that the death of Anselmo Feleppa had been the final catalyst: "I wrote them a four-page letter which was the easiest thing I've ever written considering it was the only unresolved issue – to come out to my parents. My mum said it was the most beautiful letter she had ever read, that it explained completely how I felt and why she didn't have to worry about me. It was the easiest thing that should have been the most difficult. I should ask my dad to show it to me again."

271

Patience is the performer's most personal collection to date. 'Please Send Me Someone' is a piece of airy soft funk subtitled 'Anselmo's Song'; rather than being another tribute to his late lover, it implores him as a kind of guardian angel to provide a replacement partner ("send me someone just to hold me now that you're gone"). 'American Angel' is the other side of that equation; even more laid-back and ethereal, it celebrates Kenny, "my US of Angel", and begs him not to leave ("I don't think that I could love and lose again").

"Whatever the record sells," opined George, "I believe that I didn't let myself down and I didn't let the people who were waiting for me down. And that really was the point of all my anxiety in the recording studio over the last four or five years."

But Andy Stephens wasn't about to let his artist off the hook quite so easily. The album needed to be sold, peddled, promoted to the public, to avoid the fate of another *Songs From The Last Century*. "George has always taken an almost entirely different view on that in the respect that less is more and even less is even more," he diplomatically observed. "I don't think George was very comfortable – I *know* he wasn't comfortable doing it. But it worked, my God it worked."

In the *A Different Life* bio-doc, *Patience* is seen rising to the top of the international *Billboard* charts in most territories. Riding up the Sunset Strip in Hollywood for a CD signing at a store, George and Kenny note a big billboard for the then up-and-coming Michael Bublé. "You do look a bit like him actually," George concedes to Kenny, "only without the voice or the talent." (Ooh, the *bitch!*)

To the interviewer off-camera, George describes the promotional process: "It's been like pulling teeth actually, some of the promotion in Europe that I haven't done for... phh, the best part of 20 years, I think, some of those countries. Some of it was beyond belief, it was so soul-destroying. But I know the way it works now, you can't really rely on the quality of your music at all now in what you do, and you have to give a piece of music a certain amount of television coverage or you're just not going to sell records.

"So I'm trying to tread the thin line between adapting to the modern world of media and compromising myself. The general lack of compassion and humanity on television terrifies me in the way that tabloid sensationalism used to. But at the same time, it won't kill me."

Unlike the overearnest young superstar of the late eighties, George could now afford to laugh at himself. Setting up for some promo filming, he asked the crew, "Have I got time for a wank?"

The man who, in the words of his manager, "really hates cameras" was shown in front of a whole phalanx of them. "Funnily enough," claimed George, "in the last year I'm just starting to become comfortable with the way I look – which is really fucking disastrous, isn't it? What's the point in discovering that you look okay when you're 41? You know what I mean?"

It seems so incongruous, to be a superstar and yet stricken by self-consciousness. But George seemed to be handling the promo treadmill better, as witnessed by the film crew in tow for the documentary. It would put *Patience* at number one in the UK and in various continental countries. (In the US, where it seemed he still hadn't been forgiven, it would peak at number 12 – and then only after George conceded to promote the record by going on *Oprah*.)

Most incongruous of all, however, was the record label promoting and distributing the album – Sony BMG, a subsidiary of the corporation which the performer had sunk many months of his life and literally millions of dollars into escaping from. He was well aware of the irony; but then, what George (and any other savvy pro performer) had discovered over the last several years was that the record industry, as he'd known it ever since leaving school, was rapidly ceasing to exist.

His disappointment with both DreamWorks and Virgin aside, there was little point in searching for a fresh new label if it was going to be fighting the same losing battle against the advance of Napster, or any of the less reputable musical download sites. He'd signed his prodigal son deal with Sony in the November of 2003, the previous year; but it would be a one-off this time, as the singer had his own ideas about how to properly approach the meltdown in the music industry.

In late April 2004, towards the end of his promotional itinerary, George was presented with an award by the Radio Academy in London for Most Played Artist on British radio. He was well aware of the favouritism he'd been shown by DJ and public alike. "I've only made six albums in 22 years so I don't know how this happened," he happily conceded, "I'm the luckiest writer on earth."

Running in an honourable second and third position were his old friend Elton John and relative new boy Robbie Williams. As a former member of boy band Take That, Williams had indicated the direction he wanted to head in with his choice of first solo single: a cover of 'Freedom 90'. After building up some credibility with a spate of well-crafted singles like 'Millennium', the likeably gauche Robbie – with all his girlfriend and drug problems – had become, as David Bowie said, the UK's favourite "end of pier act".

"I send a cheque to Robbie Williams like once a month and say, 'Keep up the good work,'" joked George during his promotional itinerary. "You know, 'Keep 'em off my back.' He needs to start sleeping with men," laughed the elder statesman of pop, "that'd really help me out."

As much as he was a key figure in noughties pop, Robbie would be less of a perennial than the old boy from Wham! As Robbie gradually faded throughout the decade into semi-reclusiveness and a futile attempt to break America, George Michael would find it increasingly hard to keep himself out of the papers.

For now though, the veteran Brit pop star was turning to face the future with what seemed at the time like a refreshing breath of realism. After a string of singles were released from *Patience*, he announced in early 2005 that the last of them would be 'John And Elvis Are Dead'. This time, however, it wouldn't be released to CD but as a download only. Pre-empting Radiohead and their radical gamble on letting listeners pay what they considered appropriate for downloads, George Michael was embracing the reality of the new technology. *Patience*, he suggested, might become his last ever CD release. As he explained to Kirsty Wark in their BBC interview at that time: "The idea is to release all of my new music online and give people immediate access while making a donation to charity at the same time."

So are you absolutely definite you're not going to release any more material for sale in shops?

"This is pretty much an experiment. The charity was supposed to start afresh with brand new material, what I've got is new recordings and a couple of pieces of new material. But the whole idea is to start the next phase of my career with that."

It's an experiment, you say, so if people don't download, don't click on charity, are you going to go back to the old way?

"I'm quite sure what I'd do is I'd release singles for charity in the conventional way if this didn't work. So basically, it's an experiment as far as the online part is concerned, absolutely. I don't know, maybe nobody will give me any money for any music and I'll be so cheesed off I'll say, 'Sod it, I'll charge you more than ever next time.'"

For now it seemed he had the present sussed, so why not move forward to greet the future too?

The resurgent singer appeared to be at peace with himself – and yet an air of melancholy remained. It manifested in his recurring (and perhaps psychosomatic) back pain; it came howling back in the mini-tragedy of the drowning of his little Labrador puppy, which he had bought to replace his faithful old dog Hippy – now deceased.

And it played out in the dreamy wistfulness of his long-term dope-smoking habit, which took him, in his mind, to anywhere but round here.

CHAPTER 18

25-Year Itch

In an age when celebrity has attained the status of a religion, fame can attract the kind of fanaticism previously only displayed by religious devotees. After having to be coaxed back into the routine of promoting his own music, George Michael would have his own close shave with pathological fandom on return from his promo tour.

When he came home to Hampstead on October 27, 2004, he was startled to find a 29-year-old admirer, Slovenian immigrant Lucy Nowak, on the premises. By then Ms Nowak – normally a resident of Kentish Town, just a couple of miles down the road – had been hiding in her idol's north London home for four days, apparently awaiting his return while taking shelter under the floorboards.

As shaken as George and Kenny were to find their living space invaded, they were reluctant to press criminal charges once they'd alerted the police. Instead, George stressed his hope that the young Eastern European would be given appropriate psychiatric care as a matter of urgency. It was a characteristically humane sentiment, but it also overlooked what he could not possibly have known at the time.

Lucy Nowak had a history of psychiatric care stretching back several years, which included time spent in mental hospitals. In her time spent awaiting George's return home, she'd also gained access to his private email address and the address of his new home in the West Country.

Two days after the incident, she turned up at the singer's personal assistant's office in Hampstead, distinctly unnerving the PA. She left when threatened with the police, but then sent five increasingly unhinged email messages to the object of her obsession over the next few days. On November 10, she was arrested again after being found hiding in the grounds of George's riverside mansion in Goring-on-Thames in Oxfordshire. When questioned by the press, neighbours on her council estate said the unfortunate woman played 'Faith' and 'Freedom 90' at full blast all day until the early morning. She was also said to do her best to replicate the *Faith* look, complete with tasselled leather jacket and cowboy boots – though presumably she omitted the beard.

Having already been psychiatrically assessed and bailed in London on the condition that she did not approach George Michael, Ms Nowak faced charges at Highbury Magistrates Court in February 2005. It was there that the object of her disturbed affections had a statement read to the court on his behalf; once again, he argued that incarceration would do no good (and might do harm) to Lucy Nowak. In the interests of justice and humanity, he argued that she should receive expert psychiatric attention rather than punitive sentencing.

The court was only too glad to agree and issued Ms Nowak (who at the last minute pleaded guilty to criminal damage and trespass) with a two-year conditional discharge, on the basis that she must not approach the singer again. What George failed to predict was that, having been briefly 'sectioned' (admitted to a mental hospital) for assessment, she would soon be deemed fit for release and discharged. In effect, while she wouldn't be going to prison, she wouldn't be going back to hospital either.

Neither would she keep her distance. "The emails were quite affectionate in tone, not threatening at all, but they were obviously the work of an unbalanced mind," said a police source to the press about the initial messages she'd bombarded George with. The emails had not yet ceased, however, and they now became more disturbing.

By mid-2005, a disgruntled George felt more able to complain about the intrusion and harassment that had been going on for much longer than anyone realised – in fact, for longer than he himself had initially been aware: "In the last year and a half, I've had the CPS [Crown Prosecution Service] release a stalker who basically was sending me death threats and breaking into my houses. She broke into my house on seven occasions. Once she was living there for a week without me knowing. She's smashed windows. She's stolen money. She wore my clothes. I've seen her in my clothes on the street. The police arrested her on two occasions and put her in a cell, and on both occasions the CPS let her go. At the time, I didn't want to make too much noise about it. But she was very ill and I should know I am safe from someone like that who's sending me notes about Mark Chapman and John Lennon. It's terrifying. I have to have locks put on windows and things like that, but the CPS didn't see fit to make me safe from her."

In fairness, the complainant himself had argued against punitive measures and effectively left Lucy Nowak in the hands of the medical authorities. But he was feeling the chill now. Ms Nowak had been diagnosed as a schizophrenic and drew a macabre analogy between herself and the despised Chapman, the ultimate psycho-stalker-fan who had tried to usurp his idol Lennon's fame by shooting him dead. John (and indeed Elvis) may have been dead, but George Michael had no inclination to join him anytime soon.

It was during the time of the Nowak case that George described the lifestyle of a celebrity as "unbearable", and indicated that he was poised to leave it all behind. But he would also soon become engaged in his own ongoing dialogue with the Crown Prosecution Service, and would find it harder than ever to escape the wrong kind of press attention.

The documentary film *George Michael: A Different Life* was given its premiere at the Berlin Film Festival in mid-February 2005, just before

Lucy Nowak was due to appear in court for intruding on its subject's life. It would receive a limited showing on the festival circuit before being broadcast on BBC1.

In the documentary, George goes to some lengths to stress how the subject of his own celebrity had become such a vexed question. "To be part of people's lives as an artist," says George, looking quite stoned as he semi-reclines on a couch, "that's what I dreamed of and that's what I'm still grateful for. But my God, I wish I could cope with the other stuff the way that other people do. I wish I'd been born with that particular suit of armour, you know, but I don't have it."

"Most artists are out there all the time, promoting or on tour, on the road and enjoying it," observes the ever-diplomatic Andy Stephens. "It's just not what George wants to do, it's not what he enjoys." As if in further validation, George is seen cringing in a chauffeured car when experiencing the attentions of Italian fans in Milan. "Bloody hell," he draws a sharp breath as they halt the vehicle en masse with their body weight and press their faces against the glass. The fanaticism of a few can't be doubted – but still, it's not quite Beatlemania.

"If I could stay at home and just watch the album going to number one in various territories," expounds George, filmed on a plane, "without ever having to sit in front of a camera or deal with it, oh my God, that would be my dream come true! So no, I don't need that bit. Much as it appeals to a tiny little part of my ego, I've so successfully crushed that part of my ego that it just scares me. It just *scares* me."

Later in the doc, George is seen in the Cornwall home of old best friend and early mentor Andrew Ridgeley. Thinner of pate but no less easygoing in nature, his old chum makes it clear to Andrew just who he thought got the best deal. "Put it this way, I know whose life I'd rather have led," insists George. "I think anybody would."

"But on balance..." Andrew tries to demur.

"Yeah, I'm very blessed in different ways," interrupts George, "but I think that ultimately and touch wood you've had a really good life."

Later in the same film, veteran BBC rock commentator Paul

Gambaccini reflects on how, "I wish [George would] do a few gigs. After all, fans aren't there just to buy your records and to love you."

But, despite the international rounds of radio stations and CD stores, a promotional concert tour was still a bridge too far for the artist at that time. As the man himself tried to explain: "If I loved adulation I would tour. Because believe me, touring is the most ego-stroking thing you can ever do in your life. You live in a completely isolated place. That's so not me. I'm not pretending that I'll ever not be 'George Michael' and I know I'll be famous, but there are levels. I know already, because I already stepped down one. And if I can take another step down and still make music for the people who want it, that would be fantastic. That's the plan for the next ten years."

As far as the artist himself was concerned, he would become a receding dot on the cultural landscape, working ever more introspectively for those fans who wanted to purchase his music on download. "I thought I should explain myself before I disappear," he announced of his intention when he appeared in Berlin to promote the bio-doc. "It's almost as much for me as for my fans, in terms of trying to make sense of the last 22 years and bring it to a close in a proper way."

In terms of the pop-music industry, in an interview with *Sunday Times* critic James Christopher, the star opined, "It's been killed off by corporate thinking. And I'm not interested in sparring with pop acts like Robbie Williams, Rachel Stevens and Will Young." The pop landscape was now dominated by the middle-aged managerial figure of Simon Cowell and his coterie of karaoke crooners. It was like a return to the era which predated his parents' rock'n'roll years, and George saw no place for himself in it.

"I don't think I've ever been good at the job of being a celebrity," he said of a mainstream media world where celebrity was now everything and original talent counted for nothing. (Though, he also conceded, "A bit has to do with being outed.")

The performer would make his last public appearance for some while at the Hyde Park branch of the international Live 8 concerts, on Saturday July 2, 2005. Organised by Bob Geldof and concert promoter

Harvey Goldsmith in an echo of their Live Aid triumph, two decades earlier, its intention was to influence the Western governments and financial organisations convening at the following week's G8 economic conference in Scotland, urging them to cancel much of the Third World's debt – in the words of the slogan, to "make poverty history".

If the campaign fell far short of its target and failed to remain in the public consciousness as Live Aid had done, it at least proved a memorable event for the old guard of rock and pop music. Pink Floyd reformed for what turned out to be the final performance of their career and The Who – perhaps best described as 'The Two', given the number of original surviving members – preceded them on stage. Paul McCartney, who joined U2 on stage at the start of proceedings, also closed the show.

George Michael was scheduled to give a solo performance of his rich man's guilt anthem, 'Praying For Time', although in the event an irritated throat put paid to that. Instead, he took a guest slot in the grand finale, duetting with McCartney on 'Let It Be', the Beatles classic that had formed part of the climax of Live Aid. By his own account George just about made it, as he described to Kirsty Wark: "You know the man forgot to introduce me? Everyone thought that I ran on, I've got this great piece of footage that my best friend had who was filming at the side of the stage. I was in a bad mood anyway, cos they'd got me there 20 minutes early so I was standing at the side of the stage...

"I heard the beginning of 'Baby You Can Drive My Car' start and thought, "Just a minute, you're supposed to be doing a different song!" They cut out a song from the set and he forgot to introduce me. So there's this great bit of film of me going, "Nobody told me to fuckin' go on!" and my mate going, "Just run on for the chorus, run on for the chorus!" [laughs] So that's what I did, I just ran on before I was supposed to sing the chorus. But otherwise I nearly didn't make it to Live 8. Paul thought it was hysterical.

In retrospect, over the coming months, the Hyde Park locale might seem a little ironic, while the title of the song ('Drive My Car') would be outright hilarious to some.

So what should a songsmith, now in his early forties, do with his time once he steps out of the spotlight? In George's case, part of the answer was to become more concerned with the social issues that affected him directly. In his debut as a 'serious' writer (rather than as a composer of pop songs), he had an article entitled 'Is It Time The English Were More Afraid Of God?' published in the late June 2005 issue of US gay lifestyle magazine *The Advocate*.

In it, George happily recounted how on Christmas Eve he, Kenny and three equally tipsy or stoned friends had visited an Anglican church near his 16th-century Thames-side mansion in Oxfordshire. Ostensibly there for a bit of a laugh, the writer was sympathetic to the more traditional congregation members: "As my trashed mates and I shuffled noisily into the pew closest to the church door, I looked at the sea of grey heads ahead of me and suddenly felt a little guilty. There were five of us, and none of us ever went to church ordinarily. We were there to add a little romance to our drunken Christmas break, but (despite the weakness of heart in their singing) these men and women were at midnight mass because they believed."

Acknowledging that "five tipsy queens" were no nearer to mainstream Middle England than the devout old congregation before him, the writer mused on the loss of English identity. Part of this, he conceded, was due to the retreat of the Anglican Church in the face of materialism ("on the day of rest, [the public] are all at IKEA"); much of this loss of identity he also attributed to his own personal bugbears, bland celebrity culture and American corporatism.

But he was also honest enough to express fear about the newest form of fundamentalism that had started to fill modern Britain's spiritual void. "I've never had a problem with God," stated George who, while far from being a Bible-basher, had consistently used the imagery of Christianity to express himself. "The God that Americans are presented with day after day would, I think, have a few problems with me," he conceded.

As would the new influx of religious fundamentalists who, while formerly welcomed by George and his peers in the best tradition of British liberalism, saw no onus on themselves to return the sentiment: "In a sick twist, immigration, the very thing that watered down the Church of England and protected English gay men from the ferocity of religious persecution, has become the new enemy to watch out for... Muslim clerics here are beginning to spout some very scary stuff indeed in public, the kind of rhetoric that bishops and archbishops have had to stifle for the past 40 years."

In the modern day, the United Kingdom had become a realm of very mixed blessings. The Civil Partnership Act of 2004 had opened the doors for gay couples to make a commitment to each other under the eyes of the law (often referred to as 'gay marriage'), though the first such union would not take place until the end of 2005. Meanwhile, the radical Muslim imams of whom George wrote could promise death in this world and damnation in the next to gay people, all in the name of the sharia law they hoped to bring to their adopted nation.

It was the essence of the liberal nightmare: newly incoming members of society, treated with tolerance or acceptance (though not universally so – there are of course bigots on all sides), were now intent on imposing an intolerant agenda. In writing openly and accessibly about such a social dilemma (many liberals remained silent as criticism of Islam – a religion, not a race – was seen as somehow 'racist'), George showed promise that he might one day tackle a more sustained autobiographical work, or perhaps even some serious themes that didn't pertain directly to his own life.

As he'd explained to Kirsty Wark, the increasing polarisation and atomisation of society was an increasing concern to him: "I had a bit of a row the other night. I went to my sister's birthday party and her friends were sitting in a restaurant, things got a bit heated because I'd had a couple of glasses of wine – because I have such a problem with separatism of any kind. I feel there's a horrible connection between separatism and fundamentalism in general and I think the area of society which struggles for identity is obviously the most vulnerable, and I think the working class in this country – and what is developing as an underclass – is being pulled into these religious ways of thinking simply by their lack of identity – whether they be unemployed, whether they struggle in this country or whether their family isn't integrated properly, I just believe that there's this horrible thing going on where people retreat into their corners. I do think the reason I had a fight about this is because it's a confusing issue for the individual. A lot of people feel that the strongest way to move forward is to look back and find their heritage. And I think that this only seems to divide us; I don't really approve of having the MOBO [Music of Black Origin] Awards, I think it's ludicrous that we don't acknowledge black artists within the Brit Awards.

In any case, in the mid-noughties it was his lifestyle – rather than any lyrical, thematic or social concerns – which would keep George Michael in the public eye. In late November, he confirmed to the BBC that he and long-term partner Kenny (then respectively 42 and 47 years old) would most likely take advantage of the new partnership act early in the New Year. Jokily promising a small private ceremony "without the whole veil and gown thing", in the meantime he and Kenny would be attending the ceremony for the historic union of his friend Sir Elton John (knighted in the wake of his performance at Diana's funeral service) and boyfriend David Furnish, on December 21, 2005.

But before the intended nuptials could take place, as would become increasingly common over the next several years, a curved ball came spinning out of the leftfield of George Michael's extraordinary private life.

On Sunday February 26, 2006, the Metropolitan Police made the following statement to the press: "We were called by a member of the public to a man seen slumped over the steering wheel of a car on the street close to Hyde Park Corner.

"An ambulance attended, but the man was not suffering from any injuries so was not conveyed to hospital. Police attended and spoke to

285

the man, aged 42. A search of the man revealed what was believed to be controlled substances.

"He was arrested on suspicion of possession of controlled substances of category C and on suspicion of being unfit to drive. Following an examination by the duty doctor in the custody suite he was de-arrested for the driving offence. He has been released on bail to return to a central London police station on a date in late March pending analysis of the substances recovered."

'Category C' substances at this time related to cannabis – downgraded from its usual prohibition status of category B by Prime Minister Blair, as a sop to his faintly embarrassed former 'Cool Britannia' acolytes. (Blair's more socially conservative successor would reinstate the weed's former status, all of it to little avail.) At this time it was extremely rare for possession to be treated as an arrestable offence for adults – although a driver slumped unconscious over the wheel was obviously an exceptional factor.

The fact that the driver was identified in the press as George Michael obviously excited tabloid interest. Less remarked upon, though also recorded, was the fact that the boot was found to contain sex toys and an S&M mask – no business of the law, of course – though the driver's impairment certainly was.

In its report of the incident, *The Sun* could barely conceal its glee, running pictures of a startled-looking George snapped at the driver's wheel of his Range Rover. "George was completely out of it – he was all over the place," it quoted an unnamed witness at Hyde Park. "He was found with his head slumped against the wheel. He was virtually unconscious. When the police came he could hardly speak."

Which makes it all the more remarkable is that no charge of being unfit to drive was brought, particularly as the singer was found in possession of GHB – gamma-hydroxybutyric acid, also classified as class C. Known as 'liquid ecstasy', unlike MDMA it provides its euphoric high via a powerful 'downer' that can easily slip into overdose. It certainly proffered an explanation as to why George, a seasoned and experienced dope smoker, was almost asleep at the wheel.

George was released from custody at 9 am that same morning, to be issued with an official caution in late March. According to the tabloids, he matter-of-factly acknowledged the incident as, "my own stupid fault, as usual" – harking back to the LA toilet arrest of 1998. While he joked that he was tempted to make another tie-in record and video satirising the situation, even he could have had little inkling that this would be just the first of a series of motor-vehicular mishaps.

On the morning of Sunday April 17, three neighbours within a mile of his Hampstead home were irate to find their cars had been 'pranged' by someone driving apparently the worse for wear. It didn't take long for the closest neighbour to find a suspect, when George's dented Range Rover was seen parked at an odd angle outside his house.

It took another 24 hours before representatives of the singer contacted the Met to invite them to interview George about the incident in his own home. After two officers were witnessed leaving by the press, a Scotland Yard spokeswoman announced: "The registered owner [of the Range Rover] has now been spoken to. He was not arrested. He was interviewed under caution and a file will be submitted to the Metropolitan Police's Operational Command Unit." The singer was building up quite a portfolio.

It seemed to have given the tabloid press their first real whiff of blood in several years. A furore would blow up after the night of Monday/Tuesday July 17/18, when *News Of The World* photographers descended on George as he cruised Hampstead Heath at 2.30am – a bizarre attempt to 'out' an openly gay man. Photographed emerging from the bushes, wide-eyed with surprise and wearing a baseball cap, according to the tabloid he was followed by a pot-bellied middle-aged man he'd been having sex with.

"I don't believe it!" the paper described the singer's outraged reaction. "Fuck off! If you put those pictures in the paper I'll sue! I'm not doing anything illegal. The police don't even come up here any more. I'm a free man, I can do whatever I want. I'm not harming anyone."

"Are you gay?" the tabloid claimed he continued, almost hysterically. "No? Then fuck off! This is my culture!" They also claimed to have followed the other man, an unemployed van driver, to his home after the incident. According to the *NOTW* and sister paper *The Sun*, 58-year-old Norman Kirtland had arranged a liaison with George via the Gaydar website – despite supposedly being unsure that he was meeting a modern musical superstar. ("I'm more of a soul music fan," was his priceless quote.)

After the story ran in the *NOTW* the following Sunday, George and his PR people went into overdrive. "This story is total bullshit but it's nice to know the *News Of The World* is still so concerned by my well-being," the singer announced, almost nonchalantly. This was the opening shot of a mini-counteroffensive.

According to what George told BBC News, "I'm suing the individual involved who I have never, ever seen, let alone wanted to have any kind of sexual encounter with, and I'm currently investigating suing the secondary sources of libel." The star was happy enough to admit he lived a sexually open gay lifestyle which included cruising the Heath – but seemed mortified by the suggestion that his penchant for men of the same age, or a little older than himself, meant that he'd get off with someone he claimed resembled the late, overweight club comedian Bernard Manning.

The 'secondary sources' were those press outlets who'd added to the story by claiming that the long mooted Michael-Goss civil partnership had been called off by Kenny, in disgust at his partner's antics. According to them, it was only the gift of £1 million – to fund the modern art lover's Goss Gallery project in his native Dallas – that had repaired the relationship.

George was having none of it. He also spoke of suing the photographers who set up the story in the first place. But what he would categorically *not* do was attempt to sue News International – parent company of the *NOTW/The Sun*, owned by his personal *bête noire*, Rupert Murdoch. "I'm not talking about money," he inferred darkly, "I'm talking about [if] you want to be destroyed." In the defence he gave of himself and his lifestyle, however, George seemed to mirror both the sentiment and the language used in the original *NOTW* article: "I have done nothing this year against the law, I've done nothing to encourage talk about my sex life. The question is not whether I bring it to the public, but it is why do I have to defend it in public because I don't want to talk about it at all?

"I don't know anybody who actually goes to Hampstead Heath at two o'clock in the morning for anything other than the reason of playing about with another member of the human race. If they are there, then they are a little bit strange or they just don't know the local area.

"A very large part of the male population, gay or straight, totally understands the idea of anonymous and no-strings sex. The fact that I choose to do that on a warm night in the best cruising ground in London – which happens to be about half a mile from my home – I don't think would be that shocking to that many gay people. Until such time as the straight world is not attacking people for cruising, I'd say the gay world could actually keep that to themselves, just for a little bit longer."

George's call for his right to cruise for sex unmolested was taken by many as a forthright statement of his gay rights. Not everyone was entirely convinced by the argument. Former Wham! manager Simon Napier-Bell, himself out of the closet for many years, was asked in an interview for the delightfully entitled *Butt* magazine, "What do you think of him yelling, 'This is my culture!' when he was caught cruising on Hampstead Heath?":

"He didn't say, 'This is my culture.'"

"But the truth is, cruising has gone on as long as there have been men trying to hide their sexuality," to quote George himself. And his own sexuality, having previously been hidden for many years, seemed to have attached itself to the furtive, clandestine thrill of being part of an unofficial underworld.

At the end of July, George completed his morning stoner's waking-up ritual of watching the *Richard & Judy* show by calling up to deny the incident had impacted on his relationship with Kenny. "I've got no issue with cruising," he asserted, perhaps forgetting to use the collective 'we've'. "I've talked about it many times. It's never been an issue between us.

289

"We had a lovely 10th anniversary party [in June of that year]. My present to him was a million quid so I think I should get away with so-called fooling around with 'Bernard Manning'. I've no idea who that guy was but thank you very much, whoever he was."

If it was rather charmless of George to suggest that he'd paid Kenny off, it also underlined some of the allegations he'd previously threatened to litigate against. For now, he insisted, the civil ceremony which would join them was on ice, until such a time as the press would permit sufficient privacy. "There can't be shame unless the people involved are ashamed and I'm certainly not that," he asserted. The threat of legal action would soon fade.

Over two years later, George would return to the subject with sympathetic interviewer Simon Hattenstone of *The Guardian*. "The handful of times a year it's bloody warm enough, I'll do it," he said of cruising on the Heath. "I'll do it on a nice summer evening. Quite often there are campfires up there. It's a much nicer place to get some quick and honest sex than standing in a bar, E'd off your tits shouting at somebody and hoping they want the same thing as you do in bed... I like a bit of everything. I have friends up there, I have a laugh."

He even had some kinder words for Mr Kirtland: "The poor bastard. His only crime was being the least fortunate-looking person to come off the Heath after me. They chased him down. Poor man had never met me..." If it's hard to reconcile the fortysomething George with the young man who warned against promiscuity and espoused safe sex, it can probably be taken for granted that he carried a pack of condoms to cover any eventuality.

For now, however, George Michael had a more novel activity to keep him occupied. He was actually making some music.

Twenty Five would be George Michael's second greatest hits collection in the space of one decade. Scheduled for release in November 2006 (just in time for the still-lucrative Christmas collections market), it pre-empted the March 2007 25th anniversary of the young artist entering the music industry. Among its 25 tracks encapsulating 25 years, the two-CD set also included the extra three new tracks Sony BMG had patiently waited the best part of a decade for, while George had been stranded in an internal world of pain and loss.

'An Easier Affair', the first of the new tracks, was a footloose but self-referential piece of electro-funk. Predating the album with a June 2006 single release, it's less a song than a personal statement of defiance to the press ("I've had too much *Sun*" – just weeks before his Hampstead Heath outing made the Murdoch press) and a celebration of "dancing with the freaks". Its cheerfully naughty video shows just that, middle-aged George strutting his stuff with a cross-section of young/old gay/straight dancers, including one girl(?) whose apparently implanted breasts predictably kept the video away from most network screens.

For all his heartfelt talk about not wanting to engage with the modern pop scene, George's duet with ex-Sugababe Mutya Buena is sublime. 'This Is Not Real Love' is a danceable heartbreak ballad, with the two partners locked in a sexual relationship out of habit. "Don't wait for me like some angel of tragedy," George implores Mutya, while in the promo video an androgynously thin young longhaired man embraces his similarly built girlfriend on the bed. Released simultaneously with the album, 'This Is Not Real Love' followed 'An Easier Affair' to become a UK Top 20 hit without even receiving a release in the US. (It would become a club hit when made available there 18 months later.) *Twenty Five* itself went straight to number one on the UK albums chart.

(*Twenty Five* also features a new recording of 'Heal The Pain', one of the lesser singles from *Listen Without Prejudice*. A pretty slight statement of love, its addition of George's Live 8 mate 'Macca' on vocal harmonies makes it sound even more Beatles-ish, like an outtake from a digitally remastered *Rubber Soul*.)

The advent of *Twenty Five* would also require a full promotional push; both the management and the record label made sure that they got it this time. Scheduled to begin in Barcelona during September 2006, George Michael would embark on the most extensive world tour of his career – climaxing in a series of major US city dates the following year, his first full American tour since the late eighties. For a man who, only 18 months previously, had announced his semi-retirement from the world of pop music, it was pretty good going.

But then, on the eve of the album's release, life served to intervene once again.

In the early hours of Monday October 2, 2006, traffic police were called to the junction of two main roads in northwest London. The Metropolitan Police's statement to the press ran as follows: "At approximately 3.22am this morning officers were informed of a stationary vehicle with a driver inside causing an obstruction at traffic lights in Cricklewood Lane near its junction with Hendon Way, NW2.

"Officers arrested a 43-year-old man on suspicion of being unfit to drive and possession of a controlled substance believed to be cannabis.

"The London Ambulance Service attended and the man was taken to a west London hospital as a precautionary measure.

"He was later taken into custody at a west London police station and received a caution for possession of cannabis and was bailed to return at a date in November pending further inquiries on the allegation of being unfit to drive."

Given the incident's proximity to Hampstead, many might have guessed the identity of the unconscious driver even if they hadn't been told it. There seemed to be a theme developing in the life of George Michael, and its combination of drug abuse and reckless driving was a disturbingly destructive theme at that.

As if on cue for controversy, ITV's *The South Bank Show* aired its second cosy profile of George Michael since 1990 at the end of October. Subtitled 'I'm Your Man', it was filmed during the opening dates of the 25 Live world tour. One section features George pre-show in Madrid, smoking a joint while being made up backstage: "This stuff keeps me sane and happy. I could do without it – if I was sane and happy! [giggles] The thing I would say about it is that it's very good for creative people, but it's a terrible, terrible drug in terms of, you know... You've got to be in the right position in life to take it, you've got to have achieved most of your ambitions, because it chills you out to the point where you could lose your ambitions. So I would absolutely say it's a great drug – though obviously it's not very healthy. But if you're going to take any kind of drug, this [holds up joint] is the only kind of drug I've ever thought was worth taking, and you have to wait. It never occurred to me to take even this until I was about 22, 23, by which time, strangely enough, I'd achieved quite a lot of what I wanted to – though obviously not quite enough. But yeah, you just can't afford to smoke it if you've got anything to do. If you've got anything to do at all, you're really being foolish. [He takes a sip of wine] Not that I count this interview as anything to do."

The sentiment was clear enough, if a little bit cheeky toward his audience: those who hadn't become a superstar by their early-to-mid-twenties should give the weed a wide berth. But as for good old George, he'd earned his right to herbal indulgence.

Just a few years previously, outside the pages of the *Daily Mail*, George's stoned moralising would not have attracted much ire. But, just as there had been a sea change in public attitudes toward gay people (who, with the success of *Pop Idol*'s oddly neutral Will Young, were no longer seen as defined by the sex act), so there was a reversal of tolerance toward the drug user, even among people who regarded themselves as liberal. At the heart of this change was disturbing evidence which suggested that around 10 percent of young cannabis users under a certain age – that is, a minority of a minority – were vulnerable to frightening states of psychosis which might become permanent.

After George had given such a relaxed display of his dope-smoking habit on *The South Bank Show*, he became an immediate target for anti-drugs campaigners and pressure groups such as the mental health charity MIND. On Sky News, one spokeswoman vehemently challenged his views by asserting, "It makes some people *in*sane and a lot of families very *un*happy."

It seemed unlikely material for a media shitstorm ('Stop Press – pop star smokes pot'), but, after a very short period of governmental liberalisation, the 'anti' view was becoming predominant again in English society. Liberal newspaper *The Independent* even made a front-page *mea culpa* apologising for its former campaign to legalise cannabis.

But this was occurring in the midst of George Michael's sell-out world tour and the release of his greatest hits album – neither of which, given his largely thirtysomething audience, seemed to be affected by it either negatively or positively. His fans were old enough to have made up their own minds on the subject of cannabis a long time ago.

Formally charged by police in November, George was bailed to enter a plea at Brent Magistrates' Court in January 2007. The end of the year 2006 would be a more positive time for the artist – acclaimed as Gay Man of the Year by *Boyz* magazine; and the central attraction at a New Year's Eve party held by billionaire Vladimir Potanin, believed to be the ninth richest man in Russia, at his 20-acre estate just outside Moscow. For the latter 75-minute performance (making only the slightest dent in his world tour schedules and with provisions made for Kenny and an entourage of 40 to attend), the singer was paid the record-breaking sum of $3 million (approximately £1.7 million – or £23,823 per minute).

It was after this lucrative step into the world of the rich and the powerful that George had to return to court, on January 11, 2007 – at which his solicitors entered a plea of 'not guilty' to the charge of driving while unfit, disputing some of the police evidence.

The singer and his legal representatives would appear again at court in early May, whereupon the disputed evidence was now accepted and the formal plea changed to 'guilty'. Still deep into the itinerary of his record-breaking tour, he began the next European leg (comprising 29 dates) two weeks later, in Coimbra, Portugal.

At the end of that same month, George rescheduled a date in Germany in order to perform in Sofia, Bulgaria, in aid of the 'You Are Not Alone' campaign formed to support five wrongfully imprisoned Bulgarian nurses and a Palestinian doctor – all held in Colonel Gaddafi's Libya under the bizarre, trumped-up charge that they had purposely infected hundreds of children with HIV. Reverting to type, George couldn't resist a swipe at the US during 'Shoot The Dog', where he undid the fly of a caricature-balloon George Bush to reveal a British bulldog where his penis should be.

At the same time, spring 2007 saw an oddly low-key and strangely touching mini-tour in parallel across the USA. Having been formerly showcased for view at Kenny's Goss Gallery in Dallas, the Lennon-'Imagine' piano was now being transported across the States. As gallery curator Caroline True said, "We are taking the piano on tour of America and other places in the world where horrific acts of violence have occurred and spreading a very simple message, which is peace."

The tragic venues included the Washington theatre where President Lincoln was assassinated in 1865 and the Memphis hotel where Martin Luther King was shot in 1968; the site in Waco, Texas where up to 80 members of cult leader David Koresh's congregation were killed by a heavy-handed 1993 FBI intervention; and the site of the FBI building in Oklahoma where anti-government zealot Timothy McVeigh sought to avenge the massacre in kind two years later, with a massive terrorist bombing. It was a naïve though good-hearted concept, with a number of local people encouraged to play 'Imagine' at the various venues. Notable by its apparent omission was the Dakota apartment building in New York City where John Lennon had come into fatal contact with the kind of pathological fandom experienced by George Michael in more recent years.

Back in the UK, the presiding judge at his trial was lenient enough to allow George to attend only the start and the end of proceedings, in deference to his busy schedule. On Tuesday May 8, 2007 he had to enter his formal plea and, according to the Sky News correspondent present, seemed disorientated by proceedings. Instructed by the judge to stand in the dock rather than sitting next to his lawyer, the singer initially had trouble figuring which way to plead.

"Not guilty? Oh hang on, no," he looked to his solicitor for help. "Actually I plead guilty due to tiredness and prescription drugs." It was as if the singer had just invented a specially mitigated variant on 'not guilty' or 'guilty'. But the admission of using prescription drugs (specifically sleeping pills) in combination with cannabis and, more lethally, motor vehicles would become part of the strange theme that was now running through the singer's life: "I really have been very distressed by this whole thing. I am perfectly aware that I did something very wrong and got into my car when I was unfit to drive. I was not in my normal physical state and I'm perfectly prepared to accept the correct punishment for that. It was fairly predictable considering how much work I had done that week."

His inferences were clear – the star was genuinely contrite about having put other road users or pedestrians at risk. But all the same, it wasn't so much *him* who was responsible as his currently prodigious workload.

All the same, he was called to give a blood sample to show his current state of sobriety (or otherwise); the police had noted that GHB was once again among the powerful cocktail of drugs found in the singer's bloodstream. (Unlike the law in some other countries, drugs in the bloodstream do not equate with 'possession' in the UK. The singer was therefore not charged on that count.)

George was recalled to court on June 8, 2007, for sentencing. He was shown relative leniency – banned from driving for two years and ordered to perform 100 hours of community service, which in his case would mean gardening at a homeless hostel during gaps in the tour's itinerary. As he'd later insist in his 2009 *Guardian* interview: "For all the doctored [tabloid] pictures, every single breathalyser test I've taken in my life has read 0.0, and I've never failed a sobriety test. I always preface this with, 'I deserved to lose my licence, I *needed* to lose my licence.' I had a problem with sleeping pills for about a year and a half, and I fucked up really badly. I got in the car twice when I'd forgotten I'd already downed something to try to get me to sleep. It doesn't matter that it wasn't deliberate – ultimately, I did it a second time, and I could have killed somebody. But the fact remains I was never accused of driving under the influence. I got done for exhaustion and sleeping pills."

It read as heartfelt regret; but, like other aspects of the singer's seemingly compulsive behaviour, the words of contrition would themselves become a recurring theme.

However, for now, as the judge recognised, George was still a very busy man – on the following day, he would be the first musical performer to play at the newly rebuilt Wembley Stadium, on the same site where he had first seen Elton John perform as a boy. George's celebrated June 2007 gig was filmed for posterity and is regularly repeated on TV up to the present day. The audience adored him and the singer completely wowed them – though his sense of recent personal embarrassment was still in evidence in the between-song banter at his 2007 UK gigs. ("According to the press, my idea of a night out is a Bernard Manning lookalike.")

At Wembley on June 9, George and his management would be fined a massive £130,000 by Brent Council for allowing the programme to run 13 minutes over. But by now it scarcely mattered. In fact, by the time that year's section of the 25 Live tour was completed, it was calculated that its overall total of 80 dates would have granted the singer exposure to 1.3 million fans worldwide.

This was success on a stratospheric scale, and it was accomplished by a man who'd claimed his intention was to fade from the pop-cultural landscape. What it could *not* achieve, however, was to ease George's state of mind or call a halt to the habitual behaviour that threatened to overtake him.

CHAPTER 19

A Quiet Life?

In September 2007, while still approaching the climactic section of his 25 Live world tour, a baggy-eyed George was photographed with BBC presenter Kirsty Young. Ms Young, the sexy-voiced presenter of Radio 4's revitalised *Desert Island Discs*, drew a relaxed interview out of her guest that encapsulated small but vital pieces of his life and career thus far.

Among George's more contemporary choice of records for his hypothetical desert island was 'Love Is A Losing Game' by twentysomething north London songstress Amy Winehouse; the song's production meshed a fifties torch ballad and a more technologically sophisticated modern tune in a manner that George (who most notably collided the styles of different eras on *Older*) could appreciate. The delectable Ms Winehouse was becoming as notorious for her serious habits – graduating from smoking weed to more serious drugs – as for her music. But for George, she was "the best female vocalist I've heard in my entire career. And one of the best writers.

"I wish her every success in the future. I know she can get past the media. I don't know if she can get past other things, but she's a fantastic talent and we should support her. All I can say is, please, please understand how brilliant you are," he indirectly pleaded with Amy. Although George's own drug habit appeared to be down at the softer end of the scale, it would later become apparent as to how much he might empathise with her waywardness.

His other choices included the haunting ballad 'Going To A Town' by gay singer Rufus Wainwright ("It really lays into the Bush administration, talking about America soaking the body of Jesus Christ in blood. Fantastic lyrics") and, surprisingly for a soul man, the raw grunge rock of Nirvana's 'Smells Like Teen Spirit', which he acclaimed as the best-produced rock record ever.

On a much more personal level, he admitted to Ms Young that, having studiously sought to avoid questions about his sexuality for years, he was "ridiculously ready to say these things now... What people have to acknowledge... is that there's a level of honesty that's natural to me... I'm uncomfortable with anything else. So firstly, understand how much I love my family and that AIDS was the predominant feature of being gay in the eighties and early nineties as far as any parent was concerned... My mother was still alive and every single day would have been a nightmare for her thinking what I might have been subjected to.

"I'd been out to a lot of people since 19. I wish to God it had happened then. I don't think I would have the same career – my ego might not have been satisfied in some areas – but I think I would have been a happier man."

Besides Andrew and Shirlie of Wham!, George stressed that he'd also come out at the end of his teens to one of his sisters. It was a simple statement, but it threw into sharp relief all the years of evasion and the stress of having to live out his early career behind a constructed front.

As for his own prodigious use of cannabis, the singer conceded, "Absolutely I would like to take less, no question. To that degree, it's a problem." At the same time, however, he did not believe his weed intake was "getting in the way of my life... I'm a happy man and I can afford my marijuana so that's not a problem."

In terms of the various little controversies and scandals which had dotted (and continued to mark) his career, George claimed: "I never had any feeling that my talent was going to let me down. In a strange way I've spent the last 10 or 15 years trying to derail my own career because it never seems to suffer. I suffer around it – bereavement, public humiliations – but my career just seems to right itself like a duck in the bath."

As perverse a statement as this may have seemed, it was a fact that the career of George Michael had avoided becoming a total car wreck (so to speak), despite the often fragmented state of his emotions. Whether that would remain the case was about to be sorely put to the test.

In mid-January 2008, it was announced that George Michael had signed a seven-figure deal to write his autobiography for HarperCollins. Estimates would place his advance at anything up to £3.5 million.

"I am particularly thrilled by this deal as I have long been a fan of George's," effused Belinda Budge, MD of Harper Non-Fiction UK. "Most importantly this really will be a truly authentic book and an exceptional one as he's going to be writing it entirely himself."

"George has promised HarperCollins a no-holds barred biography," seconded manager Andy Stephens, "and it's certainly going to be that." The book was scheduled to be published in the autumn of 2009. In the eventuality, at this time of writing it has still not been published; as was so often the case with the Anglo-Greek superstar, his life would intervene in his plans.

In the late March of 2008, it was announced that the final leg of the 25 Live tour would return the performer to the USA for 22 dates – formerly the region where he enjoyed his greatest popularity, more latterly where he had become one of the more contentious figures in the entertainment world. It would be predated in early April by the release of the *Twenty Five* compilation to the US, its release date staggered by a year to reflect how Wham! first broke in America in '83.

Prior to his return to US auditoriums, George explained himself in an interview with Steve Baltin of online music magazine *Spinner*. "Well, the incredible thing is I really didn't think I would do it again.

I've so kind of detached myself from a professional life in America. Ultimately, when I took on Sony in the early nineties I had a very good idea that I was shooting myself in the foot when it came to my career in America. Luckily for me, the people who decided I really should no longer be a part of the industry in America or should be seen to have paid a price for what I did didn't give a shit about the world outside of America. So my career just carried on beautifully outside of America, and in a way I was prepared to let that happen because ultimately I really do believe that if there are things that are bad about being famous, then they're worse in America. In terms of the way your life changes, it can be very distorting, especially for an English kid. It all very much overwhelmed me when I was younger. And I was perfectly prepared to give that up..."

While George appeared to put his semi-estrangement from the US purely down to the Sony battle of the mid-nineties, sidestepping the whole 'Shoot The Dog' furore, he did acknowledge the unusual route he'd taken back into the heart of American pop culture.

"I really didn't know I was going to be touring; that was something that only really occurred to me a couple of years ago. And yeah, ultimately, the truth is, the things that used to annoy me cos I'd lost them in America are actually not things I chase any more. And I'm much less angry than I was; I was so angry in the nineties. I was just angry about losing my partner and losing my mother. Those feelings of anger are completely gone. I just understand it and I feel really blessed to be able to come back and I feel very blessed that the whole *Eli Stone* thing happened."

In the latter half of 2007, during gaps in his 25 Live schedule (and his court appearances), George had responded to a very singular invitation to rejoin the world of American showbusiness. According to Greg Berlanti, who created the TV show along with co-writer/co-producer Marc Guggenheim, *Eli Stone* was "a *Field Of Dreams*-type drama set in a law firm where a thirty-something attorney, whose name is the title of the show, begins having larger-than-life visions that compel him to do out-of-the-ordinary things."

The title character was played by Jonny Lee Miller, one of the Brit actors from acclaimed nineties black comedy *Trainspotting*. Eli's visions come via an inoperable brain aneurysm, a potentially fatal condition. These prophecies include such events as a modern San Francisco earthquake – communicated to him via a guardian angel, in the form of near-forgotten (in the US) superstar George Michael playing himself.

Berlanti, one of US TV's few openly gay executives, then in his mid-thirties, was both relieved and thrilled to get his favourite singer's agreement to take on a such a wacky project. But then George was a self-proclaimed 'TV junkie', and he'd already shown himself to be a good enough sport to send up his public image on the small screen.

In February 2005, he'd appeared on a special segment of black-comic sketch show *Little Britain*, filmed for the BBC's biannual *Comic Relief* appeal. In it, comedians Matt Lucas and David Walliams appear as idle fake paraplegic Andy and his soft-hearted/soft-headed carer Lou; as a birthday treat, Lou has improbably arranged for superstar 'George Michaels' to meet them for dinner at the local Harvester. But George meets self-absorbed Andy's standard response ("I don't like him"); crestfallen, he leaves the Harvester to a volley of criticism from the idiot savant: "Tell him that, apart from 'Jesus To A Child', I find his output emotionally vapid!"

Around the time he was shooting *Eli Stone*, George also made a cameo appearance in the Christmas 2007 edition of Ricky Gervais' *Extras*. Continuing his spate of persuading major stars to parody their public images, Gervais' hapless actor character Andy runs into George at 'the gay bench' on Hampstead Heath. "Any action?" asks the baseball-hatted superstar, drawing on a joint and finishing a kebab. George explains that he only has 20 minutes as he's on lunch break from his latest round of community service. ("No, not that one, I'm on another one now.") When George takes off to avoid a tabloid photographer, the old queen who frequents the bench tells Andy, "I've had him before. In his car."

"Wasn't that a bit cramped?"

"Yes, and he was swerving all over the road too!"

That same Christmas, TV junkie George showed he was game for a further laugh via an appearance on *The Catherine Tate Show*. Licentious Irish nurse Bernie is overcome that 'Sir George' should show up as a ward patient in time for the Christmas karaoke party (for which she's practising by bawling out, "Jitterbug!"). "Do you want my sex?" pants red-haired Bernie. "Don't you read the papers, love?" retorts George.

Eli Stone, a specifically American phenomenon, first started airing in the following month, January 2008. In episode one, lawyer Eli's first otherworldly epiphany comes with a hallucination that George Michael is performing 'Faith' in chambers (the solid, square-jawed George of early middle age miming in rhythm to the big hit of his youth). When Eli comes to, he realises it's only him who's been swaying around to George's celestial tones, while the rest of the corporation's lawyers look on in bemusement.

'Faith' becomes a psychic motif that follows Eli around. Even when he's having sex with a blonde babe lawyer from his corporation, he gets off the job when he hears George performing the song in his living room. As the singer himself said of the show's first season, in which he would be a recurring figure: "The story apparently goes that Greg wrote the first draft, the initial idea for the series, and I was included in that original draft. The studio apparently didn't think that I'd say yes, so they wrote it again for Phil Collins or somebody else. But they didn't realise I was a telly addict – I am a telly addict, so I love American TV drama. The minute I heard, I said, 'Yes, I'd like to know what this concept is, I am interested,' and of course, after they said they wanted to name each episode after a song of mine, that's flattering to the ego, isn't it? So Greg came down to Dallas where I was staying with my partner, Kenny, he went over the basic idea for me, we stayed in contact – and here I am."

Responding to ABC News' probing as to why George Michael should be the show's linking plot device, he stated: " Because I've been absent from America for the best part of 15 years. I think that because Eli's initial memories are supposed to be attached to his childhood, it needed to be someone who was successful in the eighties. I think I most like the idea that the viewer is supposed to be constantly torn between the spiritual and the real. I don't want to give too much away, but the pilot shows that Eli is going through something very surreal, as it were, he keeps seeing and hearing things that aren't there – like me. And I think all the way through you're supposed to be balancing whether or not he's supposed to be going through some very important metamorphosis or whether he's ill. So I like that idea a lot."

In a similar twist to hit UK sci-fi series *Life On Mars*, Eli finds at the end of the first season that the earthly and mystical adventures he's been drawn into have all been occurring in his head, as he lies in an intensive care ward. But before that, he puts the ultimate question to the guardian angel figure of George Michael: "Are you God?" ("Some have said so," replies George, sanguine, sending himself up rather more subtly than in the UK comedy shows.) Before coming to in the hospital bed, Eli is given hope for the future by George leading the law firm's senior partners in belting out a cover of the Nina Simone standard 'Feeling Good'.

Before the end of the first season, which features episode titles like 'Father Figure' and 'Patience', George also takes a bona fide acting role – portraying himself, rather than the mystical singing cipher he otherwise appears. In episode nine, George approaches Eli Stone's firm (having been instructed via his own prophetic dream) to defend a girl threatened with expulsion from a high school with a 'sexual abstinence policy', on account of playing his 'I Want Your Sex'. For a pop star taking on one of those potentially embarrassing 'as himself' roles, George acquits himself admirably. As even Simon Napier-Bell concedes: "Anything I've said that was less than flattering about George has certainly not been about his music. That was always his great strength. And I have to say his acting looks pretty good too. I've only seen the small clip on YouTube, but I suddenly saw the possibility for him in a lead part in one of those classic American sitcom movies. Well... maybe not the lead, as he's not quite Grant-Everett in the face department. But he seems genuinely at ease with his part. And really funny."

Eli Stone first aired from late January to mid-April 2008. It would run to a second season without the participation of George Michael, whom it had helped find his way back into primetime US TV entertainment – albeit as a kind of lost star resurrected from the eighties.

His next tentative step back toward Middle America's heartland came via Simon Cowell – the man who he formerly claimed, via *Pop Idol* and *The X-Factor*, had done as much as anyone in recent times to devalue the currency of pop music. With the Cowell brand now successfully exported to the USA, US variant *American Idol* ran a charity-thon entitled *American Idol Gives Back* in early April. It was on this edition that the show's greatest success, country balladeer Carrie Underwood, sang an angst-ridden, heavily orchestrated cover of 'Praying For Time'; to repay the tribute, George accepted an invitation onto the show's grand finale in late May, whereby he would sing the song himself. When asked by *Spinner* how Simon Cowell, impresario of the new Tin Pan Alley, might regard his performance, George laughed, "I think he'll probably tell me I shouldn't have done a George Michael song. He's told plenty of people that in the past, so I think that'd be quite funny."

In the event, the singer revisited his greatest early performance with tender restraint. Against a plain piano backing, he articulated the pained lyric soulfully but without any of the strangulated vowels or elongated syllables that the modern R&B audience has come to expect. It was too subtle for some, but in terms of putting him back on the American entertainment map it worked beautifully – all courtesy of the Fox Network, owned by George's professed nemesis Rupert Murdoch. Clearly, a few little compromises had to be made on the road back.

Within a month, on June 17, 2008, George began a tour of major American cities that opened in San Diego on the West Coast and ended in New York seven weeks later. "You can't imagine what it's like playing to people who have been loyal to you for 25 years and haven't seen you for 15," the once reluctant performer told an interviewer. "That's been the most life-affirming thing I could have done. I'm so glad I did it."

On his return to the UK in August, he had scheduled two last shows for the cavernous Earl's Court – entitled 'The Final Two', in an apparent echo of Wham!'s farewell 22 year earlier. According to estimates for the *Sunday Times* 'Rich List', the 25 Live tour had added £48.5 million to George's personal fortune, bringing it up to a total of at least £90m.

The Final Two were triumphant, with the last date filmed for posterity and often repeated on cable TV up until the present day. ("Let's hear it for my partner, Kenny!" George calls out between songs, and his adoring female audience gladly oblige.) Yet the urge to disappear was never far away.

While still on its US leg, the singer had expressed his wish to a BBC interviewer to lead "a quieter life" once the monumental tour was over with:

I've got lots of other things I want to do – they're just not of this nature, really.

Outside of music?

I still want to continue making music, but definitely I've things to do outside of music – not acting, in case anyone's wondering. [Laughs] But yeah, things to do and just a quieter life to lead, I think would be nice.

So are you retiring?

No, no, I'll never retire, but in terms of 'bells and whistles', this year is very definitely the last tour, yeah.

Why, what's brought you to that decision?

Various things which I probably shouldn't talk about now, so I won't. But various things. It's starting to become more and more strange to be in the public eye these days, I think the world's going completely mental, and I just don't really want to be in the thick of it any more, really. So if I can stay away from my own idiocy, if I can try and behave – not behave myself, but if I can live further from the spotlight then I think that'll be better for all really.

You seem to be saying you can't help but get into trouble.

No, I'm just saying that I'm obviously someone who's of interest to the public for various reasons, and I'm saying that I think those things, the kind of celebrity we're talking about, is very damaging to us in other ways. I think we're all watching each other make stupid mistakes while people change the world around us, and I think people like me are a great cover these days – for other people, you see my meaning?

If George's theory that his naughtier antics were used to cover up the darker deeds of the powerful verged on paranoia, his stated intent still seemed noble. It wouldn't be long, however, before it was put to the test and found wanting.

In late September, the Metropolitan Police issued one of their by now familiar press statements: "A 45-year-old man was arrested in the Hampstead Heath area on September 19 on suspicion of the possession of drugs.

"He was taken to a north London police station, where he was interviewed and received a caution for possession of Class A and Class C drugs. He was released and no further action will be taken."

The presence of hard drugs aside, the defining detail here was the venue where George was arrested: the public toilets on Hampstead Heath, where he'd been reported for his behaviour by an attendant that Friday afternoon. As he himself jokingly said in the *Different Life* film, "I'm not presuming that cruising in itself is dysfunctional, because I don't think it is as a gay man. But cruising as George Michael, there was obviously something dysfunctional about that," he laughed. He was speaking at the time about the 1998 LA incident, but ten years on the dysfunction seemed to be building up in layers.

"Well, gay men do love a bit of rough trade, that's true," reflects Fiona Russell Powell, who knew George when he was a gay teenager frequenting Soho clubs. "I think the whole toilet thing is really quick, it's anonymous, quite often you don't even see [the other men], you've got the 'glory holes' and everything. There is a turn-on in that the environment is quite squalid. Also there's an excitement about being caught, there definitely is an element of that. And also I think it's habit – he'd been doing it for so long."

More controversial to the mainstream press was that George had been arrested, cautioned and discharged not only for possession of his beloved weed, but also crack cocaine. "The biggest message is that drugs are wrong and people will be punished," rationalised a Home Office minister, "but it must be right that there is flexiblity in the law."

But how much more flexible was the law for a major entertainer rather than for the average street-drug user? In the *Mail On Sunday*, Middle England's champion of what its editor promotes as middle-class values, right-wing polemicist Peter Hitchens thundered, "The law sets a penalty of up to seven years in prison for Mr Michael's offence. How is it 'flexible' to let him off completely without even bothering with a trial?… If he had been tried and convicted, four years breaking rocks would have been 'flexible', the full seven a very good idea."

(The fact that British penal law abandoned hard labour decades ago makes no difference to Mr Hitchens, whose journalistic shtick is predicated on the phrase 'holier than thou' and consists in part of prescribing imagined punishments.)

Even George seemed to realise things were not looking good this time. "I want to apologise to my fans for screwing up again," ran an embarrassed-sounding press statement read on his behalf, "and to promise them I'll sort myself out. And to say sorry to everybody else, just for boring them."

For once, it seemed to be the fans who were taking it the worst. *The Sunday Times* printed a short selection of dismayed responses from the internet. "I'm sick of him spending our hard-earned money on drugs," bewailed a woman calling herself janelovesgeorge. It probably never occurred to the singer that, in this democratised age of blogging and *Pop Idol* votes, the faithful might feel they had the right to say how he lived his life.

"He totally doesn't know what to do with himself now the tour is over and we aren't there any more for him to throw himself upon our mercy to fill his void," wrote someone called Tex, rather more realistically, of the artist's post-touring comedown.

One year hence, when interviewed by Simon Hattenstone for *The Guardian*, George complained, "People want to see me as tragic with all the cottaging and drug-taking... those things are not what most people aspire to, and I think it removes people's envy to see your weaknesses. I don't even see them as weaknesses any more," he claimed defensively. "It's just who I am."

One critic of George's current lifestyle who was openly stating his concerns was Elton John. Having previously opined, "George Michael needs to lighten up," at the time of the bio-documentary's release and its subject's agonising about touring, the elder superstar and one-time mentor had become increasingly concerned about George's behaviour since his first drug-driving arrest. By the time of the Hampstead cottaging and crack incident the two were no longer talking, although reformed coke addict Elton would still have something to say about it.

But the essential point that none of his fans could ignore – whether they were disapproving or apologetic on his behalf – was that George had been caught using the most downmarket, damaging drug (crack – a very violent stimulant for a man who claimed to suffer sleeping problems) in the sleaziest environment imaginable, a public toilet. Next to this, all the controversy about his heavy use of weed seemed almost like a pungent smokescreen. George's drug problems of the time seemed to be going deeper and becoming more compulsive.

CHAPTER 20

Wham!

It was the first concert after the very last one – or at least the only scheduled performance after the Final Two. The first of December 2008 found George in Abu Dhabi, capital of the United Arab Emirates, topping the bill at the Zayed Sports City Stadium with American singer-songwriter Alicia Keys.

There had been much online fan chatter about whether the Earls Court gigs would really constitute his last ever performances, or whether it just meant that sightings of the performer would become rarer than reindeer droppings under the Christmas tree. Abu Dhabi seemed to give the lie to ideas of retirement – although a purported fee of $1.7 million for one night might be enough to tempt anyone temporarily back to the stage.

In any case, the oil-rich Middle Eastern state seemed a slightly unlikely host nation for a man recently cautioned on multiple drug possession – and on its 37th National Day holiday, no less. If asked, however, George might have been able to persuade the Muslim law enforcers that rarely does a drop of alcohol pass his lips these days, which certainly seems to have been the case.

On returning home to the UK, his next recording, 'December Song', would be released in time for Christmas as an internet download only – at no fee, but with fans urged to make a charity contribution. It was the first original George Michael material issued since *Patience*, four and a half years before, and part of an ongoing experiment.

"The strange thing is I don't know how this will work out," the singer had admitted in a BBC interview several years previously, when he'd first made the decision to issue new material by download only. "If the charity site is inspirationally successful, I don't really know what my limitations in terms of promotion are, because I know what my limitations are in terms of promotion as to whether I sell more records or not – which is that I hate doing it, yeah, and I feel very un–British and see hard–sell promotion as kind of prostituting myself, that's how I see it. Even if it's a complete fallacy, I'm of that generation. But it's confusing. If I can do it for charity and I can make money for other people then maybe I won't mind, I don't know."

'December Song' was the artist's first seasonal single since 'Last Christmas' in 1984. It was issued via the official georgemichael. com website, with online prompts given to the purchaser to make a contribution to the Breast Cancer Campaign, Nordoff Robbins Music Therapy, the National Society for the Prevention of Cruelty to Children or, indeed, any registered charity of the buyer's choice.

Despite George's stated 'downloads only' policy, a CD single issued by veteran independent label Island Records went on sale in mid-December, as part of the race to establish the official Christmas number one single in the UK. That previous Saturday, December 13, he took his wares to the marketplace that, just a few years previously, he'd spoken of as anathema to classic pop music.

'December Song' opened to the joyous sound of a gospel choir singing a sample from Frank Sinatra's 'Christmas Waltz', when it debuted on the final edition of the 2008 season of *The X Factor*. As they wished the audience a New Year in which all their dreams came true, George entered from the back of the stage in his now customary dark suit, crucifix and shades, to the moderate applause of an audience more used to hearing his songs rendered by the karaoke artists on the show.

The new song was both sentimental and self-knowing, with the artist reflecting on how his mum and dad would make the world stop once a year to create a domestic heaven for their kids. Prominent among the band was his co-composer and oldest friend, David Austin, seated at the piano – a man who'd shared those magical childhood Christmases with George since they were at primary school in Kingsbury together. The artist who lived in a privileged state of deferred adolescence sang gently but evocatively of Christmas as a time when, "I could believe in peace on earth and I could watch TV all day," seasonally reaching out to all children with the empathy of a man who'd never quite grown old inside.

It was a genuinely heart-warming performance and it drew a standing ovation from the *X Factor* panel of Simon Cowell, Louis Walsh, Dannii Minogue and Cheryl Cole. However orchestrated the response may have been by Cowell – George's one-time detractor, now his occasional TV collaborator – it was still deserved. The closing applause from the audience followed their effusive cue, and for a moment it looked as if George Michael had returned to the heart of British pop culture.

If the song's commercial performance didn't match its initial reception, it was due to factors outside of the track itself. Island Records had failed to print enough CDs to fulfil the demand of every fan who'd first heard it on *The X Factor* (which attracted 18 million viewers that week), with all available copies sold out in one day during the crucial pre-Christmas week; though available for download on a number of legitimate (and pirate) sites, its most obvious point of access as a free download on George's own site lasted only for as long as Christmas Day and Boxing Day.

'December Song' peaked at 14 on the UK singles chart. In the years before downloads eclipsed the record industry, there's little doubt that it would have made the primary position – a position now held most years by whichever singing mimic wins *The X Factor*, despite the occasional grass-roots campaign against Cowell's monopolisation of the Christmas number one.

In the last couple of years, it has become a tradition of its own for George Michael to re-release 'December Song' at Christmas, though it seems to fare a little worse each time. It would be the artist's last original material released in that decade; over the ensuing months he would become less famous for his musical output than for an accelerating loss of control over his life.

In 2009, an ever less productive George Michael was the great missing presence on the pop scene. It's tempting to think of him withdrawing into a self-indulgent reclusiveness, a veritable hermitage suffused with smoggy spliff smoke and anonymous gay sex. By his own account there may be some grains of truth in that. As made clear by some of his closest friends in the *Different Life* documentary, it didn't require any massively decadent lifestyle to make George pull down the blinds or draw the curtains.

"Nothing like a bit of success to get you out of the house," grumbled old Elton, the friend and mentor who was growing increasingly estranged from his one-time protégé.

"Sometimes he's bloody sad, I tell you!" laughed David Austin. "Sometimes I've been round there and it's like, 'Are we going out anywhere?' and he's like, 'Tonight I think we'll eat local.' That means me going round and getting a pizza."

"He's never liked leaving home," confirmed former Wham! girl Pepsi. "There must be something good there," reflected her former singing partner Shirlie. "*EastEnders!*" they both chimed in simultaneously, reflecting their old friend's love of the soap opera that Shirlie's husband, Martin, used to star in.

In fact, George's long-standing love of the BBC's faux-East End melodrama was well known – there had been rumours since the late nineties that he would consummate his love via a guest appearance, and he'd also been instrumental in getting the producers to cast Martin Kemp as fringe gangster Steve Owen.

To date, the much-mooted guest appearance has never taken place. In 2009, however, the writers of *EastEnders* reciprocated the singer's affection with a rather odd storyline. In February, haplessly unlucky-in-love chubby girl Heather Trott (played by Cheryl Fergison) would be aided and abetted by her friend Shirley (Linda Carter) in stalking her personal pop idol, George Michael. Shades of the macabre Nowak affair were diminished only by Heather's essential harmlessness and the overall silliness of the story.

(Shirley realises that the Hampstead house they're loitering outside is not George's home at all, but doesn't shatter Heather's illusion. The big girl has to content herself with rooting among what she believes to be the star's rubbish – finding happiness in retrieving one of Yog's own Greek yoghurt cartons. As tabloid TV critic Garry Bushell mercilessly put it, "If you really wanted to meet George Michael, wouldn't it be easier just to dress as a bloke and hang about on Hampstead Heath with a spliff on for a night?")

On the domestic front George lived an increasingly reclusive life, still recording but making few of the results available to the public, uncertain of what their ultimate outlet would be. His only public performance for many months would come unannounced on June 9, 2009, when R&B singer/ex-Destiny's Child vocalist Beyoncé was playing the O2 (now eclipsing Wembley as London's major stadium venue).

For her performance of rocky late 2008 hit 'If I Were A Boy', Beyoncé Knowles and her dancers dragged up in androgynous black leather jackets and shades, like a kinky all-female variation on Wham!. The gasps of those old enough to recognise him were audible when George took the stage for the second verse. Singing in a less histrionic fashion than Ms Knowles, he brought a thoughtful ambiguity to the young diva's lyric about what it would be like to live as a male – or to have a girlfriend and treat her kindly, because she'd know what her pain was like.

It was an impromptu performance, apparently arranged in little more time than it took the singer to jump in his car and drive to Greenwich, having recently regained his licence. It was apparently all the more perplexing to manager Andy Stephens, who was reputedly having trouble making contact with his client at all. When he did finally contact George, apparently to question the wisdom of giving unofficial and unpublicised performances, the blow-up between the two men resulted in the star sacking his universally respected manager.

Stephens, who had handled George's affairs unwaveringly for 14 years, has remained diplomatically silent about the break ever since. It seems, however, that he was the singer's conduit to the formerly disdained world of *Pop Idol* and *The X Factor* reigned over by Simon Cowell; knowing which side the modern pop manager's bread was buttered on, Andy Stephens would take on the running of temperamentally fragile *X Factor* winner Susan Boyle, the singing Scottish spinster who'd become a transatlantic reality TV sensation.

Life for George, now without a manager, remained on a less than even keel. On the late night/early morning of Thursday/Friday 13/14 August, he was driving between Oxfordshire and London when he was involved in a potentially serious accident. At approximately 1am, his silver Land Rover collided with an articulated lorry on the southbound carriageway of the A34 back road.

Fortunately, neither driver was injured, but police on the scene regarded the singer as potentially culpable. After giving a negative breathalyser test, he was driven off to Lodden Valley police station near Reading to be tested for drug intoxication. He was finally released without charge just before dawn.

"Neither of us was charged because we were both stone cold sober," George told the press. "We both think the other is to blame so this is just an insurance fight."

When interviewed by *The Sun*, lorry driver Lawrie Rowe claimed, "His car went spinning across the outside lane and into the central barrier before bouncing back into my cab. He then hit the barrier again." According to Rowe, the driver of the Land Rover took at least 10 minutes to emerge, dazed, from the driver's seat. "He was absolutely not with it."

Interviewed by *The Guardian* several months later, George had a different take on events. "[Rowe] came into my lane, and I had nowhere to go and ended up being battered between him and the central reservation, and I have to say it's fucking amazing that I'm alive.

"If that juggernaut had killed me," he paused to reflect, "I think I'd be perfectly happy with the amount of quality music I have left in the world. My ego is sated." Both parties at least agreed that they were lucky to come through it unscathed. They may have begged to differ as to whether it was a boon or a curse that the performer was now legally out on the road again.

By October 2009, devoted *EastEnders* viewer and skunk smoker George may have found himself becoming mildly paranoid when the Heather character christened her newborn baby (father initially unknown) George Michael Trott. In the meantime, however, sightings of him outside his own home were becoming increasingly scarce.

Strange rumours of a life lived increasingly far from human contact emanated from the sacking of Andy Stephens in the late spring of '09. George would supposedly rise at his Hampstead mansion around 2pm every day, smoke a couple of potent joints of skunk and spend his time off in a private world, playing computer games until 7am the next morning. According to a *Daily Mirror* informant, the singer had gone into internal retreat after the much-guarded dissolution of his relationship with Kenny Goss, which had supposedly occurred as long ago as the previous December. Having endured his boyfriend's promiscuity, drug-suffused lifestyle and related motoring mishaps, the more sober Kenny had allegedly said enough was enough after George's late September drug arrest while cottaging on the heath.

Not so, claimed George's PA. "There is no truth in the matter at all. Kenny has been away in Dallas where he owns a gallery but is scheduled to return home this Friday. They are planning a lovely weekend together." (After many months of preparation, the Goss Gallery had finally opened in May 2009 with an exhibition by photographer and video director David LaChappelle, whose style fused surrealist and symbolist imagery with more commercial concerns. George was in attendance at the launch party.)

In his disarmingly candid December 2009 *Guardian* interview with Simon Hattenstone, George pooh-poohed the rumours that he and Kenny had split – as apparently evidenced by the big 'George' and 'Kenny' cushions in his lounge. He also tried to give a more balanced view of the way he lived his life: "I normally get up about 10am, my PA will bring me a Starbucks, I'll have a look at my emails... Then, if I'm in the mood, I'll come up to the office in Highgate, do some work, writing, backing tracks or whatever. Come home. Kenny will be here, the dogs are here. Maybe eat locally, hang out, and then probably go off and have a shag or have someone come here and have a shag.

"It's not typical," he laughed, "that's probably a couple of times a week."

Asked if he was referring to sex with Kenny, he rather tartly answered, "If it was shagging with Kenny, I wouldn't have to invite him round, would I? Kenny gets his, believe me." In his 12th year as an 'out' gay man, George Michael had developed a take-it-or-leave-it attitude to the modern tradition that said casual sex was not cheating within a gay relationship.

As to the chemically indulgent side of the singer's lifestyle, Hattenstone noted how a bagful of skunk and a handful of pills were on constant display, with the singer rolling and smoking a couple of joints during the interview. Admitting to smoking about 25 spliffs a day during his most profoundly stoned years, he noted casually, "I probably do about seven or eight a day now." Relieved to find that his voice had stayed intact during his heaviest period of indulgence, the singer was rather more coy about the more serious drug abuse indicated by his September 2008 arrest:

It's hard not to worry about Michael – for all his paranoia, recklessness and self-absorption, he exudes intelligence, warmth and generosity. "Look me in the eye," I say. "Were you smoking crack?"
Was I? On that occasion? Yeah.
"When was the last time you smoked it?"
I'm not going to tell you that. But I am going to tell you, whatever

I do, I did 105 really good performances, and none of my musicians can ever say they've seen me wasted.

For all his evasiveness on this point, it seemed that crack cocaine had been a reckless dalliance rather than a full-fledged habit. More of a constant in his life were the painkillers he had to take since an operation on his long-suffering back, immediately prior to the 25 Live Tour. ("I had 10 years where I could barely walk, because I had two discs out of place and I had them removed," he'd later explain, "so I now have literally a foot's worth of aluminium in my back and six big screws like you see in your dad's garage.")

Then there were the various kinds of sedatives to aid his sleep, which he must have been using since the point when he realised that super-strong cannabis is not always a soporific but often a hallucinogen – leaving the user trippy and only half-awake but still conscious. Put them all together and George had quite a potent cocktail flowing around his bloodstream.

As to the cumulative effect on his productivity, the performer was honest enough to admit, "The best answer for me is to keep busy. If I'm busy I don't sit around puffing." But still, little headway had been made on the autobiography and he confessed he was in a position where he might have to repay the advance to HarperCollins – whose owner, he had belatedly realised, was Rupert Murdoch, the all-powerful mogul he only half-jokingly referred to as 'the Devil'.

"There are things I need to resolve," he digressed. "And I think I'll be a much better writer when I've got through those things." Even at that stage, he can have had little idea as to how his life would hand him both the raw material and the impetus to finally get around to telling his own story.

But as for the former friend and lifelong mentor he'd fallen out with, George was altogether less sanguine about Elton. The growing estrangement dated back to the *Different Life* film in 2004, when his former idol had mocked George by saying, "You should get out more". Expressing disappointment with the *Patience* album, former coke addict Elton (who was snorting a line every four minutes at the height of his addiction and later paid the price with angina) blamed it on George's prodigious weed intake, observing that his younger friend was "in a strange place" and seemed to be suffering "a deep-rooted unhappiness".

To coin a popular cliché, George went ballistic. His answer had come in the form of an open letter to *Heat* magazine, directly addressing the celebrity-obsessed readership: "Elton John knows very little about George Michael… to this day, most of what Elton thinks he knows about my life is pretty much limited to the gossip he hears on what you would call the 'gay grapevine' which, as you can imagine, is lovely stuff indeed. Other than that, he knows that I don't like to tour, that I smoke too much pot, and that my albums still have a habit of going to number one."

Meow! In the mid-noughties, some kind of rapprochement was achieved by celebrity chef Gordon Ramsay cooking a meal for the two former friends at George's house in Hampstead. But now, towards the end of the decade, contact had decreased to the point that all George ever heard from Elton were second-hand statements of intent to intervene in what he saw as the younger man's growing personal crisis.

"Elton lives on that," George complained to Simon Hattenstone. "He will not be happy until I bang on his door in the middle of the night saying, 'Please, please, help me, Elton. Take me to rehab.' It's not going to happen. You know what I heard last week?

"Geri [Halliwell, ex-Spice Girl] told Kenny that Bono [of U2], having spoken to Elton, had approached Geri to say, 'What can we do for George?' This is what I have to deal with because I don't want to be part of that social clique. All I'd have to do to stop it is hang out in London, so people realise I don't look close to death."

On the December 2009 day that the *Guardian* interview was published, Sir Elton apparently deputised his significant other, David Furnish, to make a statement to Radio Five Live on both of their behalves: "The difficult thing for Elton and me is a lot of George's friends keep calling us saying, 'You have to do something, George is in a bad way, he's in a bad state.' We're only reacting to what his close friends say to us.

"They're saying that they're very concerned. A lot of people are saying it to us, we get it very, very regularly, that they are concerned about his health, concerned about his state of mind and his wellbeing and that as Elton has been there and experienced sobriety now for 19 years, that perhaps he's best positioned to be able to help out.

"But if George feels he doesn't need help and his life is in check and balance, then maybe his friends are wrong. I haven't seen him in such a long time, it's difficult to judge and pass comment. I respect George, I love George, I think he's a huge talent. I just hope he's fine. I just hope he's well and happy and continues to be the great artist he is. George has to want to help himself. If he wants help we're here for him. If he doesn't want help that's fine, that's his choice too."

"Elton just needs to shut his mouth and get on with his own life," George groused to Hattentstone. "Look, if people choose to believe that I'm sitting here in my ivory tower, Howard Hughesing myself with long fingernails and loads of drugs, then I can't do anything about that, can I?"

Of all subjects in this apparently least guarded of interviews, it was, perhaps ironically, his little-heard music that George was least forthcoming about. Treating it almost as a fearful secret, he made cryptic reference to unreleased material which "uses my supposed infamy on my own terms", and which still has not been heard to date.

As to his own state of mind, he candidly admitted, "Most visible traces of self-loathing have gone. I'm surprised that I've survived my own dysfunction, really." Regarding his own seclusion and reluctance to engage with the modern music industry, he was honest enough to observe how his Hampstead mansion sometimes took on the function of a luxury prison. "Mind you," he reflected, "if you're going to live in a prison, it might as well be a good one."

★★★

On Saturday December 12, 2009, the apparently media-shy George Michael made one of his sporadic, almost paradoxical returns to *The X Factor*. On the following evening's contest final he would once again perform 'December Song', whose annual re-release had already become a tradition. For this first night though, he was there to play the celebrity game and buddy up with a young hopeful for a duet.

Young Newcastle singer Joe McElderry was visibly thrilled to be accompanied by the elder vocalist. In their rendition of the celebrated George & Elton hit, 'Don't Let The Sun Go Down On Me', the older man articulated the song's angst subtly while the young contestant went all-out for the kind of vowel-strangling effect that talent shows regard as proper singing. He would win the contest.

(Sadly, he wouldn't win much of a career. The deal for any *X Factor* winner was a contract with Simon Cowell's record label; Syco. In April 2011, Syco announced it was not renewing McElderry's contract. It served to demonstrate the crucial difference between karaoke singers who have learned to hit all the right notes – of whom there are many – and an original artist like George Michael.)

Away from the celebrity show circus, the year 2010 seemed to promise different – and possibly better – things for the now veteran performer. After a lengthy layoff from live performance, in the early New Year George announced an Australian tour that would take in the key cities of Sydney, Melbourne and Perth.

On February 20, 2010, George played the Bushwood Dome in Perth to an audience of 15,000. It was a very modest crowd size for him, but they responded to the occasion accordingly. "Are we ready to make up after 22 years?" he teased the crowd at the opening of his set. All the shouted cries were in the affirmative. For the singer had neglected the Antipodes after the *Faith* tour of 1988, and he was there to make up for it.

Modern Australia was a land of many parts that suited the mature George Michael. Long seen as the macho outgrowth of colonial Britain, which had once transported its convicts and dispossessed orphans, it was now a pluralistic society with a celebrated gay culture in its biggest city.

On March 5, George was an esteemed guest at the Sydney Gay and Lesbian Mardi Gras After Party, capping several sell-out shows in the city by playing a 1am set. According to the Sydney *Daily Telegraph*, the performer "ditched industry invitations on the night of the Gay and Lesbian Mardi Gras parade to visit Oxford St cafés and make new friends." In fact, he was making new friends the entire time he was out there. According to a gay website source, George signed up for Grindr, an iPhone app that allowed gay men to meet up for no-strings sex, under the profile name 'Back for Wood'.

He appeared to be having the time of his life. At the end of the tour, he stayed on for a planned two-week holiday that extended closer to two months. It also extended the number of personal homes that the superstar had secreted around the world. In May 2010, George put down AUD$5 million for a three-storey, five-bedroom house situated, according to the estate agent's blurb, on a "dramatic headland position overlooking cliffs and crashing waves". Its ocean view and glass walls must have reminded him of his former modernistic dream home in Santa Barbara, which he had since sold.

It was Australia which would become his new second home. Back home in London, over a month later, less of the decreasingly visible star's time would be spent in the pop media and more of it on the gay social circuit. On Saturday July 3, 2010, he would attend the London-wide celebrations that constituted the annual Gay Pride march, ending with street parties at the central London landmarks of Trafalgar Square and Piccadilly Circus. It was at the end of this day that the strands of his life which had been gradually coming undone over the last several years would suddenly unravel, in one careless action.

It happened in the early hours of the following morning, as described in the following Metropolitan Police press release: "Police were called at approximately 03:35 hrs on Sunday 4 July to reports of a vehicle in collision with a building on Hampstead High Street. Officers attended and a man in his forties was arrested on suspicion of being unfit to drive. He was taken to a north London police station and later bailed to return during August pending further inquiries."

The cops were called by a local resident who'd heard the crash as £80,000 worth of heavy Range Rover smashed into the shop-front of a local Snappy Snaps photographic store. There was a full record of the accident preserved on CCTV. When George Michael, the driver of the car, later appeared to answer charges in court, the Crown's prosecutor would describe his condition:

"The engine was still running. Officers saw Mr Michael slumped in the vehicle. When officers knocked on the window he jumped up. He was trying to get the car into gear. He looked at the officers with his eyes wide open and the officers could see that his pupils were dilated. They opened the door and could see he was dripping with sweat.

"Officers asked him to get out of the car but he remained where he was. They placed him in handcuffs within the car. He still did not respond and, in their words, appeared to be spaced out and did not know what was happening."

On George's person were found two ready-rolled joints – damning in the eyes of the law, perhaps, but hardly an explanation for what had happened. When initially told of the result of his recklessness, the disorientated driver was supposedly in denial. "No I didn't," the cops claimed he insisted. "I didn't crash into anything."

Taken to his local police station at Hampstead, George predictably failed the test to determine whether he was fit to drive. He gave a blood test which would later yield a combination of THC (the psychoactive ingredient in cannabis) and prescription drugs. There was no trace of alcohol. More coherent now, the singer admitted to smoking a "small quantity" of weed at 10 pm; perhaps just as crucially, he said that he'd taken the prescribed anti-anxiety pill Amitriptyline when he'd got home from the Gay Pride celebrations, to combat his sleeping problems, but was unmindful enough to go out driving between his house in Hampstead and second home in Highgate, where he intended to meet a friend. George would be bailed later in the day.

When the press converged on Hampstead High Street that following Monday morning, they found a section of the glass façade of Snappy Snaps and its yellow wooden panelling smashed. Scrawled across the latter, a local wag had written the word "WHAM!" over the indentation.

By the time that George – looking chastened, sober-suited and grey-bearded, as though the seriousness of the occasion had urged him to lay off of the hair dye – appeared at Highbury Magistrates' Court on Monday August 23, with the ever-loyal Kenny in tow, he'd already imposed an unofficial driving ban on himself. Entering pleas of guilty via his lawyers to driving while unfit and possession of a class-B controlled substance (cannabis having been returned to its former criminal status), the surrender of his licence was already a foregone conclusion. His discomfort was heightened further when District Judge Robin McPhee confirmed he was deferring sentencing for three weeks, to consider all his options.

When George returned to court for sentencing, on Tuesday September 14, 2010, it was under the jurisdiction of District Judge John Perkins. Up to a couple of dozen faithful fans were seated in the public gallery. His barrister, Mukul Chawla QC, sought to mitigate on his client's behalf, stressing the performer's "profound shame and horror of having repeated the conduct of 2006".

There can be little doubt of the personal agony the singer felt over his own actions. But still, the language of regret was much the same as that expressed inside and outside court two years earlier; the offending behaviour had been just as reckless. "He acknowledges his actions of driving had the effect of causing other road users to be in danger and that stark fact is something about which he is greatly ashamed," stressed Mr Chawla. "The prospect he could have put anyone else in danger is an appalling prospect to him."

It was also stressed that the accident had been a "wake-up call" to the contrite serial offender, motivating him finally to seek help for what he now saw was an addiction to cannabis. After the accident, he'd sought immediate and ongoing psychological counselling and had spent two weeks at a detoxification clinic. "For the first time in many years he has started writing again," emphasised the QC of how his client was turning his life around. "His creativity, so long hampered by his drug dependence, is re-emerging."

Acknowledging that the star did not merely have a psychological addiction to one substance to contend with, Mr Chawla also stressed that George had tried to get off of the various pills he was prescribed for insomnia and anxiety early in 2010; when his self-prescribed 'cold turkey' approach failed to work, he'd then been prescribed the powerful relaxant Amitriptyline only eight days before the crash – trying to fight dependency to other drugs, it seemed, had only led to another.

For all the mitigation in the star's defence, Judge Perkins had reached the decision that only a custodial sentence was appropriate. "You drove your motor vehicle about a mile while suffering from a severe impairment as a result of mixing not only a prescription treatment with which you were unfamiliar but also with cannabis," he pronounced in his summing up. "That's a dangerous and unpredictable mix and something which for you is dangerous given your record.

"It does not appear that you took proper steps to deal with what is clearly an addiction to cannabis. That's a mistake which puts you and, on this occasion, the public at risk."

The legal view was that the presence of an illicit substance during a criminal act was an aggravating factor. Many habitual cannabis smokers might argue the point – it's well-known that THC is retained in the body's fatty tissues for up to a month, and it will inevitably show up in users' systems even when they're not intoxicated. It also seems more likely that George's semi-conscious disorientation and sweating were a side effect of Amitryptiline, a particularly disorientating chemical.

But for all that – being permanently semi-stoned and adding a heavy downer to the mix should be no one's idea of an alternative Highway Code.

The judge acknowledged that, along with his addiction problem, the defendant was also undergoing counselling for depression and long-standing bereavement issues. "I accept entirely that you have shown remorse for the offence, that you are ashamed of it, that you admitted it."

In fact, without the defendant's cooperation and contrition, the judge said, his term would inevitably have been longer. He could not, however, concur with the defence's plea that their client be allowed to serve another term of community service. Judge Perkins thereby sentenced George Michael (whom he addressed by that name, rather than as 'Mr Panayiotou', at the defendant's request) to eight weeks – half of which was to be served in prison, with the final four weeks on parole. He was also banned from driving for five years and fined £1,250, with £100 costs and a £15 victim surcharge.*

George flinched and tossed his head as he heard sentence pronounced. One faithful fan could be heard sobbing upstairs in the public gallery. Kenny Goss dropped his head into his hands – seemingly as much in exasperation at where his partner's behaviour had led as in despair at the sentence.

Taken down from the dock, George was driven away in a prison van to HMP Pentonville – just off of the Caledonian Road, not far from the north London neighbourhood where his mother grew up. It had been a home away from home for London's miscreants and debtors since the time of Charles Dickens, and not even the baying tabloid press would have accused the singer of passing his time comfortably there.

Other commentators were more reflective on how one of the modern entertainment industry's premier talents had come to such a pass, oft conjecturing on Sir Elton's diagnosis of 'deep-rooted unhappiness'. "When people get rich and famous it's supposed to be the be-all and end-all, isn't it?" Fiona Russell Powell, George's early eighties contemporary, remarked to this writer. "They strive to get it and then they get there and it's, 'Is that all there is?' That's another reason why many of them go off the deep end, because it doesn't satisfy the soul, it's not very nourishing really in any deep way."

---

* The latter presumably went to Snappy Snaps – although the total damage would obviously come to more, George having approached the store's manager via his lawyer to meet the costs himself.

Another voice from that early Wham! era, Simon Napier-Bell, regarded George's downfall in a rather different – if notably tolerant – context. As he wrote in *The Sunday Times*:

It's a long time since I managed George Michael – 24 years – and almost that long since I last spoke to him. I'm not sure that the person I knew then is the same person we saw in court this week. Seems to me, nowadays he's more relaxed, more amusing, more casual, more forgiving. And he's prepared to show regret.

He once said to me: "I've never done anything I could regret later." He certainly wasn't talking from the point of view of Je ne regrette rien. It was more the statement of a control freak – a 'self-control freak' – but I didn't really believe it. It sounded hopeful rather than true, though it's certainly true that George is the most in-charge-of-his-own-life person I've ever met.

He's also the most creatively complete person I ever managed; the only solo artist who can produce his own records alone better than with anyone else. There is virtually no other singer who can do that – not McCartney, nor Madonna, nor Björk.

George knows himself perfectly. And he safeguards himself perfectly. He never writes a song for anyone else because if he did, and it wasn't a hit, it would look as if his songwriting was failing. He is cautious, and thinks ahead in every instance with regard to his career. When Wham! were in China, reporters were there in their hundreds, inconsiderate and intrusive, giving George and Andrew no time to themselves. Every time they lifted a camera, George, who loathed them, smiled sweetly. But Andrew would pull a face. George told him: "You shouldn't do that. When you get home you'll hate every picture you see of yourself." And he did. But George's pictures were beautiful.

It was this ability always to think ahead that so impressed me about George, and he never gave any sign that one day he might lose it, which is what contrasts so hugely with his impulsive behaviour these days with regard to sex and drugs.

But then, drugs and sex should be impulsive – that's the fun of them.

328

Just as jumping in your car and going somewhere should be. For me, it's impossible to condemn his desire to carry on doing all these things, except when it's a hazard to other people. Crashing into Snappy Snaps was hilarious. Crashing into a baby in a pram outside might have been less so.

It's difficult to think of George sitting in a prison cell without feeling sorry for him. And I'm sure he feels sorry for himself too. But I'm also certain he'll come out smiling, saying he's a better person for it, just as Boy George did last year, and Jonathan King the year before. Whether they really were or not is up to us to decide, but on their part it's a reasonable defensive position to take — a safe stance — and career-wise, George will surely play safe.

But not too safe, please! He needs to think carefully before he rushes to change himself too much. For a manager faced with an artist whose addictive behaviour is disruptive it's important to remember that the causes of his addiction are probably the same as the causes of his creativity. Send your artist off to be cured of drug or drink or sex addiction and you may end up with an artist who is no longer creative. As a manager, I always look back at what my original terms of engagement were. To parent the artist? To make him successful? To maximise his earnings?

Well, definitely not to parent him. Most probably to create a successful career and earn the most from it. And normally, if drug addiction gets in the way, I've found it safer to live with it than to try and cure it. Only if it brings creativity to a full stop would I consider getting it cured. But it's a fine balance. Tiger Woods went off for addiction therapy because he was addicted to sex. He was also addicted to winning. Cured of one addictive behaviour, he may never again find the other.

My advice to George would be: if you enjoy the way you live, keep right on as you are — smoke all the cannabis you like, and have sex the way you like it too. But don't drive. Galling as it may be to give up that freedom, get a tight-lipped chauffeur (or two, or three) and make sure there's one on duty at all times. But other than that, don't rush to change your life too much. If your addictive behaviour is the source of your creativity, adjustments are made at your own peril.

The comment by Napier-Bell received an online response from a woman named Jo Gray, who said she used to work for George and "never ceased to admire his generous spirit and creative talent". She was in definite agreement with the former Wham! manager: "Let the man be a man and toot as much as he likes – point taken about the chauffeur requirement – wouldn't you want to forget that yellow bouffant?"

But George himself was way ahead of either of them. Ever since the accident he'd known that, if it wasn't to be seen as anything other than a temporary fall from grace, then his road back would have to feature drug detoxification among its first mileposts.

At first, the tabloid press were positively gleeful about George Michael's prison sentence. In his first couple of days, after the universally humiliating strip search and the customary short period of suicide watch, the *Daily Mirror* was somehow able to access an 'inmate' who claimed, "when he was taken to shower they sang, 'guilty George has got no freedom' to the tune of 'Careless Whisper' ...

"When the cells were unlocked in the morning he just sat there and refused to come out. Everyone was peering out of their windows overlooking the exercise yard expecting to see him but he didn't show."

According to the *Mirror*, "Michael, 47, was whisked straight into the G Wing vulnerable prisoners unit when he arrived at tough Pentonville in North London on Tuesday night. It was thought he would be safer among the paedophiles and sex offenders ..." *Which is where he belongs,* you could almost hear the paper sneering.

When George himself was finally able to describe his prison sentence, it sounded altogether less melodramatic:

"I know people think it must have been a horrific experience, but for me anyway I think it's much easier to take any form of punishment if you actually deserve it. And I did, there's no question about that. The reason I went to prison – apart from the fact that I'm George Michael and I've become the poster boy for cannabis – is that it was the second time I had a conviction. If people actually take the time to look back then they'll realise there wasn't even any cannabis involved in the first conviction... By the time I got to court, in my own head I'd been released from a very, very dark chapter of my life anyway – I'd had some counselling, I'm in ongoing therapy about drug abuse and stuff. So I think what people need to know is I took it very seriously. I didn't understand my own behaviour; then I *did* understand my behaviour, but felt that by the time I went to court this was never going to happen again regardless. I knew I was going to lose my licence; I was assured I wasn't going to prison, but I thought I was. And like I said, it was much easier to take because I thought it was deserved. I honestly am someone who was brought up with such a principle of 'do unto others' that this was a shameful thing to have done repeatedly. So karmically I felt like I had a bill to pay: I went to prison, I paid my bill; that's the way I felt. I hope that whole period of my life where I felt a bit lost is over for good."

It was spoken like the composer of 'Praying For Time', the neo-Buddhist New Ager with the karmic debt to repay. And this time, if God was keeping score, George wanted him to know that all debts would be honoured. But then, he wouldn't be spending his time alone on a hillside, seeking nirvana. The beginning of his time would be served at a grotty old Victorian London prison.

"Of course it was Pentonville, I knew it wasn't a weekend break. What did I think? Well, I didn't feel sorry for myself really. I thought, 'Oh my God, this place is absolutely filthy.' But I just thought, 'You get your head down; it's an eight-week sentence, it's the natural way of doing things if you misbehave yourself, four weeks of your life.' Nobody *told* me I wasn't in Pentonville for four weeks – they were nice enough to keep that from me. That actually was like a clearing house, because it was the closest prison to the magistrate's court. That's the way it works. But they didn't tell me so I thought I was in there for four weeks, which wouldn't have been great, and I probably would have come out with a terrible back, because the beds are about 80 years old and they're made of metal. You're lying on about an inch and a half of foam.

"I've been through so many things in my life that have been emotionally torturous that, ultimately, four weeks of however bad it was going to be, I didn't find that daunting. All these stories about me crying, that was just the usual rubbish. They *wish* that was me, but that's not me."

Somehow, George's own words carry the greater air of authenticity. Despite whatever images the press may present, most prisoners are just people who have made bad choices and messed up – just like you, or I, or George are capable of doing. The idea that his fellow cons would be offended to suddenly have a famous gay pop star in their midst does not hold up. Most of the older lags – thirties, forties and beyond – have wives or girlfriends just like everybody else; they wouldn't want to be refused sex on their release because they'd been a party to something bad that happened to George Michael.

(Even the tabloids' adapted lyric of 'Careless Whisper' sounded like a sub-editor's contrivance. Why not the more obvious "George ain't got no freedom!", to paraphrase the song of that name?)

According to George's matter-of-fact version of events, in the isolation of his prison sentence he was no longer feeling quite so alienated. Going by the amount of correspondence he received, it seemed he was on more people's minds than ever:

"[Elton] wrote to me in the nick, which was nice. So did Boy George, he wrote me a lovely letter; we spoke in the last couple of days; one of the guys from Frankie [Goes to Hollywood] I have to say thank you to, I can't remember which one it was. And I got a letter from Paul McCartney, which was lovely, because of course he'd got done in Japan. Andrew got to me through regular channels; George got through to me on emailaprisoner.com, which I thought was fantastic. There's a service, you pay £5 or something, and anyone you know who's in prison, you can write to."

(In 2009, an ageing Boy George had served four months of a 15-month sentence relating to a bizarre incident almost two years earlier – when he handcuffed and imprisoned a male escort in his East End flat, threatening him over stolen images from his laptop. As with his namesake, George O'Dowd began his sentence at Pentonville and was said to be terrified; in the eventuality, it seems he did his time well. He is alleged to have put the word out among his former prison contacts to ensure that George Michael was holding up well, dispelling two and a half decades of bitching about him.)

At the end of his first week in prison, it was rumoured that inmate number A8365AW would be appealing via his lawyers against the sentence. The appeal never took place – which was probably for the best, as George may have risked having his sentence increased. Instead, he was moved from the allocation point of Pentonville to the more relaxed environment of HMP Highpoint in Suffolk, housing security category 'C' prisoners. It was where he would serve the bulk of his sentence and, while not the 'holiday camp' that the yellow press might make it out to be, it was clearly no bad place to do his time either. As George would relate soon after:

"The last night was great actually. And the strange thing about it was that the whole wing I was on had been told they couldn't come near me for an autograph – and of course every single one of them did *and* every single staff member as well, every single one. But on the last night, a guy came into the room and asked me sign this guitar – he'd managed to get hold of a guitar. So I signed it to him. I used to say to them all, 'Go and get a piece of prison paper – then it'll be *worth* something.' Do you know what I mean? Especially a few years down the line. 'Go and get a piece of Her Majesty's Service prison paper with a George Michael signature on it.' [laughs] This guy came in with a guitar and he wanted me to write the date. He said, 'It's the 10th of the 10th of the 10th.' I thought that's just so fitting, it's like the clock rolling round to the end of something before I start again, do you know what I mean?"

George Michael saw release from Highpoint Prison on the 11th of the 10th, 2010. With reporters encamped around his Hampstead home, he momentarily decamped from his friends and family to issue a short statement that, in its bright breeziness, was almost a form of quiet defiance.

"I'm coming out here on my own so that you'll realise I just want to start again," he promised the ladies and gentlemen of the press. "I'm going to try to stop running away from you guys. You'll get sick of me. You'll see me about."

It seemed almost deflating to the tabloids, all of whom seemed to prefer the buzz around the singer when there was a disaster or tragedy in the offing. In fact though, the promise took a little time to be fulfilled. Part of his next few months would be spent in Australia, where George was picking up the pieces of the new life he'd started to make before he so rudely interrupted it.

But he was also productive in a way that he hadn't been in years – creating music that he intended for release, rather than storing it away on a DAT tape or MP3 file somewhere. In early March of 2011, ready to embark on a new wave of activity, he'd drop in on his old cohort, Radio Two DJ Chris Evans, for their third full-length interview in a decade in a half. In it, George spoke about his transition from a permanently semi-stoned state to sobriety:

"I hope it's self-evident [laughs], just in the fact that I've dropped about 15 pounds, I'm not eating as much any more, which should tell you a lot. None of my trousers fit any more – for the right reasons, for a change...

"Even though [the driving accidents were] a mistake rather than a conscious decision each time, I still didn't understand why it wasn't hitting my subconscious hard enough to stop that mistake happening again. And then [I] went into proper, proper therapy with a completely clean system – when I say clean, I mean clear of antidepressants as well. Because antidepressants, although they're miraculous in some situations, sometimes they can really cloak what's going on. I think I really had proper therapy for the first time about bereavement without antidepressants...

"It really wasn't a case of me stumbling from place to place and getting it together. It's different but it's the same for everybody – if you use drugs to escape a situation, then eventually it's the drugs you can't escape. It's the same as anybody else's story one way or another."

Most remarkable about the beginning of this new spate of activity was the choice of material. To an extent it seemed like cheating, as the first 'original' George Michael release in over two years was a cover version; it's in the original source material – the song 'True Faith' by electro band New Order – that he was confounding expectations:

"I came out of the nick, sat around chatting with my mates for a couple of hours then switched on VH1. What was playing on the TV was 'Freedom' by Wham! – which was quite remarkable in the first place, you know that video of us in China? And then suddenly afterwards they played 'True Faith' – I suddenly heard the lyric for what it was for the first time; what a fantastic lyric it was about addiction. And I thought, 'How perfect is that?' And I recorded the vocal for it within 24 hours. Literally almost all of this is one take done at home – and this is the kind of musicality I only show when I'm completely joyful, you know. You would be a bit cheerful, getting out of prison – for a bit."

Maybe we shouldn't be so surprised at the choice of material. In recent years, George has talked about how, in the Wham! days, he and Andrew used to listen to Joy Division – the intense, doom-laden post-punk band that New Order grew out of, after the suicide of original singer Ian Curtis. New Order took the electronic textures and tones of Joy Division's final album, *Closer* (a favourite of George's – and of dope smokers everywhere), and made something more danceable out of it.

The original version of 'True Faith' is typical in that sense – a catchy, almost ethereal song, it's only on closer consideration that you realise vocalist/songwriter Bernard Sumner is singing a non-judgmental lyric about a young man whose illusory sense of freedom depends on taking a drug (possibly heroin) every day. The faith of the title is not in any recognisable religion, but in "the thing that costs you too much".

George was obviously coming at the song from a more personal angle – as evidenced by his performance. In the accompanying video released in time for 2011's Comic Relief (to which all proceeds from the download would be donated), the older, grey-bearded, crop-haired guy with the receding hairline sings the ambiguous lyric slowed down to a lazy R&B/swing beat. Amid druggy clouds of smoke, from which robotic animated characters rise and disappear, George halts the original song for a while to slur out that he has "a big fucking question" about what's going on. He puts his moral uncertainty about his former lifestyle on display for all to see.

The most controversial point about 'True Faith' among music fans (particularly outraged fans of the original) is how George broke the back of the song and reconstructed it. It's true that the languid beat doesn't really suit what was previously an urgent lyric that communicated "a feeling [that] I'm in motion" – but what seems to have offended most is the channelling of his famous vocal tones, just about recognisable for a brief moment, through an electronic vocoder.

It was not without precedent – Stevie Wonder and Neil Young had used the device, while George himself used it previously on a cover of Joni Mitchell's sinister love song 'Edith And The King Pin', recorded around the time of *Patience* and finally issued on the 'December Song' CD. It's also perhaps the one element of George's cover that would have suited New Order's electro-based original.

But then, how perverse is it that having rid himself of all his chemical addictions, George Michael should record a new single that sounds so far out there that you'd think its maker must be on drugs?

EPILOGUE

Unfinished Symphony

Newly ensconced in his luxury $5 million Sydney Harbour home, George Michael withdrew from the scrutiny of the British press after spending Christmas 2010 with Kenny Goss and his own family. In early 2011, hazardous nocturnal drives around north London became a thing of the past, given up in favour of an anonymous chauffeured red car and a glass of white wine in the afternoon at the Hunky Dory Social Club on Sydney's Oxford Street.

Embracing Sydney's Northern Beaches gay scene, George became something of a born-again Aussie. According to the Sydney *Daily Telegraph*, he'd also signed up to Scruff, a new iPhone social networking service that promises, "Meet hundreds of thousands of scruffy gay guys in your neighbourhood." It seems one of the world's greatest living exponents of the love song may still like a bit of rough. (George did not respond to the paper, which had previously outed him as a gay social-network user one year before. But if the guy in the profile photo isn't him, he has a promising career beckoning on the lookalike circuit.)

Small wonder perhaps that he should be forced to defend the state of his relationship when he came back to Hampstead in the early spring. "It is complete bullshit about myself and Kenny breaking up," he emphatically told Channel 5's *The Wright Stuff* when he phoned them to contradict a *Sun* report in mid-March. "We've had our problems but he's never had a problem with my lifestyle."

It all had a touch of *déjà vu* about it, even if it wasn't his former morning TV mouthpiece. (With *Richard & Judy* shunted off to an obscure cable channel, what else was a boy to do?) But there again, George, the reformed pot and pill head, was still enough of a TV junkie to have an ongoing relationship with that medium.

As far back as the end of the previous year, an apparent evening of bonhomie, backslapping and vino was shared chez Michael with Simon Cowell and Jonathan Ross – the east London-bred chat show host who'd been George's near-neighbour in Hampstead for many years. He'd also conducted a long TV interview with the young George back in the days of *Faith*, and it was mooted that 'Wossy' might provide the vehicle that brought both him and George back to primetime entertainment. It all sounded perfect: after blotting his BBC copybook engaging in a puerile jape with comic Russell Brand, Ross would launch a new Saturday night ITV series immediately after *The X Factor*, featuring an exclusive one-to-one interview with George and the man himself singing some of his most celebrated tunes.

But by mid-January, Cowell had nixed it. He decided that the content would be somehow too adult for the six-to-70 kiddies of all ages who tuned into his regular show.

"We were talking about the kind of areas that would be tough in the interview and the kind of tone of the interview, and would it be right to follow a show like *The X Factor* with a show that potentially deals with a lot of emotion," Ross felt compelled to explain the cancellation to interviewers on Gaydar Radio. "Some of the things George has told me about the last few years of his life and his childhood, which we would have covered in this interview, were very moving. At times, quite shocking. I think it would have been, perhaps, inappropriate."

As the most reliable word suggests that George's spell in prison has finally galvanised him into writing his autobiography, we can only assume that these personal revelations will finally see print, even if they're never broadcast. It bodes less well for the state of the commercial TV industry, of course.

In March, George made his actual return to the small screen with his contribution to the 2011 *Comic Relief*. "Even in the darkest periods I've been through, I truly appreciate comedy," he told Chris Evans. "It keeps you alive! Some days the only thing that got you through the day was a good episode of something. So I'm very drawn to comedians, the people I tend to stay in touch with are comedians rather than actors or singers. I think probably because they're the only people who put themselves out there more; I'd say singing is the second bravest thing you can do onstage. Being a comedian is ranked up at number one. The video is going to be played on the night of *Comic Relief*, and there's a little extra from me but I don't think we should go any further. I don't want to spoil anyone's fun."

'True Faith', the New Order cover, made its official debut on *Comic Relief*. Despite its likeably out-of-leftfield nature, by that point it had failed to make much of an impact on the UK charts (though, as George told the fans on Twitter, his most recently embraced mode of contact, it had raised £74,000 for the charity). As in 2005, George also participated as a guest star in the linking comedy sketches; sadly, there was nothing here to match the classic *Little Britain*/Andy & Lou routine. Instead, George played foil to the Smithy character (popular chubby boy James Corden) from *Gavin And Stacey*, who was reluctant to do his bit for the charity because he was driving around in his plumber's van with "a mate who's been away" (Smithy and George in matching tracksuit tops). It did at least tickle the funny bone when Smithy got George excited by playing Wham!'s old hits in the motor – a scenario that people who remember him from back in the day claim isn't so far from the truth.

In the wake of *Comic Relief*, rumours kept bubbling to the surface about George's curious on/off working relationship with Simon Cowell, the 'Dark Lord' of British TV. Despite Cowell cancelling the promising Michael-Ross show, rumours were circulating that George would come onboard *X Factor USA* as a judge for a purported £1 million fee. When that was turned down (George's apparent Brit replacement being Cheryl Cole, which would all end in tears), then he was mooted as a guest judge on the original UK show for a one-off £75,000.

Neither, it seems, was ever a realistic prospect, as he testified when he phoned in to another of his favourite daytime TV shows, *Loose Women*. "I couldn't be involved in the bit where they take the mickey out of people," he earnestly confessed. "I understand how terrifying and heartbreaking auditions are, particularly if you're really young. I could never be involved in that part – maybe some mentoring thing, I don't know, but I couldn't be involved in the cruel part."

George's own comeback plans were rather more interesting, and they slipped out in the public domain in the most casual manner. His latest addiction was undoubtedly Twitter; he'd sent his very first tweet from Chris Evans' radio show early in March. Later that month he sent out a blast against all those who were writing off the single:

"'True Faith' at no2 in the UK iTunes video chart, CD no1 for the 18th day on Amazon UK, and went from 55 to 18 on the airplay chart. So thank you all, and fuck the journos who are trying to kill the record. Which, by the way, they do pretty much every time, lol :).

"Face it paps, hacks and haters," he continued, "the album will sell great, the tour will sell out, and the fans remain some of the loyalest in the world." It was a lot of promises made for one short message: a new album by the man who, just over two years earlier, had branded albums "passé" and a full tour by a performer who had supposedly retired from the stage.

Later, he sent the following stream of joyful invective aimed at the press:

"Hey everyone ... something important to say ... WHAT THE FUCK!!!!!!!

"This is why I love twitter! MEDIA PAY ATTENTION!

"I HAVE NEVER AND WILL NEVER APOLOGISE FOR MY SEX LIFE ! GAY SEX IS NATURAL, GAY SEX IS GOOD! NOT EVERYBODY DOES IT, BUT ... HA HA!

"I apologised for my driving accidents and the homophobic language that they induced in a HOMOPHOBIC PRESS!"

He was, to all extents and purposes, just a boy with a new toy. But while the 47-year-old man was busy embracing post-internet modes of communication and sounding like a kid on ecstasy, he was also taking the first tentative steps to rehabilitating himself in the public eye.

In mid-April, he told chat show host Piers Morgan (a former editor of the *Daily Mirror*, ironically enough) that he was making a major goodwill gesture for the Royal Wedding of England's Prince William to his fiancée Kate Middleton. As a present to the couple (and one suspects in memory of the prince's much beloved mother, George's friend Diana), the singer had recorded a cover of Stevie Wonder's 'You And I', a deeply romantic ballad from the Motown legend's classic 1972 *Talking Book* album.

The intention was to present the song as a gratis gesture to the royal couple, whose wedding at Westminster Abbey on April 29 was declared a public holiday in the UK – and indeed to all the public, who were to be able to download the track free from George's website. But then commerce got in the way of the artist's goodwill.

"Those fuckers at EMI wanted to charge me for every download," he complained on Twitter of the song's copyright holders, "[but] I'd like Will and Kate to know I was prepared to do that." The composer himself came to the rescue when Stevie Wonder waived all royalty payments on the song, at least until what he promised would be a long time after the wedding.

'You And I', as a piece of music, returned George Michael to the electronically orchestrated, slightly maudlin emotions of 'A Different Corner'. If 'True Faith' was him getting with the times, then the Wonder cover was a reassurance to his audience that the old George was still there below the surface.

It might have made for a strange hybrid of emotions, if George had come to pay tribute to the happy couple at the same monolithic Abbey where he'd once cried his eyes out over the groom's late mother. But in any case, it was not to be. William and Kate accepted his gift in the manner in which it was intended, while George urged his fans to make a donation to the Royal Wedding charity trust for downloading the single.

All the same, an invitation from Buckingham Palace was not forthcoming. The performer apparently took it in stride. "They should

[be] surrounded by people they love," he acknowledged with realism and good humour, "not dodgy ex-con pop stars."

(Elton, on the other hand, was present in the chapel where he'd once lamented Diana. According to the press, in their new-found status as Britain's alternative royal couple, David Furnish had complained that the John-Furnishes were not seated prominently enough. "We all earn the right to get a little more grumpy as we get older," said George of his lifelong musical hero and latter-day accuser, "but he's getting terribly close to Nan territory, you know the Nan from *Catherine Tate*." George did at least have the good grace to congratulate the gay couple on the birth of their son Zachary, while asserting that he could never do any such thing: "Can you imagine being George Michael's son at school? I don't think [Elton is] quite as embarrassing as George Michael as a potential father.")

But for all his acceptance of himself as pop culture's wise fool, George was still clearly yearning to be taken back to its bosom. Quizzed by an interviewer about the ceremony for the 2012 Olympics in east London, he conceded that he would love to perform but hadn't been asked. In any case, in career terms he had bigger fish to fry – as he first announced in the March 2011 interview with Chris Evans: "Someone said to me, 'This album is going to be like a more electronic *Faith*. Because you're writing with that kind of directness again.' I think there's a lot more joy to put into the writing this time around, and since I've been out as a gay man house music is more of an influence in my life.

"So ultimately, as a gay man you don't really stop listening to club music as early as straight people do, do you know what I mean? And I wanted the album to reflect that, but also this other project that I'm doing reflects somebody that's getting older as a singer and interpreter as well. So what I thought was, 'What do you want at this point in life?' I can honestly say I have no interest in just repeating my successes. There are other aspects to the new material that I think are progress. Once you've reached a certain point and had a certain type of success again and again, ultimately, to drive you forward as an artist, I think what you look for is authenticity. And if I'm going to be authentic, then authenticity is to do the type of tour I'm about to do, which I've never done before, and then expressing more personal truths about the things that I now think about, having lived as a gay man for 12 years."

The album, which George said had come about in part due to his burst of confidence at leaving his drug dependency behind, would subsequently be described by him as the work of "a gay collective on which some of the records are sung by myself, some by other artists, possibly unknown ones, but there will be collaborations with a lot of artists." It was as if he was seeking to make up for half a life's worth of denial and lost time. When George announced in May 2011 that he had "a really serious problem with the fact that when I brought myself down, I felt I was letting young gay kids down," it remained a matter of conjecture as to whether he really had in mind the gay kids of today, who have the verbal support of a liberal establishment but the threat of a more macho culture on the street, or his own peers when he refused to come out for so many years.

The great irony remains that, when he was forced out of the closet, the star found that the last people to give a damn about his personal sexuality were the majority of George Michael fans. And so it remains to this day.

The live tour would be a different thing altogether. Under the heading *Symphonica*, he would kick off 47 European dates at Prague's State Opera House in August 2011, before returning in the autumn and winter to perform in London at the Royal Opera House, the Royal Albert Hall and the O2 – all with the backing of a full orchestra, reinterpreting his life's works. "This new classical setting will give each song added layers and new nuances. It's unmistakeably George Michael, but not as we've ever known him," said the tour's spokesman.

It's an intriguing concept – the potential richness of 'Praying For Time' and 'Jesus To A Child' with full orchestral backing is obvious. But what of the dance-orientated numbers? 'Outside'? 'Freeek'? 'Shoot The Dog' even?

But then this is the resurgent George Michael – the crop-headed, black-spectacled and respectable-looking gentleman who's preparing a gay house-orientated album at the same time. With much time to make up for and his youth long gone, the performer is behaving both as one thing and as its opposite.

It's a career renaissance on a major scale. (At time of writing, two more London dates have been added at Earls Court at the end of 2011, due to intense demand.) As a multifaceted and often contradictory human being, George Michael still has the potential to fuck up on a human level – as he surely knows better than anyone else. But he is engaged in an almost manic spate of creative activity that has its origin in a day when he almost let everything go. One careless moment and one slipped foot on the clutch could have ended his career; as it stands now, it looks as if it finally gave him the resolve to make the most of everything he nearly threw away.

On Monday, August 22, 2011, the first chapter of that career renaissance took place at the State Opera House in Prague. Chatting in confessional mode to a capacity audience, garrulous George spoke to the Czech crowd as if they were old pals who'd loyally supported him throughout every episode of the soap opera that was his life. He also dropped a casual little bombshell. "In truth, Kenny and I haven't been together for two and a half years," he confessed as a preamble to a recently penned autobiographical ballad, 'Where I Hope You Are Now' – which features a tearjerkingly regretful line about, "Some place warm we could hang out when we're old."

"This man has brought me a lot of joy and pain," he confided to his several thousand close friends. "My love life has been a lot more turbulent than I've ever let on, and I'm so sad about my relationship with Kenny." With a similarly light touch, George made his lover's own substance addiction into an open secret. According to a teary-eyed George, the man he still called "my partner" had descended into alcoholism since the death of his parents in Texas several years previously. It was, said the singer, the scariest thing he'd ever witnessed.

The twinning of mourning and addiction was a syndrome he could only sympathise with – even if admission of their fractured relationship belied all his recent denials, throwing into sharp relief Kenny's anguished attendance at his September 2010 trial. But if there was a personal agenda, it was that George Michael had reclaimed the right to control information about his own life. In a manner perhaps not witnessed since his solo heyday of the late eighties, there was little doubt about just who was in control now.

Acknowledgements

In any unauthorised biography, it's always a challenge for the author to find voices of authority to bolster authorial opinion. I must therefore express my gratitude firstly to Simon Napier-Bell, former manager of Wham! and many other artists (some of whose names continue to resonate). Simon declined to offer a new interview, having in his opinion already written or said enough – or too much – about George Michael. Instead, in an act of kindness, he offered carte blanche quotation rights from his works and interviews, which was gratefully accepted. It may come as a (hopefully pleasant) surprise to Simon to find how thoroughly his words have been utilised; rather than merely quoting from Napier-Bell's books, however, your author has transcribed much of the material from the pop legend and *bon viveur*'s TV interviews of the last 25 years, as well as quoting from email correspondence that relates to this book's subject. Much of this wealth of material has never seen print before.

I also gratefully acknowledge Fiona Russell Powell, a very fine writer in her own right. As a contemporary of George's who came on the London club scene at the same time, Fiona is well placed to recall the double life led by the young singer "when he first started whammering". I'm grateful for her recollections of the early-mid eighties and her observations and opinions relating to the years that followed. Her candour about those early days created a rift between her and George's social circle after he was 'outed' in 1998. The points she made in a controversial magazine article of the time are expanded here and inform several sections of this book. In the light of George's subsequent admission that he first tried to leave the closet aged 19, I hope Fiona's testimony will now be appreciated for what it is – the missing piece in the narrative of George Michael's life.

In terms of the 'narrative spine', reference to the authorised (and highly recommended) bio-documentary *George Michael: A Different Life* proved invaluable in terms of comparing the relaxed, self-deprecating figure of the last decade with the more controlled (and controlling) young man described by his eighties contemporaries. Transcribing interviews from the film helped to give a more rounded, human view of his story, as did a number of other broadcast interviews (many of them produced by the BBC) – most notably two lengthy sessions with Chris Evans for Radio 2 (1996 and 2011) and a *Desert Island Discs* interview with Kirsty Young for Radio 4 (2007), plus TV interviews with Kirsty Wark (2004), Michael Parkinson (1998 and 2006); Graham Norton (2003) and Tim Sebastian for BBC4's *HardTalk* (two interviews – George Michael, 2003, and Simon Napier-Bell).

In obtaining a view of the younger George Michael and his importance to pop music in the eighties, *Bare*, co-authored by George with Tony Parsons, is still invaluable. It offers an authorised perspective of its subject quite at odds with those of the contributors to this book. In terms of the events of the nineties, the unauthorised *George Michael: Older* by Tim and Nicholas Wapshott provides a useful sequence of facts and figures (even if it's on shakier ground with the subject of pop music). The ups and downs of the last decade have been well documented in the UK press – both the broadsheets and the tabloid papers disdained by this book's subject. (Where George's account of events differs from that of the press, the author has acknowledged this.)

Lastly, an acknowledgement of the close acquaintances of our subject who were approached by the author – including those who initially agreed to an interview but later withdrew. Your loyalty to George Michael is appreciated, as is the wish not to participate in 'competition' with his long-mooted autobiography (awaited with interest by many, including this writer). I hope it will be conceded that the following work is merely a less subjective account, rather than some kind of enemy action. The author has sought to balance the more colourful or contradictory aspects of the man and his life with respect for him as a creative artist and a human being.

Discography

Wham! singles

A – WHAM RAP! (ENJOY WHAT YOU DO – 7″ version)
(Panayiotou/Ridgeley)
B – WHAM RAP! (ENJOY WHAT YOU DO – Club Mix)
Innervision 7″ IVL A2442, June 1982

A – WHAM RAP! (Social Mix)
B – WHAM RAP! (Unsocial Mix)
Innervision 12″ IVLA 13 2442, June 1982

A – YOUNG GUNS (GO FOR IT!) (Michael)
B – GOING FOR IT (Michael)
Innervision 7″ IVL A2776, October 1982

A – YOUNG GUNS (GO FOR IT!)
B – GOING FOR IT
Innervision 12″ IVL A 13 2776, October 1992

A – WHAM RAP! (ENJOY WHAT YOU DO – Special US
Remix Part One) (Michael/Ridgeley)
B – WHAM RAP! (ENJOY WHAT YOU DO – Special US
Remix Part Two)
Innervision 7″ IVL A 2442, January 1983

A – WHAM RAP! (ENJOY WHAT YOU DO – Special US
Remix)
B – WHAM RAP! (ENJOY WHAT YOU DO – Special Club
Remix)
Innervision 12″ IVL A 13 2442, January 1983

A – BAD BOYS (Michael)
B – BAD BOYS (Instrumental)
Innervision 7″ A 3143, April 1983

A – BAD BOYS (12″ Mix)
B – BAD BOYS (Instrumental)
Innervision 12″ TA 3143, April 1983

A – CLUB TROPICANA (Michael/Ridgeley)
B – BLUE (ARMED WITH LOVE) (Michael)
Innervision 7″ A 3613, July 1983

A – CLUB TROPICANA
B – BLUE; CLUB TROPICANA (Instrumental)
Innervision 12″ TA 3613, July 1983

A – CLUB FANTASTIC MEGAMIX (Michael/Moore/Griffin)
B – A RAY OF SUNSHINE (Instrumental Mix) (Michael)
Innervision 7″ A 3586, November 1983

A – CLUB FANTASTIC MEGAMIX
B – A RAY OF SUNSHINE (Instrumental Remix)
Innervision 12″ TA 3586, November 1983

A – WAKE ME UP BEFORE YOU GO-GO (Michael)
B – WAKE ME UP BEFORE YOU GO-GO (Instrumental)
UK EPIC 7″ A 4440, May 1984

A – WAKE ME UP BEFORE YOU GO-GO
B – A RAY OF SUNSHINE (live on *The Tube*); WAKE ME UP
BEFORE YOU G0-GO (Instrumental)
UK EPIC 12″ TA 4440, May 1984

A – FREEDOM (Michael)
B – FREEDOM (Instrumental)
UK EPIC 7″ A 4743, August 1984

A – FREEDOM (Long Mix)
B – FREEDOM (Instrumental)
UK EPIC 12″ TA 4743, August 1984

A – EVERYTHING SHE WANTS (7″ Remix) (Michael)
A – LAST CHRISTMAS (Michael)
UK EPIC 7″ QA 4949, December 1984

A – EVERYTHING SHE WANTS (12″ Remix)
A – LAST CHRISTMAS (Pudding Mix)
UK EPIC 12″ QTA 4949, December 1984

A – I'M YOUR MAN (Michael)
B – DO IT RIGHT (Michael)
EPIC 7″ A 6716, November 1985

A – I'M YOUR MAN (Extended Stimulation)
B – DO IT RIGHT; I'M YOUR MAN (A Cappella)
EPIC 12″ TA 6716, November 1985

A – THE EDGE OF HEAVEN (Michael)
B – WHAM RAP! '86
EPIC 7" A FIN 1, June 1986

A – THE EDGE OF HEAVEN
B – WHAM RAP! '86
A – BATTLESTATIONS (Michael)
B – WHERE DID YOUR HEART GO? (David and Don Was)
EPIC limited edition double-7" FIN 1, June 1986

A – BATTLESTATIONS; WHERE DID YOUR HEART GO?
B – THE EDGE OF HEAVEN; WHAM RAP! '86
EPIC 12" FIN T1, June 1986

Wham! albums

FANTASTIC

Bad Boys; A Ray Of Sunshine; Love Machine (Moore/Griffin);
Wham Rap! (Enjoy What You Do); Club Tropicana; Nothing Looks
The Same In The Light (Michael); Come On (Michael); Young
Guns (Go For It!)
INNERVISION vinyl IVL25328 July 1983

FANTASTIC

Bad Boys; A Ray Of Sunshine; Love Machine; Wham Rap! (Enjoy
What You Do); A Ray Of Sunshine (Instrumental Remix); Love
Machine (Instrumental Remix); Club Tropicana; Nothing Looks
The Same In The Light; Come On; Young Guns (Go For It!);
Nothing Looks The Same In The Light (Instrumental Remix)
SONY CD 4500902, 1999

MAKE IT BIG

Wake Me Up Before You Go-Go; Everything She Wants; Heartbeat (Michael); Like A Baby (Michael); Freedom; If You Were There (Isley Brothers); Credit Card Baby (Michael); Careless Whisper (Michael/Ridgeley)
EPIC vinyl EPC 86311, October 1984

MAKE IT BIG

Track listing as above.
SONY CD 4655762, 1998

MUSIC FROM THE EDGE OF HEAVEN

The Edge of Heaven, Battlestations, I'm Your Man (Extended Version), Wham Rap, A Different Corner (With Introduction), Blue (Live in China), Where Did Your Heart Go?, Last Christmas. Columbia, 1986. US and Japan only.

WHAM! – THE FINAL

Wham Rap! (Enjoy What You Do); Young Guns (Go For It!); Bad Boys; Club Tropicana; Blue (Armed With Love); Wake Me Up Before You Go-Go; Careless Whisper; Freedom; Last Christmas (Pudding Mix); Everything She Wants; I'm Your Man; A Different Corner (Michael); Battlestations; Where Did Your Heart Go?; The Edge Of Heaven
EPIC vinyl double album EPC 88681, April 1986

WHAM! – THE FINAL

Track listing as above.
EPIC CD CDEPC 88681, April 1986

THE BEST OF WHAM!: IF YOU WERE THERE

If You Were There; I'm Your Man; Everything She Wants; Club Tropicana; Wake Me Up Before You Go-Go; Like A Baby; Freedom; The Edge Of Heaven; Wham Rap! (Enjoy What You Do); Young Guns (Go For It!); Last Christmas; Where Did Your Heart Go?; Everything She Wants '97; I'm Your Man '96
SONY CD 4890202, November 1997

George Michael singles

A – CARELESS WHISPER
B – CARELESS WHISPER (Instrumental)
EPIC 7" A 4603 June 1984

A – CARELESS WHISPER (Extended Mix)
B – CARELESS WHISPER (Instrumental)
EPIC 12" TA 4603 June 1984

A – A DIFFERENT CORNER
B – A DIFFERENT CORNER (Instrumental)
EPIC 7" A 7033 April 1986

A – A DIFFERENT CORNER
B – A DIFFERENT CORNER (Instrumental)
EPIC 12" GTA 7033 April 1986

A – I WANT YOUR SEX (Rhythm 1: Lust) (Michael)
B – I WANT YOUR SEX (Rhythm 2: Brass In Love)
EPIC 7" LUST 1 June 1987

A – I WANT YOUR SEX (Monogamy Mix); I WANT YOUR
SEX (Rhythm 1: Lust); I WANT YOUR SEX ((Rhythm 2: Brass In
Love);
B – I WANT YOUR SEX (Rhythm 3: Last Request); HARD DAY
(Michael)
EPIC 12″ LUST T1, June 1987

A – FAITH (Michael)
B – HAND TO MOUTH (Michael)
EPIC 7″ EMU 3, October 1987

A – FAITH
B – FAITH (Instrumental); HAND TO MOUTH
EPIC 12″ EMU 2, October 1987

A – FATHER FIGURE (Michael)
B – LOVE'S IN NEED OF LOVE TODAY (Wonder)
EPIC 7″ EMU 4, December 1987

A – FATHER FIGURE
B – LOVE'S IN NEED OF LOVE TODAY (Live) (Wonder);
FATHER FIGURE (Instrumental)
EPIC 12″ EMU T4, December 1987
Track listing as above.
EPIC CD EMU 4, December 1987

A – ONE MORE TRY (Michael)
B – LOOK AT YOUR HANDS (Michael/Austin)
EPIC 7″ EMU 5, April 1988
Track listing as above.
EPIC 12″ EMUT5, April 1988

ONE MORE TRY (Album Version); LOOK AT YOUR HANDS
EPIC CD EPC6515322, April 1988

A – MONKEY (7″ Edit) (Michael)
B – MONKEY (A Cappella)
EPIC 7″ EMU 6, July 1988

A – MONKEY (Extended Version)
B – MONKEY (A Cappella); MONKEY (Extra Beats)
EPIC 12″ EMUT6, July 1988
Track listing as above, plus MONKEY (7″ edit).
EPIC CD EMU 6, July 1988

A – KISSING A FOOL (Michael)
B – KISSING A FOOL (Instrumental)
EPIC 7″ EMU 7, November 1988
Track listing as above.
EPIC 12″ EMU T7, November 1988.

KISSING A FOOL; KISSING A FOOL (Instrumental); A LAST
REQUEST (I WANT YOUR SEX PART III) (Michael)
EPIC CD EMU 7, November 1988

A – PRAYING FOR TIME (Michael)
B – IF YOU WERE MY WOMAN (Michael)
EPIC 7″ GEO 1, August 1990

A – PRAYING FOR TIME
B – IF YOU WERE MY WOMAN; WAITING (Reprise) (Michael)
EPIC 12″ GEO T1, August 1990
Track listing as above.
EPIC CD GEO C1, August 1990

A – FREEDOM! '90 (Michael)
B – FREEDOM! (Back To Reality Mix)
EPIC 7″ GEO 3, October 1990
Track listing as above.
EPIC 12″ GEO T3, October 1990

FREEDOM! '90; MOTHER'S PRIDE (Michael); FREEDOM!
'90 (Back To Reality Mix)
EPIC CD GEO C3, October 1990

A – WAITING FOR THAT DAY (Michael/Jagger/Richards)
B – FANTASY (Michael)
EPIC 7″ GEO 2, December 1990
Track listing as above.
EPIC 12″ GEO T2, December 1990
WAITING FOR THAT DAY; FANTASY; FATHER FIGURE;
KISSING A FOOL
EPIC CD GEO C2, December 1990

A – HEAL THE PAIN (Michael)
B – SOUL FREE (Michael)
EPIC 7″ EPC 656647 7, February 1991
Track listing as above.
EPIC 12″ EPC 656647 6, February 1991
Track listing as above.
EPIC CD EPC 656647 2, February 1991

A – COWBOYS AND ANGELS (Edit) (Michael)
B – SOMETHING TO SAVE (Michael)
EPIC 7″ EPC 6567774 7, March 1991

A – COWBOYS AND ANGELS (LP Version)
B – COWBOYS AND ANGELS (Edit); SOMETHING TO SAVE
EPIC 12″ EPC 656774 8, March 1991
Track listing as above.
EPIC CD 656774 5, March 1991

A – TOO FUNKY (Michael)
B – CRAZYMAN DANCE (Michael)
EPIC 7″ EPC 658058 7, June 1992

A – TOO FUNKY (Extended Mix)
B – CRAZYMAN DANCE
EPIC 12″ EPC 658058 6, June 1992

A – TOO FUNKY (Extended Mix)
B – CRAZYMAN DANCE; TOO FUNKY
EPIC CD EPC 658058 2, June 1992

JESUS TO A CHILD (Michael); ONE MORE TRY (Live);
OLDER (Instrumental) (Michael)
VIRGIN CD VSCDG 1571, January 1996

A – JESUS TO A CHILD; FREEDOM! '94
B – ONE MORE TRY (Live); OLDER (Instrumental)
EPIC double CD VSCDX 1571, January 1996

FASTLOVE★ (Part 1) (Michael/McFadden/Rushen/Washington);
I'M YOUR MAN; FASTLOVE (Part 2 – Fully Extended Mix)
Includes sample: 'Forget Me Nots' – Patrice Rushen.
VIRGIN CD VSCDG 1579, April 1996

SPINNING THE WHEEL (Radio Edit) (Michael/Douglas); YOU
KNOW THAT I WANT TO (Michael/Douglas); SAFE (Michael);
SPINNING THE WHEEL (Forthright Edit)
VIRGIN CD VSCDG 1595, February 1997

OLDER; I CAN'T MAKE YOU LOVE ME (Reid/Shamblin);
DESAFINADO (Jobim/Mendonca/Cavanaugh/Hendricks); THE
STRANGEST THING (Live) (Michael)
VIRGIN/AEGEAN CD VSCDG 1626, March 1997

STAR PEOPLE '97 (Michael); EVERYTHING SHE WANTS
(Unplugged); STAR PEOPLE (Unplugged)
VIRGIN CD 1641, April 1997

YOU HAVE BEEN LOVED (Michael/Austin); THE
STRANGEST THING '97 (Radio Mix); FATHER FIGURE
(Unplugged); PRAYING FOR TIME (Unplugged)
VIRGIN CD 7243 8 94586 2 6, October 1997

OUTSIDE (Michael); FANTASY '98; OUTSIDE (Jon Douglas
Remix)
EPIC CD 666249 2, November 1998

FREEEK! (*Michael/Moogymen); FREEEK! (The Scumfrogs
Mix); FREEEK! (Moogymen Mix)
*Includes samples: 'Try Again' – Aaliyah; 'Breathe And Stop' –
Q-Tip; 'NT' – Kool and the Gang.
POLYDOR CD 570-681-2, March 2002

SHOOT THE DOG (Explicit Album Version) (*Michael/Oakey/
Burden); SHOOT THE DOG (Moogymen Mix)
*Includes sample: 'Love Action (I Believe In Love)' – The Human
League.
POLYDOR CD 570-927-2, August 2002

FLAWLESS (GO TO THE CITY) (Radio Edit) (*Michael/
Alexander/Wooden/Turnier/Matthew/Stumm); PLEASE SEND
ME SOMEONE (ANSELMO'S SONG) (Alternative Version –
Edit) (**Michael/Barry/David)
*Includes sample: 'Flawless' – The Ones.
**Includes sample: 'Moonraker' – Shirley Bassey.
SONY CD 675068 1, March 2004

AMAZING (Michael/Douglas); FREEEK! '04
SONY CD 674726 2, May 2004

ROUND HERE (Michael); PATIENCE (Michael)
SONY CD 675470 2, November 2004

JOHN AND ELVIS ARE DEAD (Michael/Austin); EDITH AND
THE KINGPIN (Live at Abbey Road) (Mitchell); PRAYING FOR
TIME (Live at Abbey Road); FOR THE LOVE (OF YOU) (Isley
Brothers); PRECIOUS BOX (Shapeshifters Remix) (Michael)
October 2005. Download only.

AN EASIER AFFAIR (Michael/Ambrose/Flynn/Cushnan);
BROTHER, CAN YOU SPARE A DIME? (Harburg/Gorney)
SONY CD 82876869462, July 2006

DECEMBER SONG (I DREAMED OF CHRISTMAS)
(*Michael/Austin); JINGLE (A MUSICAL INTERLEWD)
(Michael); EDITH AND THE KINGPIN (Live at Abbey Road);
PRAYING FOR TIME (Live at Abbey Road)
*Features sample: 'Christmas Waltz' – Frank Sinatra.
ISLAND/AEGEAN CD 2732142/2729330, December 2008
Also available as a download.

TRUE FAITH (New Order)
March 2011. Download only.

YOU AND I (WE CAN CONQUER THE WORLD) (Wonder)
April 2011. Download only.

George Michael albums

FAITH

Faith; Father Figure; I Want Your Sex (Parts I & II); One More Try;
Hard Day; Hand To Mouth; Look At Your Hands; Monkey; Kissing
A Fool; Hard Day (Shep Pettibone Remix); A Last Request (I Want
Your Sex Part III)
EPIC vinyl EPC 460000 1/EPIC CD EPC 460000 2, October
1987

LISTEN WITHOUT PREJUDICE VOL. 1

Praying For Time; Freedom! '90; They Won't Go When I Go
(Wonder); Something To Save; Cowboys And Angels; Waiting
For That Day; Mother's Pride; Heal The Pain; Soul Free; Waiting
(reprise)
EPIC vinyl 467295 1/EPIC CD EPC 467295 2, September 1990

OLDER

Jesus To A Child; Fastlove; Older; Spinning The Wheel; It Doesn't
Really Matter; The Strangest Thing; To Be Forgiven (Michael);
Move On (Michael); Star People; You Have Been Loved; Free
(Michael)
Virgin vinyl V 2802/Virgin CD CDV 2802, May 1996

LADIES & GENTLEMEN – THE BEST OF GEORGE MICHAEL

Disc One (For The Heart):
Jesus To A Child; Father Figure; Careless Whisper; Don't Let The
Sun Go Down On Me (John/Taupin); You Have Been Loved;
Kissing A Fool; I Can't Make You Love Me; Heal The Pain; A
Moment With You (Michael); Desafinado; Cowboys And Angels;
Praying For Time; One More Try; A Different Corner
Disc Two (For The Feet):
Outside; As (Wonder); Fastlove; Too Funky; Freedom! '90; Star
People '97; Killer (Adamski/Seal)/Papa Was A Rollin' Stone
(Whitfield/Strong); I Want Your Sex (Part II); The Strangest Thing
'97; Fantasy; Spinning The Wheel; Waiting For That Day; I Knew
You Were Waiting (For Me) (Morgan/Climie); Faith; Somebody To
Love (Mercury)
EPIC double CD 491705 2, December 1998

SONGS FROM THE LAST CENTURY

Brother, Can You Spare A Dime?; Roxanne (Sting); You've Changed (Carey/Fischer); My Baby Just Cares For Me (Donaldson/Kahn); The First Time Ever I Saw Your Face (MacColl); Miss Sarajevo (Hewson/Evans/Clayton/Mullen/Eno); I Remember You (Schertzinger/Mercer); Secret Love (Fain/Webster); Wild Is The Wind (Tiomkin/Washington); Where Or When (Rodgers/Hart); It's Alright With Me (instrumental – hidden track) (Porter)
VIRGIN/AEGEAN CD 7243 8 48741 2 4/CDVX2920, December 1999

PATIENCE

Patience; Amazing; John And Elvis Are Dead; Cars And Trains (Michael/Douglas); Round Here; Shoot The Dog; My Mother Had A Brother (Michael); Flawless (Go To The City); American Angel (Michael); Precious Box; Please Send Me Someone (Anselmo's Song); Freeek! '04; Through (Michael); Patience (Part II) [hidden track]
SONY/AEGEAN CD 515402 2, May 2004

TWENTY FIVE

Disc One (For Living):

Everything She Wants (Remix); Wake Me Up Before You Go-Go; Freedom; Faith; Too Funky; Fastlove; Freedom! '90; Spinning The Wheel; Outside; As; Freeek!; Shoot The Dog; Amazing; Flawless (Go To The City); An Easier Affair

Disc Two (For Loving):

Careless Whisper; Last Christmas; A Different Corner; Father Figure; One More Try; Praying For Time; Heal The Pain; Don't Let The Sun Go Down On Me; Jesus To A Child; Older; Round Here; You Have Been Loved; John And Elvis Are Dead; This Is Not Real Love (Michael/Jackman/Cushnan)

Disc Three (For the Loyal – limited edition only):

Understand (Michael); Precious Box; Roxanne; Fantasy; Cars And Trains; Patience; You Know That I Want To; My Mother Had A

Brother; If You Were There; Safe; American Angel; My Baby Just
Cares For Me; Brother, Can You Spare A Dime?; Please Send Me
Someone (Anselmo's Song); Through
AEGEAN/SONY BMG double (or limited edition treble) CD
88697009002/88697009012, November 2006

FAITH REMASTERED
Disc One:
Faith; Father Figure; I Want Your Sex (Parts 1 & 2); One More Try;
Hard Day; Hand To Mouth; Look At Your Hands; Monkey; Kissing
A Fool; A Last Request (I Want Your Sex Part 3)
Disc Two:
Faith (Instrumental); Fantasy; Hard Day (Shep Pettibone Mix); I
Believe (When I Fall In Love It Will Be Forever) (Wonder/Wright);
Kissing A Fool (Instrumental); Love's In Need Of Love Today (Live);
Monkey (7″ Edit Version); Monkey (A Cappella & Beats); Monkey
(Jam & Lewis Remix)
Disc Three (DVD):
George Michael & Jonathan Ross Have Words (1987); Music Money
Love Faith (February 1988); I Want Your Sex (re-synced with re-
mastered audio); I Want Your Sex (Uncensored); Faith; Father Figure;
One More Try; Monkey; Kissing A Fool
EPIC/LEGACY CD/DVD SPECIAL EDITION 088697753202/3,
January 2011

Singles as a collaborator/duettist

BAND AID:
A – DO THEY KNOW IT'S CHRISTMAS? (Geldof/Ure)
B – FEED THE WORLD (Geldof/Ure)
MERCURY 7″ FEED 1, December 1984
A – DO THEY KNOW IT'S CHRISTMAS? (Trevor Horn Mix)
B – FEED THE WORLD; DO THEY KNOW IT'S
CHRISTMAS? (Regular Mix)
MERCURY 12″ 880 502-1 Q, December 1984

ARETHA FRANKLIN & GEORGE MICHAEL:
A – I KNEW YOU WERE WAITING (FOR ME)
B – I KNEW YOU WERE WAITING (FOR ME) (Instrumental)
EPIC 7" DUET 2, January 1987
A – I KNEW YOU WERE WAITING (FOR ME) (Extended Remix)
B – I KNEW YOU WERE WAITING (FOR ME) (A Cappella); I KNEW YOU WERE WAITING (FOR ME) (Edited Remix)
EPIC 12" EPC 650253 6, January 1987

DEON ESTUS (with GEORGE MICHAEL):
HEAVEN HELP ME (Estus/Michael)
POLYDOR 12" MIKAZ 2 871 539, January 1989

GEORGE MICHAEL & ELTON JOHN:
A – DON'T LET THE SUN GO DOWN ON ME (Live)
B – I BELIEVE (WHEN I FALL IN LOVE IT WILL BE FOREVER)
EPIC 7" 31-657646-04, November 1991
A – DON'T LET THE SUN GO DOWN ON ME (Live
B – I BELIEVE (WHEN I FALL IN LOVE IT WILL BE FOREVER); LAST CHRISTMAS
EPIC 12" 657646-5, November 1991
DON'T LET THE SUN GO DOWN ON ME; I BELIEVE (WHEN I FALL IN LOVE IT WILL BE FOREVER); IF YOU WERE MY WOMAN; FANTASY
EPIC CD 657646-2, November 1991

GEORGE MICHAEL & QUEEN (with LISA STANSFIELD):
FIVE LIVE
Somebody To Love; Killer/Papa Was A Rollin' Stone (PM Dawn Remix); These Are The Days of Our Lives; Calling You (Telson); Dear Friends (May) (extra track)
PARLOPHONE CD CDR 6340, April 1993

TOBY BOURKE (featuring GEORGE MICHAEL):
WALTZ AWAY DREAMING (Bourke/Michael)
AEGEAN CD AECDE01, May 1997

GEORGE MICHAEL & MARY J. BLIGE:
AS; A DIFFERENT CORNER (Live at <i>Parkinson</i>);
AS (Full Crew Mix)
EPIC CD EPC 666701, April 1999

WHITNEY HOUSTON & GEORGE MICHAEL
IF I TOLD YOU THAT (Album Version) (Jerkins/Jerkins/Daniels/
Estes); IF I TOLD YOU THAT (Johnny Douglas Mix)
ARISTA CD 74321 76628 2, July 2000

GEORGE MICHAEL & MUTYA:
THIS IS NOT REAL LOVE (Main Mix); EVERYTHING SHE
WANTS (Remix); I'M YOUR MAN (Extended Stimulation)
SONY BMG/AEGEAN CD 88697020702, November 2006

Album tracks as a collaborator

VARIOUS ARTISTS:
TWO ROOMS – CELEBRATING THE SONGS OF ELTON
JOHN & BERNIE TAUPIN
Tonight (John/Taupin)
MERCURY Vinyl 8457491/CD 8457592, September 1991

VARIOUS ARTISTS:
RED HOT + DANCE
Too Funky; Do You Really Want To Know? (Michael); Happy
(Michael)
EPIC CD 47 18212, July 1992

GEORGE MICHAEL & VARIOUS ARTISTS:
Title to be confirmed late 2011/early 2012.

Index

BC	1/12